Innovation and Small Firms

Innovation and Small Firms

Zoltan J. Acs
David B. Audretsch

The MIT Press
Cambridge, Massachusetts
London, England

This book was set in Palatino
by Asco Trade Typesetting Ltd., Hong Kong
and printed and bound by Halliday Lithograph.

Library of Congress Cataloging-in-Publication Data

Acs, Zoltan J.
  Innovation and small firms / Zoltan J. Acs, David B. Audretsch.

    p.   cm.
  Includes bibliographical references.
  ISBN 0-262-01113-1
  1. Small business—United States—Technological innovations.
I. Audretsch, David B. II. Title.
HD2346.U5A62   1990   89-13734
338.6'42—dc20   CIP

Contents

List of Tables

Acknowledgments

That this book could have been written anywhere other than at a research institute such as the Wissenschaftszentrum Berlin (WZB) seems unlikely. Not only were substantial financial resources required to purchase a number of different data bases, but processing the data involved considerable expertise from computer and research assistants. While we are grateful to the WZB for providing the necessary resources, we are particularly grateful to Manfred Fleischer, who has supported this project from its incipiency. His special efforts to alleviate the usual hindrances that typically bog down research projects are greatly appreciated.

We are deeply indebted to F. M. Scherer, who directed us through three substantive revisions of the manuscript by providing us with painstakingly detailed and invaluable comments. His generosity and persistence in criticizing each of the drafts are greatly appreciated. Thanks also go to Leonard W. Weiss, who made numerous suggestions on an earlier draft of the manuscript.

We are also thankful to our colleagues here in Berlin who provided numerous comments and suggestions throughout the various stages of this manuscript. In particular, we thank George Bittlingmayer, Felix R. FitzRoy, Harris Schlesinger, J.-Matthias Graf von der Schulenburg, Joachim Schwalbach, Hideki Yamawaki, and Klaus Zimmermann.

We also thank Bo Carlsson, Axel Dahrenmöller, Mark Dodgson, Paul Geroski, Gunter Kayser, Albert Link, John R. Munkirs, Manfred Neumann, Richard R. Nelson, Keith Pavitt, Paul Reynolds, Robert Smiley, and David J. Storey for their comments and suggestions on certain parts of the mannuscript. Bruce D. Phillips and William K. Scheirer of the U.S. Small Business Administration were particularly helpful in providing us with some of the data and in making concrete criticisms. We also wish to thank participants at seminars at the University of Bonn, University of Bremen, Hungarian Academy of Science, Graduate Center of the City University of New York, Rensselaer Polytechnic Institute, University of Nuremberg, Case Western Reserve University, University of Bradford, U.S. Small Business Administration, and at the 1987 and 1988 conferences of the European Association for Research in Industrial Economics (EARIE) in Madrid and Rotterdam for their useful comments.

We wish to thank the *American Economic Review* and *Review of Economics and Statistics* for granting us permission to include parts of out articles in chapters 2 and 3. Similarly, we thank *Economica* and the *Southern Economic Journal* for giving us permission to include parts of our articles in chapter 5. Part of the material contained in chapter 6 was compiled jointly with Bo Carlsson, to whom we are deeply indebted.

We wish to thank Michael Karge, Talat Mahmood, Sigrid Raasch, and Jianping Yang for their capable computer assistance. We are also grateful for the careful typing of parts of the manuscript by Christiane Loycke de Roux. Linda von Chamier-Cieminski typed the bulk of the manuscript and also took on managing the production of the entire manuscript. Her painstaking editorial assistance extended well beyond typing. Not only did she exercise her customary care and precision during the numerous revisions of the manuscript, but she displayed a remarkable degree of patience and goodwill throughout this endeavor. Special thanks go to her.

Innovation and Small Firms

1   Introduction

That small firms should emerge as a driving force of the U.S. economy precisely when technical change seems to play an unprecedented role in the national welfare poses a paradox to at least one strand of conventional wisdom. A prevalent assumption is that technological change requires increasingly large quantities of research and development resources amassed and organized by giant corporations. With the greater internationalization of markets and the important role that technological leadership plays, this view would have predicted that small firms would recede in importance as they are increasingly overwhelmed by large enterprises able to exploit economies of scale. Such a view dates back at least to Karl Marx, who predicted that the efficiencies inherent in the corporate structure of organization, along with the exploitation of scale economies in a competitive market, would result in "a constantly diminishing number of the magnates of capital, who usurp and monopolise all advantages of this process of transformation" (Marx 1912, 836).

In fact, there is little contention that high technology is accounting for an increased share of U.S. economic activity. The U.S. Office of Technology Assessment (1984) estimated that the employment growth rate between 1976 and 1980 in high-technology industries was nearly 20 percent, while it was only about 15 percent for all manufacturing industries. Similarly, the 1989 *Economic Report of the President* (ch. 6) notes that the U.S. trade performance has been consistently superior in high-technology markets when compared to the entire economy. For example, between 1981 and 1987, the share of U.S. manufacturing exports accounted for by high-technology industries rose from 35 to 42 percent. This reflects the apparent comparative advantage of U.S. industries in high R&D and information-intensive markets (Audretsch and Yamawaki 1988; Yamawaki and Audretsch

1988). Not surprisingly, with the increased globalization of manufacturing industries, there has been a reallocation of U.S. resources from capital-intensive products toward high-technology goods.

What is perhaps more surprising has been the concomitant rise in the relative importance of small firms. This shift has not escaped the attention of the popular press. For example, *The Economist* reports:

> Despite ever-larger and noisier mergers, the biggest change coming over the world of business is that firms are getting smaller. The trend of a century is being reversed. Until the mid–1970s, the size of firms everywhere grew; the numbers of self-employed fell. Ford and General Motors replaced the carriage-marker's atelier; McDonald's, Safeway and W. H. Smith supplanted the corner shop. No longer. Now it is the big firms that are shrinking and small ones that are on the rise. The trend is unmistakable—and businessmen and policy-makers will ignore it at their peril.[1]

While the exact extent of this shift has been hotly contested (see, for example, FitzRoy 1989), the direction of the shift has not. Perhaps most striking is the convergence toward a singular conclusion, even when comparing different measures applied by different authors.

It was in the area of job generation that this recent emergence of small firms was first identified. In 1981 David Birch revealed the startling findings from his long-term study of U.S. job generation. Despite the conventional wisdom prevailing at the time, Birch (1981, 8) found that, "[W]hatever else they are doing, large firms are no longer the major providers of new jobs for Americans." Instead, he discovered that most new jobs emanated from small firms. While his exact methodology and application of the underlying data have been a source of considerable controversy (Storey and Johnson 1987; Armington and Odle 1982), as have the exact quantitative estimates, his qualitative conclusion that the bulk of new jobs has emanated from small enterprises has been largely substantiated. Of course, the entire notion and measure of job generation is not particularly well defined for analysis in industrial organization, because no information is gained about the extent to which the generated jobs subsequently disappear. This qualification also applies to the observation that the number of new businesses has been drastically increasing over time. Still, in 1976, 376,000 new businesses were formed, while in 1986 there were 703,000 new businesses. This 87-percent increase is more than twice as much as the 39-percent increase in real Gross National Product (GNP) that occurred over the same period (Brock and Evans 1989). What is perhaps more striking is that average real

GNP per firm increased by nearly two-thirds between 1947 and 1980, from $150,000 to $245,000. However, within the next seven years, it had fallen by about 14 percent to $210,000.

Although it is clear that a greater portion of enterprises are small, it also appears that these small firms account for a greater share of U.S. employment and sales. For example, the 1987 *Statistical Abstract of the United States* shows that the amount of employment in firms with between 20 and 99 employees grew annually by 3.64 percent between 1975 and 1984, but employment in firms with more than 1,000 employees grew annually by only 1.25 percent.

Of course, there is a temptation to attribute this relative increase in the number of small firms and in small-firm employment to the obvious long-term transition of employment into services and out of the manufacturing sector. That is, employment in U.S. manufacturing fell from 40 percent of the total work force in 1959 to 27.7 percent of the work force in 1984. In fact, the shift in economic activity from large to small firms has been even greater in manufacturing than in services or finance (Acs and Audretsch 1989b). Using the data that serve as one of the bases for this book, we find that manufacturing firms with fewer than 500 employees accounted for about one-fifth of total sales in 1976, but by 1986 the small-firm share of sales had risen to over one-quarter. Measured in terms of employment shares, this shift in manufacturing was even greater.

While the statistical evidence that small firms are playing a more prominent role in all sectors of the economy is quite convincing, the exact reasons for this are considerably more tentative. There are at least six factors that have been hypothesized to explain this recent emergence of small firms. The first is, in the term used by Blair (1948), the "decentralizing" effects of certain new technologies, such as numerically controlled (NC) machine tools, which have contributed to a reduction in the minimum efficient scale (MES), or the level of output required to exhaust scale economies. While there have been some systematic attempts to estimate the impact of these new technologies on MES (Carlsson 1989a; Shepherd 1982; and Diwan 1989), this notion has also received considerable attention in the popular press. For example, management consultant Tom Peters claims that, "Old ideas about economies of scale are being challenged. . . . Scale itself is being redefined. Smaller firms are gaining in almost every market, at least in America. (Even Peter Drucker, father of modern big-firm management, now advocates the 'mid-size' company.)

Even the tiniest firm can usually do some activity—from plant watering to specialised legal services—better than a giant. So we see a spreading trend toward deintegration and subcontracting."[2]

The second reason is that increased globalization has rendered markets more volatile as a result of competition from a greater number of foreign rivals as well as from exchange rate fluctuations. Thus organizational and productive flexibility, which tends to be more within the domain of smaller firms than within that of their larger counterparts, is increasingly a valuable asset. Third, William A. Brock and David Evans (1989, 1986) argue that the changing composition of the labor force may also be a catalyst for small enterprises. The increase in the labor-force participation of women and the entry of the baby-boom generation into the labor market may have increased the supply of exactly the kinds of labor that are most conducive to small firms. More than one-half of American mothers are active in the labor force. Not only is the flexibility of small firms more compatible with the schedules of working mothers, but Evans and Leighton (1989) found that between 1975 and 1985, the female self-employment rate increased by over one-third, while the male self-employment rate increased by about one-tenth. That is, women have a greater tendency to work in smaller firms and are increasingly starting their own firms. In addition, the decrease in real wage rates during the 1970s and early 1980s may also have provided smaller firms, which are presumably labor-intensive, with a competitive advantage over their larger counterparts, which are more likely to be relatively capital-intensive.

The fourth explanation is the proliferation of consumer tastes away from standardized mass-produced goods and toward stylized and personalized products. To the extent that relatively small batches of customized products are replacing long production runs of standardized goods, the inherent cost disadvantage of small-scale production will tend to decrease. The recent deregulation movement may also have contributed to the viability of small enterprises. For example, the relaxation of entry regulations in certain industries, such as telephone manufacturing and financial services, has increased the opportunities for small businesses. Finally, it has been argued that the United States is currently experiencing a period of "creative destruction," conforming to Schumpeter's (1950) analysis of the evolutionary process through which entrepreneurs develop new products and processes that ultimately displace the entrenched firms and institutions.

Most of these speculations are exactly that—speculations, which have not been subjected to rigorous systematic analysis. However, one thing seems clear: The recent emergence of small firms is likely to remain a phenomenon in search of explanations for some time.

Yet the view that larger enterprises should be promoted at the expense of smaller firms, even by public policy, seems to be the basis of at least one strand of conventional wisdom.[3] Adams and Brock (1988, 2) describe this view: "The *nouvelle vogue* among prominent U.S. public policy spokesmen is the facilitation of corporate mergers and acquisitions, the promotion of corporate bigness, and the emasculation of the anti-merger law. They claim that this kind of bold new departure is needed to enable firms in the United States to challenge large foreign rivals and regain global competitiveness."

However, this view notwithstanding, it may be that the recent emergence of small firms has occurred not *despite* the concomitant increased importance of technological change, but rather *because* of it. What is not at all clear is whether this phenomenon is the result or the cause of many of the recent innovations. There is a long-standing tradition in the field of industrial organization that, just as market structure and firm size are considered to influence innovative activity, technological change is viewed as having, at least in certain instances, an impact on the size distribution of firms. In 1948 (p. 121) Blair remarked that, "The whole subject of the comparative efficiency of different sizes of business has long raised one of the most perplexing dilemmas in the entire body of economic theory. . . . But a beginning must be made sometime in tackling this whole size-efficiency problem on an empirical basis. The first step in any such undertaking would logically be that of studying the underlying technological forces of the economy, since it is technology which largely determines the relationship between the size of plant and efficiency."

While, as Blair (1948) argued, new technologies may be responsible for shifting the MES and therefore the size distribution of firms, small firms themselves may also be active contributors to this process of technological change. That is, there is an interaction between the size distribution of firms and technological change, so that neither factor is completely exogenous nor exclusively endogenous. Dosi (1988), among others, therefore emphasizes the importance of examining the dynamic process by which technical change and market structure interact with each other in determining the direction of market evolution. In particular, Dosi (1988, 157) argues that, "Each production activity is characterized by a particular distribution of firms. . . . However, the picture of an industry that emerges at any time is itself the result of a competitive process. Thus, a satisfactory understanding of the relationship between innovation and distribution of firms' structural and performance characteristics also implies an analysis of the learning and competitive process through which an industry changes." This would suggest that small firms play an important role in contributing to the process of technological change as well as to the process by which markets respond to technological change.

While the rise of small firms has been noted in the popular press, there has been very little systematic analysis of either their contribution to technological change or their role in market processes. This lack of knowledge has led Brock and Evans (1989, 17) to observe that although, "The small-business sector—which a cynic might define as those businesses that economists hardly ever study—is a sizeable and growing part of the U.S. economy. . . . The paucity of research on small businesses together with the rising importance of small businesses in the economy has created a significant gap between what policymakers would like to know and what economists can say with some confidence."

By contrast, innovation is a subject that has enjoyed a prominent position in the research agenda of economists over the years. However, virtually all of the empirical work on innovation and technical change has focused on large firms. The reason we are interested in small firms and innovation is that the intersection of these two sets represents a significant vacuum in the economics literature, precisely at a time when there is a growing body of anecdotal evidence indicating that small firms are playing an increasing role in technical change. The purpose of this book is to fill this gap in the literature.

In light of the fact that small firms constituted an ever-decreasing share of the U.S. economy during the first half of this century, Congress passed the Small Business Act of 1953, which established the U.S. Small Business Administration (SBA). The agency was directed to help small businesses obtain government contracts and loans, along with management and technical assistance. In response to its dissatisfaction with these limitations of the SBA, Congress established the Office of Advocacy of the Small Business Administration in 1976. This led to a dramatic shift in policy. Although the earlier Act had tried to protect small enterprises from exposure to a hostile economic environment, the Office of Advocacy was given the mandate to protect small firms from a hostile bureaucracy. This added emphasis was a response to the increased regulation in the early 1970s and the concomitant increased burden on small firms.

Congress emphasized its concern about the impact of government regulation on small firms by passing three relevant legislative acts in 1980. The most important, the Economic Policy Act of 1980, mandated the president to submit to Congress an annual report on the state of small business and authorized the creation of the Small Business Data Base (SBDB). In order to understand the economic impact of the government on small business as well as the economic contribution of small firms to the economy, the SBA conducted a series of detailed studies in 1982. One of these measured the contribution of small firms to the innovation process and resulted in the creation of the Small Business Innovation Data Base (SBIDB). Both of these data bases make an indispensable contribution to this study. They provide the requisite and unprecedented data for carrying out the empirical analyses.

A study of this kind must proceed within a conceptual framework in order to advance satisfactorily and logically our understanding of the subject at hand. We are essentially concerned with two issues: (1) the role of small firms in innovation; and (2) the manner in which market structure, and the firm-size distribution in particular, respond to technological change. While our subject can be studied from many different perspectives, and from both a macro and micro framework, these topics of firm-size distribution, market structure, and technical change are at the very foundation of industrial organization. In examining these questions through the lens of industrial organization, the analysis is carried out in the context of the structure–conduct–performance paradigm. Therefore this book relies on the traditional theories of industrial organization and tests existing hypotheses, many of them never previously empirically tested due to data constraints, by applying the newly created SBA data.

In chapter 2 we begin by introducing the two new important data sources—the SBDB and SBIDB—which we use in carrying out the systematic analyses of innovation and firm size. Chapter 3 employs the SBIDB data to identify the determinants of innovative activity and to ascertain whether those determinants vary between large and small firms.

The reasons why there should be so much variation in the presence of small firms across manufacturing industries are examined in chapter 4. In particular, we consider how both the overall amount of innovative activity as well as the innovative activity of small firms have affected the viability of small firms. The purpose of chapter 5 is to apply a new measure, employment-weighted gross entry, or births, in order to compare how the patterns of entry vary across firm size, with the traditional measures of entry, and how they are affected by the innovative activity of large and small firms. Chapter 6 begins with the empirical observation that there has been a noticeable shift toward smaller firms in the group of industries comprising the metal-working sector. Following the long-standing tradition in industrial organization that such shifts may be attributable to technological change, we examine the extent to which the implementation of certain flexible technologies, such as numerically controlled machines and programmable robots, has contributed to this shift in the firm-size distribution. Chapter 7 considers the role that innovation and firm size play in intra-industry dynamics. The extent to which the growth rates of small and large firms vary, or the validity of the assumption underlying Gibrat's Law, is examined. In addition, we investigate the effect of different types of technological environments on industry turbulence, or the extent of firm movements within, into, and out of an industry. Finally, in the last chapter a summary and conclusions are presented. While it is beyond the scope of a statistical study at the broad industry level to make specific policy recommendations, we do suggest that some of the conventional wisdoms regarding innovation and firm size at least be questioned.

2

The Innovation and Firm Size Data Bases

2.1 New Sources of Data

We use two new important sources of data in this book in order to better understand the relationship between firm size and innovation. These data enable a systematic empirical analysis of innovation and firm size to be conducted, beyond that which has previously been possible. Because of the contribution these two data sources make to the analyses, this chapter is devoted to describing these data, to making comparisons with more traditional data measures, and to providing qualifications about the applicability and reliability of the data.

The innovation data are presented in the second section. There are two distinguishing features of these data when compared to the more traditional measures of technical change, such as R&D expenditures and the number of patents. First, we apply a direct measure of innovative output, the number of innovations introduced in the market in 1982, rather than a measure of innovative input, such as R&D expenditures, scientists and engineers, or a count of patents. Second, most of the previous empirical research has examined only the innovative activity contributed by relatively large firms; the innovative output of the smallest firms has received scant attention and quantification.[1] Thus, most of the inferences that have been made about the causes of innovative activity have been based on observing only the behavior of larger firms. Such inferences may be misleading, since, as we show in this chapter, about half of the number of innovations are contributed by firms that employ fewer than 500 workers.

After describing the procedure used for compiling the innovation data base, we consider the issues of variations in the importance or significance of the recorded innovations, particularly with respect to firm size, and how the innovation measures compare to more traditional measures of technological change, such as R&D expenditures and patented inventions. We then examine how the innovations are distributed according to firm size and across manufacturing industries and sectors. In order to provide some comparisons with similar attempts to create a data base of innovative activity, we briefly examine three other sets of data that provide some direct measure of innovation.

In the third section of this chapter the U.S. Small Business Administration Data Base (SBDB) is introduced. These data provide the basis for most of the analysis examining issues of firm size used throughout this book. After describing the data base and how it was compiled, several important qualifications about the applicability of the data are presented. To the extent to which it is possible, we then compare the SBDB data with several other similar data sets, including the *Enterprise Statistics* of the Bureau of the Census at the U.S. Department of Commerce, data from the Bureau of Labor Statistics, and the *County Business Patterns*, also from the Bureau of the Census.

2.2   The Innovation Data

The measure of innovative activity used throughout this book is the number of innovations in each four-digit SIC (Standard Industrial Classification) industry recorded in 1982. The data, which were only recently released by the U.S. Small Business Administration,[2] consist of 8,074 innovations introduced into the United States in 1982. Of these innovations, 4,476 were identified as occurring in manufacturing industries. These data are classified according to four-digit SIC industry in appendix D.

A private firm, The Futures Group, constructed the data base and performed quality-control analyses for the Small Business Administration by examining over 100 technology, engineering, and trade journals, covering each manufacturing industry. From the sections in each trade journal listing innovations and new products, a data base consisting of the innovations by four-digit SIC industry was formed. The entire list of trade journals used to compile these data is available from the authors. The Small Business Administration defines an innovation as "a process that begins with an invention, proceeds with the development of the invention, and results in introduction of a new product, process or service to the marketplace" (Edwards and Gordon 1984, 1).

Because the innovations recorded in 1982 were the result of inventions made, on average, 4.3 years earlier, in some sense the innovation data base represents the inventions made around 1978 that were subsequently introduced to the market in 1982. The data were also checked for duplication. In fact, 8,800 innovations were actually recorded, but it was subsequently found that 726 of them appeared either in separate issues of the same journal or else in different journals. Thus, double-counting was avoided.

The innovation data were classified according to the industry of origin based on the SIC code of the innovating enterprise. The Futures Group assigned the innovation to an industry based on the information given in the trade journal. When no such information was given and the relevant industry could not be determined from other sources, no industry was assigned to the innovation. The data were then classified into innovations by large firms, defined as firms with at least 500 employees, and innovations by small firms, defined as firms with fewer than 500 employees. For example, an innovation made by a subsidiary of a diversified firm would be classified by industry according to the SIC industry of the innovating subsidiary (establishment) and not by the SIC industry of the parent firm (enterprise). However, the innovation would be classified by size according to the size of the entire firm and not just by the size of the subsidiary. Because sixty-seven innovations could not be classified according to firm size, the number of total innovations does not always equal the sum of large- and small-firm innovations.

To determine the criteria by which editors of the trade journals decide to include a new product in their new-product section, and to determine if any systematic biases exist, The Futures Group carried out detailed interviews with five journal editors and reported the following:

The *Surgical Business* editor said that material is published on a first-come, first-served basis, regardless of firm size. However, they prefer to work with public relations departments of firms. When a company is too small to have its own public relations department, or cannot afford a public relations firm, *Surgical Business* works with the firm via personal contact to design the news item. The *Electronics* editor said that they choose material they consider significant from a pool of submitted material without regard to firm size. *Intech* receives 300–400 press releases each month and the technical editor and staff members select 50 of these products that they deem to be of special interest. The *ASHRAE Journal* also receives press releases, but their policy is to publish each one they receive, generally within a month of receipt. Information obtained from *Popular Science* indicates that they utilize the same process as does *Intech*. If these positions are characteristic of the population of the new-product editors, then the material appearing in the new-product sections of the trade journals should only be weighted to the large firm to the extent that the small firm is not sophisticated enough, or does not have the necessary resources, to produce press releases. Furthermore, the material may be biased toward the unusual or what some editors consider to be of special interest. (Edwards and Gordon 1984, 14–15)

There are several other qualifications that should be made concerning the innovation data. The trade journals report relatively few process, service, and management innovations and tend to capture mainly product innovations. The most likely effect of this bias is to underestimate the number of innovations emanating from large firms, since larger enterprises tend to produce more process innovations than do their smaller counterparts. However, because it was found that the large-firm innovations are more likely to be reported in trade journals than are small-firm innovations, the biases are perhaps at least somewhat offsetting.

Table 2.1 lists the total number of innovations in those industries that had the greatest number of innovations in 1982, along with the corresponding number of large- and small-firm innovations. In some industries, the large firms exhibit considerably more innovative activity than do their smaller counterparts, while in other industries the small firms are apparently more innovative.

Table 2.2 shows the distribution of manufacturing industries according to innovation frequency. About one-quarter of the innovating industries contributed at least sixteen innovations, while slightly more than one-half of these industries had fewer than six innovations. One potential concern might be that the significance and "quality" of the innovations vary considerably between large and small firms. Based on 4,938 of the innovations, each innovation was classified by Edwards and Gordon (1984) according to one of the following levels of significance: (1) the innovation established an entirely new category of product, (2) the innovation is the first of its type on the market in a product category already in existence, (3) the innovation represents a significant improvement in existing technology, and (4) the innovation is a modest improvement designed to update and existing product.

Table 2.1
Number of innovations for large and small firms in the most innovative industries, 1982[a]

Industry	Total innovations	Large-firm innovations	Small-firm innovations
Electronic computing equipment	395	158	227
Process control instruments	165	68	93
Radio and TV communication equipment	157	83	72
Pharmaceutical preparations	133	120	13
Electronic components	128	54	73
Engineering and scientific instruments	126	43	83
Semiconductors	122	91	29
Plastics products	107	22	82
Photographic equipment	88	79	9
Office machinery	77	67	10
Instruments to measure electricity	77	28	47
Surgical appliances and supplies	67	54	13
Surgical and medical instruments	66	30	36
Special industry machinery	64	43	21
Industrial controls	61	15	46
Toilet preparations	59	41	18
Valves and pipe fittings	54	20	33
Electric housewares and fans	53	47	6
Measuring and controlling devices	52	3	45
Food products machinery	50	37	12

Table 2.1
(continued)

Industry	Total innovations	Large-firm innovations	Small-firm innovations
Motors and generators	49	39	10
Plastic materials and resins	45	30	15
Industrial inorganic chemicals	40	32	8
Radio and TV receiving sets	40	35	4
Hand and edge tools	39	27	11
Fabricated platework	38	29	9
Fabricated structure metal	35	12	17
Pumps and pumping equipment	34	18	16
Optical instruments and lenses	34	12	21
Polishes and sanitation goods	33	13	19
Industrial trucks and tractors	33	13	20
Medicinals and botanicals	32	27	5
Aircraft	32	31	1
Environmental controls	32	22	10

a. Large- and small-firm innovations do not always sum to total innovations because several innovations could not be classified according to firm size.

Table 2.2
The distribution of manufacturing industries according to innovation frequency[a] (percentages in parentheses)

| | Number of innovations | | | | | | | |
	1–5	6–10	11–15	16–20	21–25	26–30	31	Total
Total innovations	149	36	21	13	15	6	36	276
	(53.99)	(13.04)	(7.61)	(4.71)	(5.43)	(2.17)	(13.04)	(99.99)
Large-firm innovations	127	28	24	6	7	8	18	218
	(58.26)	(12.84)	(11.01)	(2.75)	(3.21)	(3.67)	(8.26)	(100.00)
Small-firm innovations	129	33	16	9	4	1	13	205
	(62.93)	(16.10)	(7.80)	(4.39)	(1.95)	(0.49)	(6.34)	(100.00)

Source: U.S. Small Business Administration.
a. Only industries where there is at least some innovation activity are included in this table.

Table 2.3
Distribution of large- and small-firm innovations according to significance levels (percentages in parentheses)

Innovation significance	Description	Number of innovations Large firms		Small firms	
1	Establishes whole new categories	0	(0.00)	0	(0.00)
2	First of its type on the market in existing categories	50	(1.76)	30	(1.43)
3	A significant improvement in existing technology	360	(12.70)	216	(10.27)
4	Modest improvement designed to update existing products	2,424	(85.53)	1,858	(88.31)
Total		2,834	(99.99)	2,104	(100.00)

The distribution of innovative significance according to firm size is shown in table 2.3. While none of the innovations in the sample were in the highest level of significance, 80 were in the second level, 576 in the third level, and 4,282 were classified in the fourth level. Within each level of significance, the distribution between large- and small-firm innovations proved to be remarkably constant. In both the second and third significance categories, the large firms accounted for 62.5 percent of the innovations and the small firms for the remaining 37.5 percent. In the fourth significance category, the large firms accounted for a slightly smaller share of the innovations, 56.6 percent, while the small firms contributed the remaining 43.4 percent. A chi-square test for the hypothesis that there is no difference in the frequency of innovation with respect to innovation significance and firm size cannot be rejected at the 99 percent level of confidence.[3] Thus, based on the classification of the significance level of innovations, there does not appear to be a great difference in the "quality" and significance of the innovations between large and small firms.

To provide a test for any biases that might arise in the assignment of the innovation significance classification, The Futures Group undertook telephone interviews based on a subset of 600 innovating companies that were randomly selected. Of these selected companies, 529 were reached and 375 telephone interviews were actually carried out. Of those selected companies not participating in the telephone interview, the most frequent reason for not participating was the inability of The Futures Group to contact the innovating firm or targeted person responsible for the innovation. The respondents of the interviews tended to rate their innovation as being more important than the rating assigned by The Futures Group. For example, while The Futures Group did not assign any innovations to the most significant category, twenty-five of the interviewed firms considered their innovation to be worthy of the highest significance rating. Confronted with this disparity in ratings, Edwards and Gordon (1984, 66) conclude, "The liberalism on the part of the respondents, especially in the assignation of l's, may be attributed to product loyalty on the part of some respondents and, perhaps, unfamiliarity with other products on the market on the part of some of the nontechnical respondents. Alternately, The Futures Group may really have underrated the innovations."

The telephone interviews also enabled the length of time between the invention and innovation to be determined, so that it could be tested whether this time interval varies systematically with firm size. Not only was the mean number of years to innovation 4.3 for both large and small firms, but a chi-square test leads to the conclusion that the time interval between invention and innovation is independent of firm size (Edwards and Gordon 1984).

Although not listed in table 2.1, there is a fairly strong correspondence between the company R&D/sales ratio (from the 1977 Federal Trade Commission Line of Business) and the number of total innovations. For example, the industry with the greatest number of innovations, electronic computing equipment, had the second greatest amount of total R&D expenditures ($618 million). The R&D/sales ratio of 8.7 percent is also relatively high. However, there is no obvious relationship between the industry R&D/sales ratio and the relative innovative advantage between large and small firms.[4] The difference in rankings by absolute R&D levels and by R&D/sales ratios is attributable to the highly skewed distribution of the former measure.

Table 2.4 provides a more detailed comparison of the total number of innovations and the total number of patented inventions between June 1976 and March 1977 (from Scherer 1983a).[5] In order to make both data sets compatible, the patent data, which are adjusted from Scherer's unpublished appendix, are used in table 2.4. The ratio of patents to innovations is particularly interesting since it sheds some light on the productivity of patented inventions. It is apparent that

Table 2.4
Comparison of innovation data with patent measures[a]

Industry group	Total innovations	Patents	Patents/ innovations
Food and tobacco	206	455	2.21
Textiles and apparel	29	349	12.03
Lumber and furniture	83	167	2.01
Paper	61	396	6.49
Chemicals (excluding drugs)	332	3,925	11.82
Drugs	170	891	5.24
Petroleum	24	600	25.00
Rubber and plastics	129	1,649	12.78
Stone, clay, and glass	59	643	10.90
Primary metals	74	443	5.99
Fabricated metal products	340	1,052	3.09
Machinery (excluding office)	612	2,551	4.17
Computers and office equipment	566	1,012	1.79
Industrial electrical equipment[b]	444	1,888	4.25
Household appliances	64	233	3.64
Communications equipment	262	1,404	5.36
Motor vehicles and other transportation equipment[c]	152	723	4.76
Aircraft and engines	48	418	8.71
Guided missiles and ordnance	16	114	7.13
Instruments	736	2,200	2.99
Total[d]	4,407	21,113	4.79

a. Patent data for June 1976–March 1977 are from Scherer (1983a), but adjusted for sampling rates from Scherer's unpublished appendix.
b. Includes SIC 361, 362, 364, and 367.
c. Includes SIC 371, 373, 374, 375, and 379.
d. Includes only industries in this table.

the number of innovations realized per patented invention varies considerably across industries. Of particular interest is that the patent per innovation ratio in drugs is about one-half of that in the rest of the broader chemical sector. This is consistent with the frequently made observation (Nelson 1984) that the propensity to patent is particularly high in the pharmaceutical industry, and it is also remarkably similar to the pattern of patents per scientists and engineers identified by Evenson (1984). The relatively high ratios of patents per innovation in the chemical and petroleum sectors, and the relatively low ratios in the computers, electrical machinery, lumber, and instruments sectors are explained by Mansfield (1984, 462):

The value and cost of individual patents vary enormously within and across industries. . . . Many inventions are not patented. And in some industries, like electronics, there is considerable speculation that the patent system is being bypassed to a greater extent than in the past. Some types of technologies are more likely to be patented than others.

Probably the best measure of innovative intensity is the total innovation rate (TIE), which is defined as the total number of innovations per 1,000 employees in a four-digit SIC industry.[6] The large-firm innovation rate (LIE) is defined as the number of innovations made by firms with at least 500 employees, divided by the number of employees (thousands) in large firms. The small-firm innovation rate (SIE) is defined as the number of innovations contributed by firms with fewer than 500 employees, divided by the number of employees (thousands) in small firms. The innovation rates, or the number of innovations per 1,000 employees, are used here because they measure large- and small-firm innovative activity relative to the presence of large and small firms in any given industry. That is, in making a direct comparison between large- and small-firm innovative activity, the absolute number of innovations contributed by large firms and by small firms would be misleading, since it is not standardized by the relative presence of large and small firms in the industry. When a direct comparison is made between the innovative activity of large and small firms, the innovation rates are presumably a more reliable measure of innovation intensity because they are weighted by the relative presence of small and large firms in any given industry.[7] Thus, while large firms in manufacturing introduced 2,445 innovations in 1982, and small firms contributed slightly fewer, 1,954, small-firm employment was only about half as great as large-firm employment,

Table 2.5
Correlation matrix of input and output measures of innovative activity

	Total innovation rate	Large-firm innovation rate	Small-firm innovation rate	Total R&D expenditures/ sales	Company R&D expenditures/ sales
Large-firm innovation rate	0.791	—			
Small-firm innovation rate	0.752	0.340	—		
Total R&D expenditures/sales	0.354	0.262	0.353	—	
Company R&D expenditures/sales	0.526	0.435	0.502	0.699	—

yielding an average small-firm innovation rate in manufacturing of 0.309, compared to a large-firm innovation rate of 0.202.[8]

In order to compare the new innovation measures with the more traditional measures of technical change, table 2.5 provides a correlation matrix of input and output measures of innovative activity. There is a striking difference in the simple correlation of 0.354 between the total R&D/sales ratio (from the 1977 FTC Line of Business Survey) and the total innovation rate, and of 0.526 between the company R&D/sales ratio and the total innovation rate. That the correlation between company R&D and innovative activity is stronger than the correlation between total R&D and innovative activity is consistent with the findings by Griliches (1986) that privately financed R&D has a larger effect on private productivity and profitability than does government-financed R&D. This is not surprising since a much larger share of government-financed R&D is allocated toward military applications which may not necessarily have commercial uses, and this is certainly less likely to result in the type of commercialized innovation that is being recorded in our data set.

Table 2.6 shows the average innovation rates for industries aggregated to the two-digit SIC level. For example, in the food industries there was an average of 0.2119 innovations per 1,000 employees. Thus, the average innovation rate in the food sector was about three times as high as that in textiles, but only slightly higher than the rate in apparel or lumber. The lowest innovation rates were in printing (0.0426), textiles (0.0740), rubber (0.1204), and transportation equipment (0.1250). The highest total innovation rates were in instruments (1.3586), chemicals (0.7592), and nonelectrical machinery (0.6039).

Table 2.6 also shows the large-firm and small-firm average innovation rates for each of the two-digit SIC sectors. The large-firm innovation rate (LIE) is highest for rubber (2.1814), which is almost 500 times higher than the lowest LIE, for leather (0.0053). The small-firm innovation rate (SIE) is the highest for instruments (2.9987), which is considerably higher than the lowest SIE, for printing (0.0313). In general, the LIE and SIE do not seem to be closely related. While LIE is relatively high in rubber, instruments, and chemicals, SIE is relatively high in instruments, chemicals, nonelectrical machinery, and electrical equipment; while LIE is relatively low in leather, textiles, printing, and petroleum, SIE is relatively low in printing, food, rubber, and paper. Some striking contrasts emerge between the LIE and the SIE. While LIE is the highest in the rubber industry, SIE is almost

Table 2.6
Innovation rates for large and small firms, by two-digit SIC sector, 1982[a]

Sector	Total innovations	Large-firm innovations	Small-firm innovations
Food	0.2119	0.2555	0.1361*
	(0.1741)	(0.3120)	(0.1905)
Textiles	0.7040	0.0295	0.1669*
	(0.0612)	(0.0646)	(0.1723)
Apparel	0.1253	0.0639	0.1439
	(0.1553)	(0.1222)	(0.2076)
Lumber	0.1400	0.0506	0.1415
	(0.2179)	(0.0680)	(0.2662)
Furniture	0.3053	0.2412	0.2592
	(0.2917)	(0.3759)	(0.2243)
Paper	0.1616	0.1931	0.1214
	(0.1651)	(0.2821)	(0.2691)
Printing	0.0426	0.0468	0.0313
	(0.0350)	(0.0452)	(0.0552)
Chemicals	0.7592	0.6272	1.3547*
	(0.5945)	(0.6297)	(1.5641)
Petroleum	0.3386	0.0476	0.6173
	(0.3797)	(0.0824)	(0.6591)
Rubber	0.1204	2.1814	0.1129
	(0.0787)	(4.1868)	(0.1779)
Leather	0.1356	0.0053	0.1793*
	(0.1487)	(0.0106)	(0.1695)
Stone, clay, and glass	0.2130	0.1625	0.2696
	(0.1640)	(0.2116)	(0.1979)
Primary metals	0.1586	0.1624	0.3336
	(0.2905)	(0.3394)	(0.8319)
Fabricated metal products	0.3224	0.2878	0.3619
	(0.3109)	(0.3357)	(0.3862)
Machinery (nonelectrical)	0.6039	0.4860	1.1491*
	(0.6728)	(0.5673)	(1.7965)
Electrical equipment	0.3713	0.2719	0.7948*
	(0.3510)	(0.3263)	(0.7912)
Transportation equipment	0.1250	0.1182	0.1911
	(0.1289)	(0.1868)	(0.3349)
Instruments	1.3586	0.7442	2.9987*
	(0.9939)	(0.5367)	(2.5253)

Note:* The difference between the large- and small-firm innovation rates that is statistically significant at the 90 percent level of confidence.
a. Innovation rates are defined as the number of innovations divided by employment (thousands of employees). Standard deviations are listed in parentheses.

the lowest. Similarly, although LIE is relatively small in the petroleum industry, SIE is relatively high.

It is clear from table 2.6 that the difference in innovation rates between large and small firms varies considerably across industries. SIE exceeds LIE in fourteen of the two-digit sectors, but LIE exceeds SIE in four of the sectors. Just as SIE exceeds LIE by 2.2545 in instruments, LIE exceeds SIE by 2.0712 in rubber.

Besides the more traditional measures of technological change, which have already been examined in this chapter, there are three other distinct sources of data attempting to directly measure innovation activity that can be used for comparison with our innovation data. The first of these sources was compiled by the Gellman Research Associates (1976) for the National Science Foundation. Gellman identified 500 major innovations that were introduced into the market between 1953 and 1973 in the United States, the United Kingdom, Japan, West Germany, France, and Canada. According to the National Science Board (1975, 100), "The innovations were selected by an international panel of experts as representing the most significant new industrial products and processes, in terms of their technological importance and economic and social impact." Of the 319 innovations contributed by U.S. industries, nearly one-quarter were from firms with fewer than 100 employees. An additional 24 percent were contributed by firms with between 100 and 999 employees. Between 1967 and 1973, U.S. manufacturing firms with fewer than 100 employees contributed an average of 2.0 innovations per $10 billion of sales. Firms with between 100 and 999 employees also contributed an average of 2.0 innovations per $10 billion of sales, while firms with at least 1,000 employees produced only 1.5 innovations per $10 billion of sales (National Science Board 1975).[9] An average lag of 7.4 years between the invention and the innovation was identified.[10] One explanation for the longer lag identified in the Gellman study is that their data include only the most significant innovations. It is quite conceivable that a positive relationship exists between significance of innovation and the length of the lag.

The second comparable data base once again involves the Gellman Research Associates (1982), this time for the U.S. Small Business Administration. In their second study, Gellman compiled a total of 635 U.S. innovations, including 45 from the earlier study for the National Science Foundation. The additional 590 innovations were selected from fourteen industry trade journals for the period 1970–

1979. About 43 percent of the sample was selected from the award-winning innovations described in *Industrial Research & Development* magazine.

Despite the obviously different selection and significance criteria applied in the Gellman and Futures Group innovation data bases, two striking similarities emerge. The first is that the distribution of the 635 innovations compiled by the Gellman Research Associates does not differ substantially from the distribution of innovations that is shown in table 2.4. In fact, when the innovations are classified according to the industry groups listed in table 2.4, the same six industries emerge as contributing the largest number of innovations for both the Gellman data as well as for those in the U.S. Small Business Administration Innovation Data Base (compiled by The Futures Group). The rank order varies only slightly. In descending order, the most innovative industries identified in the Gellman data are instruments, machinery (excluding office), industrial electrical equipment, chemicals (excluding drugs), computers and office equipment, fabricated metal products, and motor vehicles and other transportation equipment.[11] For the innovation data we use, which are shown in table 2.4, the most innovative industries in descending order are instruments, machinery (excluding office), computers and office equipment, industrial electrical equipment, fabricated metal products, chemicals (excluding drugs), and communications equipment. While some of the slight differences can be attributed to different significance criteria of the innovations included in each data base, the different time periods may also account for at least some of the variations.

The second striking similarity between the two data bases is that they both identify about the same difference between the small-firm and large-firm innovation rates. While the Gellman data base identified small firms as contributing 2.45 times more innovations per employee than do large firms, the U.S. Small Business Administration Innovation Data Base finds that small firms introduce about 2.38 more innovations per employee than do their larger counterparts.[12]

The third other data source that has attempted to directly measure innovation activity has been compiled at the Science Policy Research Unit (SPRU) at the University of Sussex in the United Kingdom.[13] The SPRU data consist of a survey of 4,378 innovations that were assembled over a period of fifteen years. The survey was formed by writing to experts in each industry and asking them to identify "significant technical innovations that had been successfully commercialised in the United Kingdom since 1945, and to name the firm responsible" (Pavitt et al. 1987, 299). Firm-specific characteristics, including firm size, were then determined through the use of a follow-up questionnaire.

As with the Gellman data, the SPRU innovation data reveal several patterns similar to our data with respect to the distribution across manufacturing industries and across firm sizes. In descending order, the most innovative industries were mechanical engineering, nonelectrical machinery, electrical equipment, chemicals, and instruments. The least innovative industries were printing, paper, and rubber and plastics (Pavitt et al. 1987). The ratio of the share of manufacturing firms' innovations to their shares of employment for the period 1981 to 1983 was greatest (2.07) for firms with between 100 and 199 employees. The second highest ratio (1.90) was for firms with at least 50,000 employees, while the third highest ratio (1.58) was for firms with between 200 and 499 employees. The SPRU data reveal that the relatively high innovative activity of small firms is a new phenomenon that did not emerge until around 1970. That is, in the period 1956–1960 the ratio for the largest firms was about four times greater than it was for firms with between 100 and 199 employees.

U.K. firms with fewer than 200 employees accounted for 31.6 percent of the innovations in instruments, 26.2 percent in nonelectrical machinery, and 17.5 percent in electrical equipment. As table 2.6 shows for our U.S. data, the small-firm innovation share is the highest (50.6 percent) in instruments, followed by nonelectrical machinery (48.5 percent) and electrical equipment (41.1 percent).

Thus, three other data bases that have been compiled to directly measure innovative activity reveal similar patterns with respect to the distribution of innovations across manufacturing industries and between large and small firms.[14] These similarities emerge despite the obviously different methods used to compile the data, especially in terms of sampling and standard of significance. The data we use clearly tend to include innovations of less significance than do the other three data bases. Similarly, while the SPRU data were compiled from the judgments of what constitutes a significant innovation from many different independent experts representing different industries, the U.S. Small Business Administration Innovation Data Base was compiled by just a few people (The Futures Group), who were more likely to apply the same standard of judging an innovation.

2.3   The Firm Size Data Base

The data on firm size that we use throughout this book are drawn from the U.S. Small Business Administration's Small Business Data Base (SBDB). Before discussing the characteristics of the SBDB, we need to understand the reasons for a microdata base by firm size. It is unfortunate that prior to the authorization of the Office of Advocacy of the Small Business Administration by the U.S. Congress in 1976, there was no agency responsible for collecting and disseminating statistics on small firms. Various agencies of the U.S. government, such as the Census Bureau of the U.S. Department of Commerce, do publish statistics on small enterprises (firms), but only at five-year intervals, and then not for all industries. Therefore, before the Office of Advocacy came into existence, no easily accessible, current, and comprehensive data on the U.S. small business sector were available.

While other U.S. government agencies do publish data by size class on a regular basis, such as the employment data of the U.S. Bureau of Labor Statistics, this information does not identify the parent firm of each establishment and is therefore not useful for understanding the contributions of small *firms* as opposed to small *establishments*. When the Small Business Administration began looking for sources of data within the U.S. government to document the contributions of small firms, it essentially found no available current data by ownership category. The Office of Advocacy turned to the Dun and Bradstreet Corporation to fulfill its congressional mandate of disseminating statistics on the state of small business.

The SBDB data are comprised of the U.S. Establishment Longitudinal Microdata (USELM) and the U.S. Enterprise and Establishment Microdata (USEEM) files, which have been derived from the Dun and Bradstreet (DUNS) Market Identifier File (DMI). The essential unit of observation in the data base is an establishment, defined as an economic entity operating at a specific and single location. However, the firm may consist of several establishments.[15] In cases of multiproduct firms, or where the establishments operate in different industries or even sectors, each establishment is classified according to its appropriate four-digit SIC industry.[16] Establishments are then linked by ownership to their parent firms. The establishments are classified by the size of the entire firm, not just their own size.

The USEEM file provides biennial observations on about 4.5 million U.S. business establishments over the period 1976 to 1986. This cov-

ers a changing business population of nearly 20 million establishments. Each file includes the establishment location in terms of state
and county, employment, the primary and secondary industry, the
starting year, sales, organizational status and connection to other
establishments, and the employment of the entire firm (enterprise), if
the establishment belongs to a multi-establishment enterprise.

The distinction between the firm and its constituent establishments
is particularly important in manufacturing. Although over 96 percent
of manufacturing firms in 1984 were comprised of establishments
within a single industry, about 72 percent of employment in manufacturing was in firms with establishments in at least two different industries (Starr 1987).[17]

Storey and Johnson (1987) argue that because the underlying data
have been assembled by a commercial organization whose principal
purpose is to provide credit rating information, the reliability of the
data is probably enhanced. They point out that the data are not based
on confidentiality but rather are publicly available (for a fee). In addition, Dun and Bradstreet has a commercial incentive to provide data
that are both current and accurate. Similarly, the reporting firms
themselves have an incentive to provide accurate information to a
credit rating company.

Nonetheless, the Dun and Bradstreet data have been subjected to
serious criticism. Perhaps one of the most significant weaknesses in
the DUNS data is missing branch records. Because the Dun and Bradstreet files are compiled on the basis of credit rating, branches and
subsidiaries of multi-establishment firms that are unlikely to require
credit independently from the parent firm are often not recorded. It
has been estimated that nearly half of the multi-establishment firms
do not report disaggregated data for all subsidiaries (Storey and Johnson 1987). In one of the first applications of these data, Birch (1981)
dealt with this discrepancy by recalculating the total enterprise employment from the aggregation of the employment recorded in each
affiliated establishment. By contrast, Armington and Odle (1982) re-
calculated the employment level of each affiliated establishment from
the reported enterprise employment level. As Storey and Johnson
(1987) note, the effect resulting from attempts to reconcile this discrepancy between the aggregation of establishment data and the
enterprise data was that Birch tended to understate the extent of
employment in multi-establishment firms, while Armington and
Odle tended to overstate it.

A second problem with the Dun and Bradstreet data is their chronic underrepresentation in industries such as department stores; restaurants; credit agencies; insurance agencies; medical, legal, educational, and social services; and membership organizations that may operate without credit. While most of these industries actually show as many employees as identified in the *County Business Patterns* from the U.S. Bureau of the Census, there are fewer establishments identified by Dun and Bradstreet than appear in the *County Business Patterns*. This is because Dun and Bradstreet does not reveal all of the establishments to the U.S. Small Business Administration.

There are still certain other dynamic weaknesses with respect to nonupdated records in the data base (Storey and Johnson 1987). As Jacobson (1985) found, in a few cases firms and establishments are not included in the data base until several years after they have been established. This leads to a slight understatement of the number of firms and establishments, particularly in rapidly expanding industries (such as certain types of services) and in new industries (such as microcomputers and software-related industries).

In order to correct for at least some of these deficiencies in the DUNS data, the Brookings Institution in conjunction with the Small Business Administration and the National Science Foundation restructured, edited, and supplemented the USEEM with data from other sources.[18] For example, median employment levels by state and four-digit SIC industry from the *County Business Patterns* data were used to estimate the employment figures for the 2 to 3 percent of establishments that did not report data (Armington et al. 1984). More important, a "family tree" is constructed for each firm, identifying each branch and subsidiary. These family trees are then used to reconcile the organizational status and employment figures between member establishments of multi-establishment enterprises. The employment figures for the entire enterprise are compared to those reported by the individual establishments. Any discrepancy arising between the employment reported for the entire firm and the aggregation of all the individual establishments is then corrected either by increasing the total amount of employment attributed to the entire establishment to be consistant with that reported by the individual establishments, or else by imputing proxy branch establishments to represent affiliates implied by the employment reported by the enterprise (Armington and Odle 1983). Thus, it should be clearly understood that the U.S. Small Business Administration undertakes

Table 2.7
Comparison of SBDB employment (thousands of employees) with other
federal data sources according to sector, 1982 (percentages in parentheses)

Sector	Bureau of Labor Statistics (BLS)	Bureau of the Census (CBP)	Small Business Data Base (USEEM)	(USELM)
Mining	1,128	1,188	1,626	1,331
	(1.53)	(1.61)	(1.85)	(1.53)
Construction	3,905	3,941	5,165	4,921
	(5.30)	(5.33)	(5.86)	(5.66)
Manufacturing	18,781	19,572	23,078	23,084
	(25.47)	(26.49)	(26.19)	(26.56)
Transportation, communication, and public utilities	5,082	4,627	5,755	6,026
	(6.89)	(6.26)	(6.53)	(6.93)
Wholesale trade	5,728	5,235	5,916	5,743
	(7.16)	(7.09)	(6.71)	(6.61)
Retail trade	15,179	15,280	16,470	16,207
	(20.59)	(20.68)	(18.69)	(18.64)
Finance, insurance, and real estate	5,341	5,447	6,714	6,400
	(7.24)	(7.37)	(7.62)	(7.36)
Services	19,306	18,582	23,405	23,213
	(26.18)	(25.15)	(26.56)	(26.70)
Total	73,730	73,872	88,129	86,425

Sources: BLS is from the U.S. Department of Labor Statistics, *Employment and
Earnings*, March 1983, annual average data.
CBP is from U.S. Department of Commerce, Bureau of the Census, *Country
Business Patterns*, 1982 U.S. summary, table 1B.
USEEM and USELM are from the U.S. Small Business Administration Data
Base.

substantial modification procedures of the raw Dun and Bradstreet data to at least partially correct for some of the inherent flaws in the DUNS data. These procedures are also more explicitly detailed in U.S. Small Business Administration (1987).

Table 2.7 compares the U.S. Small Business Administration's Small Business Data Base employment data in 1982 with equivalent data from two other U.S. government data sources—The Bureau of Labor Statistics (BLS) employment data and the Bureau of the Census *County Business Patterns* employment data. One reason for the differences among these data sources is the way in which the USEEM file records the owner/operator of sole proprietorships that have employees. While the USEEM file includes owners of such firms as employees of their own firms, the BLS and *County Business Patterns* do not. For this reason, the employment totals in the USEEM file will tend to exceed those in the BLS and *County Business Patterns* data. The difference in aggregate employment for each sector should approximately equal the number of sole proprietorships that have employees. In 1982 there were about 14 million sole proprietorships in the United States, of which about one-third had paid employees. Thus, between 4.5 and 5 million employees account for the difference between the USEEM file and the other federal data sources (Boden and Phillips 1985).[19]

Although the major federal data sources are compared in table 2.7, based on 1982 employment for each of the major sectors of the economy, not much can be inferred regarding the consistency of these data sources in identifying the distribution of firms across different firm-size classes. Such a comparison is made possible in table 2.8, which decomposes the SBDB and BLS employment for six different size-class categories and for each of the eight major sectors. There are two important observations to be made from table 2.8. First, there is nearly an 11 percent difference between the SBDB and BLS employment counts for the entire economy (excluding agriculture, forestry, and fishing). The greatest difference is in the mining sector, while the smallest difference is in the retail trade sector. In manufacturing, which is the focus of this book, the difference in employment counts between the SBDB and BLS is considerable.

The second point is that the firm-size distribution is remarkably consistent between the two data sources. For example, there is only about a three-percentage-point difference in the employment share of large firms (with at least 500 employees) in the manufacturing sector between the SBDB and BLS. For the entire economy, the difference in

Table 2.8
Comparison of SBDB employment with Bureau of Labor Statistics (BLS) according to sectors, 1986 (percentage share listed in parentheses)[a]

	Total	Number of employees in establishments					
		1–9	10–19	20–99	100–499	1–499	500+
Total							
SBDB	90,084,040	12,580,900 (13.96)	9,608,460 (10.67)	26,475,900 (29.39)	21,004,260 (23.32)	69,669,520 (77.34)	20,414,520 (22.66)
BLS	81,203,667	11,341,211 (13.97)	7,884,654 (9.71)	22,028,061 (27.13)	20,365,024 (25.08)	61,618,950 (75.88)	19,584,717 (24.12)
Mining							
SBDB	1,137,000	124,400 (10.94)	102,600 (9.02)	324,300 (28.52)	272,100 (23.93)	823,400 (72.41)	313,600 (27.48)
BLS	832,201	76.126 (9.15)	76,285 (9.17)	244,407 (29.37)	229,784 (27.61)	626,602 (75.3)	205,599 (24.71)
Construction							
SBDB	5,011,200	1,473,500 (29.40)	753,100 (15.03)	1,846,900 (36.86)	709,600 (14.16)	4,783,100 (95.45)	228,100 (4.55)
BLS	4,414,801	1,158,110 (26.23)	760,548 (17.27)	1,597,705 (36.19)	678,870 (15.38)	4,195,233 (95.03)	219,568 (4.97)
Manufacturing							
SBDB	22,812,100	1,042,300 (4.57)	1,055,500 (4.63)	4,973,500 (21.80)	7,304,700 (32.02)	14,376,000 (63.02)	8,436,100 (36.98)
BLS	18,945,093	628,076 (3.32)	786,256 (4.15)	3,713,528 (19.60)	6,206,417 (32.76)	11,334,277 (59.83)	7,610,816 (40.17)

Table 2.8
(continued)

| | Total | Number of employees in establishments | | | | | |
		1–9	10–19	20–99	100–499	1–499	500+
Transportation, communications, and public utilities							
SBDB	6,071,500	519,900 (8.56)	514,500 (8.47)	1,733,700 (28.55)	1,614,000 (26.58)	4,382,100 (72.17)	1,689,400 (27.83)
BLS	5,200,001	427,974 (8.23)	372,126 (7.16)	1,209,909 (23.27)	1,149,911 (22.11)	3,159,920 (60.77)	2,040,081 (39.23)
Wholesale trade							
SBDB	6,261,700	1,642,500 (26.23)	1,291,200 (20.62)	2,013,300 (32.15)	903,900 (14.44)	5,850,900 (93.44)	410,800 (6.56)
BLS	5,694,999	1,114,998 (19.58)	905,969 (15.91)	2,172,454 (38.15)	1,130,058 (19.84)	5,323,479 (93.48)	371,520 (6.52)
Retail trade							
SBDB	17,142,900	3,788,300 (22.10)	2,806,300 (16.37)	6,573,700 (38.35)	3,064,900 (17.88)	16,233,200 (94.69)	909,700 (5.30)
BLS	17,326,603	2,875,548 (16.60)	2,197,709 (12.62)	6,022,943 (34.76)	3,858,302 (22.27)	14,954,502 (86.31)	2,372,101 (13.69)
Finance, insurance, and real estate							
SBDB	7,098,700	1,105,700 (15.58)	1,290,200 (18.18)	1,850,400 (26.12)	1,212,900 (17.09)	5,459,200 (76.9)	1,639,500 (23.10)
BLS	6,140,301	921,326 (15.00)	507,581 (8.27)	1,567,210 (25.52)	1,525,345 (24.84)	4,521,462 (73.63)	1,618,839 (26.36)

Services						
SBDB	24,548,700	2,884,300 (11.75)	1,795,000 (7.31)	7,160,100 (29.17)	5,922,200 (24.12)	17,761,600 (72.35)	6,787,100 (27.65)
BLS	22,649,668	4,139,053 (18.27)	2,278,180 (10.06)	5,499,905 (24.28)	5,586,337 (24.66)	17,503,475 (77.28)	5,146,193 (22.72)

Sources: U.S. Small Business Administration, Small Business Data Base (USEEM file). U.S. Department of Labor, Bureau of Labor Statistics, unpublished data prepared under contract for the U.S. Small Business Administration, 1988. Table adapted from Brown and Phillips (1989, table 1).

a. Data exclude agriculture, forestry, and fishing.

Table 2.9
Distribution of firms according to employment size for the enterprise
statistics and SBDB data, 1982[a]

Number of employees in firm	Enterprise statistics		Small Business Administration	
	Number	Percent	Number	Percent
1–19	3,606,593	91.31	3,222,523	87.97
20–99	320,370	7.53	363,620	9.93
1–99	3,926,963	98.84	3,586,143	97.90
100–499	42,468	1.00	63,667	1.74
1–499	3,969,431	99.83	3,648,810	99.63
500+	7,030	0.17	13,393	0.37
Total	3,976,461	100.00	3,663,203	100.00

Sources: U.S. Department of Commerce, Bureau of the Census, *1982 Enterprise Statistics*, ES82-1 (Washington, D.C.: U.S. Government Printing Office, October 1986), table 3, and U.S. Small Business Administration Data Base. Adapted from U.S. Small Business Administration (1988, table 5.2).
a. Data exclude farm enterprises.

the large-firm employment shares is less than two percentage points. Thus, while there are considerable differences between the absolute employment counts in the SBDB and BLS data sources, the distribution across firm-size classes is quite consistent.

While tables 2.7 and 2.8 compare the employment data of the SBDB with those from other sources, it is also possible to compare the number of U.S. enterprises recorded by different data sources. The most comprehensive source of enterprise data is the Internal Revenue Service, which listed over 17 million nonfarm enterprises in 1986. A second source of enterprise statistics is the U.S. Department of Commerce, Bureau of the Census, which surveys individual business establishments and compiles the *Enterprise Statistics*. Like the SBDB, the *Enterprise Statistics* classifies the establishment according to the size of the affiliate enterprise. The *Enterprise Statistics* generally does not record home-based businesses or business activity in transportation, communications, utilities, finance, insurance, or real estate. In 1982 the *Enterprise Statistics* recorded 4,256,143 enterprises, while the number of enterprises recorded by the SBDB was 3,663,203. One reason for this difference in enterprise counts is that the SBDB does not generally include firms that have been established for less than

Table 2.10
The small-firm employment shares[a] (percent) for the SBDB (USEEM) and
enterprise statistics data according to sector, 1982

Sector	Small Business Administration	Enterprise statistics
Agriculture	86.3	92.0
Mining	45.4	55.8
Construction	82.8	81.4
Manufacturing	30.5	28.7
Wholesale	87.0	87.6
Retail	63.1	61.7
Services	53.5	77.2

Sources: The USEEM data are from the U.S. Small Business Administration
Data Base. The Enterprise Statistics are from the U.S. Department of Commerce, Bureau of the Census, *1982 Enterprise Statistics*, ES82–1 (Washington, D.C.: U.S. Government Printing Office, October 1986).
a. A small firm is defined as an enterprise with fewer than 500 employees.

two years, while the *Enterprise Statistics* includes a greater percentage of newly established firms.

The distribution of firms according to employment size in 1982 is compared for the SBDB data and the *Enterprise Statistics* data in table 2.9. The *Enterprise Statistics* and SBDB data sources reveal very similar, although not identical, distributions of firm size. At least some of the differences have been explained by MacDonald (1986), who found that Dun and Bradstreet tends to assign more small firms to manufacturing than does the Bureau of the Census. For the large firms that he examined, however, he found the two data sources to be quite similar.

While table 2.9 compares the SBDB and *Enterprise Statistics* data on the basis of enterprise counts, it is also possible to make a comparison across different firm sizes for shares of employment. Thus, the 1982 employment shares of small firms, defined as enterprises with fewer than 500 employees, are compared across sectors for these two data sources in table 2.10. The *Enterprise Statistics* and SBDB data report similar small-firm employment shares for the construction, manufacturing, wholesale, and retail sectors. There is considerable disparity between the two data sources in agriculture, mining, and services. These differences are due to different methods of coverage used in the two sources. For example, the *Enterprise Statistics* only partially cover the service sector, while the SBDB data do not fully cover agriculture. In addition, many mining firms in the SBDB are reported in petroleum refining in the manufacturing sector.

The comparison of the SBDB data with two other major federal data sources has revealed that, while the absolute counts for employment and establishments vary considerably, the firm-size distribution is remarkably consistent between the different data sources. These results apply to both establishment and employment measures, as well as for comparisons based on the major sectors within the economy.

2.4 Conclusion

This chapter has been concerned with three major facets of the new sources of data that are the basis for the subsequent empirical analysis in this book. First, these two major data bases—one involving a direct measure of innovation activity by firm size and the other providing measures of economic activity by firm size—were introduced and described. Second, critical qualifications concerning the applicability of the new data sources were provided. Third, these new data bases were compared to more traditional sources of data that have been used to measure similar phenomena.

While this chapter has presented the new data bases on innovation and firm size, virtually no attempt was made to relate them to each other. The purpose of the following chapters is to explicitly investigate the relationships between innovation activity and firm size.

3

Innovation, Market Structure, and Firm Size

3.1 Introduction

Surprisingly little has been established in the economics literature to identify those conditions and market environments that are conducive to innovation activity and those conditions that retard it.[1] Further, as pointed out in the previous chapter, the empirical research has tended to focus upon the innovative activity of large firms while overlooking that contributed by small firms.[2] The purpose of this chapter is to identify the major determinants of innovation and to examine whether they affect small firms differently than large firms.

As Kuznets (1962) observed, perhaps the greatest obstacle to understanding the role of innovation in economic processes has been the lack of meaningful measures of innovative inputs and outputs. More recently, there has been the development of new data sources measuring different aspects of technical change. These new sources of data have included measures of patented inventions (Hall et al. 1986; Jaffe 1986; Pakes and Griliches 1980), better measures of research and development (Bound et al. 1984; and Scherer 1982a), and stock market values of inventive output (Pakes 1985). While several of these new and improved data sources have been used to test the hypotheses that innovative activity increases along with firm size and the extent to which the market can be characterized by imperfect competition, there have not been many studies able to apply a more direct measure of the innovative output. For example, the limitations of using patent data were significant enough to require supplementing them with renewal data (Pakes and Schankerman 1984).

In this chapter we extend the literature on new measures examining technical change by applying the more direct measure of innovative activity using the new data that were introduced in chapter 2. We present a model that suggests that innovative output is influenced by the amount of R&D expenditures and the extent to which the economic rents accruing from innovation can be appropriated. The econometric analysis enables three hypotheses to be tested: (1) the degree to which R&D expenditures produce innovative output is conditioned by the ease of appropriability; (2) as Winter (1984) suggests, small- and large-firm innovative activity responds to distinct technological and economic regimes; and (3) large firms have the innovative advantage in markets characterized by imperfect competition, but small firms have the innovative advantage in markets more closely approximating the competitive model.

The major hypotheses and empirical findings regarding the relationships between innovative activity and firm size, and innovative activity and market structure, are examined in the second section. Cross-section regressions are estimated for the 1982 total innovation rate, large-firm innovation rate, and the small-firm innovation rate in the third section. In the fourth section, a model is presented estimating the difference between the large- and small-firm innovation rates. In the last section, a summary and conclusion are provided. Not only do we find little support for the hypothesis that innovative activity is promoted in highly concentrated markets, but we find considerable evidence suggesting that innovative activity for small firms responds to a different technological and economic environment than does innovative activity for large firms.

3.2 Market Structure, Firm Size, and Innovation: Previous Findings

As Kamien and Schwartz (1975), Scherer (1980), Baldwin and Scott (1987), and others have pointed out, two central hypotheses regarding innovative activity have emerged. The first is that innovation activity is promoted by large firms and inhibited by small ones. The second is that a market structure characterized by imperfect competition is more conducive to technical change than is a market more closely approximating the model of perfect competition.

"Who innovates more—the large or the small firm?" This question has generally been the essential focus of the first hypothesis.[3] While neoclasical economics considered the spur of competition from an industry comprised only of small firms to be uniquely suited to promote technological change, Schumpeter (1950) provided a dissenting view. The naivety of the traditional theory has been challenged by Galbraith (1956, 86), who argues, "There is no more pleasant fiction than that technical change is the product of the matchless ingenuity of the small man forced by competition to employ his wits to better his neighbor. Unhappily, it is a fiction."

Despite Scherer's warning (1980, 418) that, "the search for a firm size uniquely and unambiguously optimal for invention and innovation is misguided," both theoretical and empirical evidence defending each side of the debate continues to accumulate. Two polemic positions have emerged regarding the relative advantages of large- and small-firm innovative activity. On the one hand, classical and neoclassical economic doctrine imply that relatively small firms, spurred by the competitive motive, are the most conducive to technological progress. On the other hand, the Schumpeterian view argues that large enterprises are uniquely endowed to exploit innovative opportunities. According to Schumpeter (1950, 106), "What we have got to accept is that (the large-scale establishment) has come to be the most powerful engine of progress."[4] The Schumpeterian[5] view argues that market predominance is a prerequisite to undertaking the risks and uncertainties associated with innovation. It is the possibility of acquiring economic quasi-rents that serves as the catalyst for large-firm innovation.

Five factors favoring the innovative advantage of large firms have been identified in the literature. First is the argument that innovative activity requires a high fixed cost. As Comanor (1967) observes, R&D typically involves a "lumpy" process that yields scale economies. Similarly, Galbraith (1956, 87) argues, "Because development is costly, it follows that it can be carried on only by a firm that has the resources which are associated with considerable size." Second, only firms that are large enough to attain at least temporary market power will choose innovation as a means for profit maximization (Kamien and Schwartz 1975). Third, R&D is a risky investment; small firms engaging in R&D make themselves vulnerable by investing a large proportion of their resources in a single project. However, their larger counterparts can reduce the risk accompanying innovation through diversification into simultaneous research projects. The larger firm is also more likely to find an economic application of the uncertain outcomes resulting from innovative activity (Nelson 1959). Fourth, scale economies in production may provide scope economies for R&D. Scherer (1980) notes that economies of scale in promotion and in distribution facilitate the penetration of new products, thus enabling larger firms to enjoy a greater profit potential from innovation. Fifth, an innovation yielding cost reductions of a given percentage results in higher profit margins for larger firms than for smaller firms.

The literature has conversely identified factors that place the small firm vis-à-vis the large firm in an advantageous position for undertaking innovative activity. These factors generally emanate from the difference in management structures between large and small firms. For example, Scherer (1980) argues that the bureaucratic organization of large firms is not conducive to undertaking risky R&D. The decision to innovate must survive layers of bureaucratic resistance, where an inertia regarding risk results in a bias against undertaking new projects. However, in the small firm the decision to innovate is made by relatively few people. Second, innovative activity may flourish the most in environments free of bureaucratic constraints. Thus, a number of small-firm ventures have benefited from the exodus of researchers who felt thwarted by the managerial restraints in a larger firm. Finally, it has been argued that while the larger firms reward the best researchers by promoting them out of research to management positions, the smaller firms place innovative activity at the center of their competitive strategy (Phillips 1965).

Scherer (1988b, 4–5) has summarized the advantages small firms may have in contributing innovations:

Smaller enterprises make their impressive contributions to innovation because of several advantages they possess compared to larger-size corporations. One important strength is that they are less bureaucratic, without layers of "abominable no-men" who block daring ventures in a more highly structured organization. Second, and something that is often overlooked, many advances in technology accumulate upon a myriad of detailed inventions involving individual components, materials, and fabrication techniques. The sales possibilities for making such narrow, detailed advances are often too modest to interest giant corporations. An individual entrepreneur's juices will flow over a new product or process with sales prospects in the millions of dollars per year, whereas few large corporations can work up much excitement over such small fish, nor can they accommodate small ventures easily into their organizational structures. Third, it is easier to sustain a fever pitch of excitement in small organizations, where the links between challenges, staff, and potential rewards are tight. "All-nighters" through which tough technical problems are solved expeditiously are common.

Most of the empirical studies examining the relationship between firm size and innovation have had to rely on a proxy measure of innovative activity. These measures have typically involved either some measure of an input into the innovative process, such as R&D, or else a proxy measure of innovative output, such as the number of patented inventions. A clear limitation in using R&D measures is that they represent only the resources allocated toward trying to produce innovative output, but not the actual amount of resulting innovative activity. That is, R&D is an input and not an output in the innovation process. The reliability of patent measures has also been questioned because not all patented inventions prove to be innovations, and many innovations are never patented. According to Scherer (1983a, 107–108)," [T]he quantity and quality of industry patenting may depend upon chance, how readily a technology lends itself to patent protection, and business decision-makers' varying perceptions of how much advantage they will derive from patent rights. Not much of a systematic nature is known about these phenomena, which can be characterized as differences in the propensity to patent."

Scherer (1983a) found the lowest propensity to patent, based on the ratio of patents to R&D expenditures, in the motor vehicles, other transportation equipment, aircraft, and office equipment industries. Thus, even as new and superior sources of patent data have been used (Hall et al. 1986; Jaffe 1986; and Pakes and Griliches 1980), the reliability of these data as measures of innovative activity has been challenged. For example, Pakes and Griliches (1980, 378) observe that "patents are a flawed measure (of innovative output) particularly since not all new innovations are patented and since patents differ greatly in their economic impact."

The plethora of empirical studies relating R&D and patents to firm size is most thoroughly reviewed in Baldwin and Scott (1987). In fact, while there are considerable ambiguities and inconsistencies in the results, it does seem that the studies relating firm size to R&D inputs have generally reached a different conclusion than have those relating firm size to the number of patented inventions. While some studies have found that expenditures on R&D increase proportionately with firm size, and others have found that they actually increase more than proportionately with firm size, there is little evidence that this relationship is anything less than proportional. Of course, different studies applying different measures of R&D for varying coverages of firm sizes have, not surprisingly, generated somewhat different results. Still, overall the empirical evidence seems to confirm Scherer's (1982b, 234–235) conclusion that the results "tilt on the side of supporting the Schumpeterian Hypothesis that size is conducive to vigorous conduct of R&D." By contrast, the scant empirical evidence relating patent activity to firm size seems to suggest that the generation of patents increases at a less than proportional rate along with firm size.

Although a complete review of the empirical literature examining the relationship between R&D and firm size is available in the Baldwin and Scott (1987) volume, several of the studies should be emphasized here. Using the U.S. Federal Trade Commission's Line of Business Data, Scherer (1984b) was able to estimate the elasticity of R&D spending with respect to firm sales for 196 industries. He found evidence of increasing returns to scale (an elasticity greater than one) for about one-fifth of the industries, constant returns to scale for 71 percent of the industries, and diminishing returns (an elasticity less than one) in 8 percent of the industries. Scherer's results were somewhat different from his 1980 (p. 420) observation that R&D effort (R&D expenditures as a percentage of sales) tends to be relatively independent of firm size within a sample of the largest U.S. firms, but consistent with the findings of Soete (1979) that R&D intensity increases along with firm size (again for a sample of the largest U.S. firms).

While the Scherer and Soete studies were restricted to relatively large firms, Bound et al. (1984) included a much wider spectrum of firm sizes in their sample of 1,492 firms from the 1976 COMPUSTAT data. They found that R&D increases more than proportionately along with firm size for smaller firms, but that a fairly linear relationship exists for larger firms. Despite the somewhat more ambiguous findings in still other studies (such as Comanor 1967; Mansfield 1968 and Mansfield et al. 1971), the empirical evidence seems to generally support Scherer's contention for mild support of the Schumpeterian hypothesis that research effort is positively associated with firm size.

The few studies relating patents to firm size are considerably less ambiguous. Here the findings unequivocally suggest that "the evidence leans weakly agains the Schumpeterian conjecture that the largest sellers are especially fecund sources of patented inventions" (Scherer 1982b, 235). In one of the most important studies, Scherer (1965b) used the *Fortune* annual survey of the 500 largest U.S. industrial corporations. He related the 1955 firm sales to the number of patents in 1959 for 448 firms. Scherer found that the number of patented inventions increases less than proportionately along with firm size. Scherer's results were confirmed by Bound et al. (1984) in the study mentioned above. Basing their study on 2,852 companies and 4,553 patenting entities, they determined that the small firms (with less than $10 million in sales) accounted for 4.3 percent of the sales from the entire sample, but 5.7 percent of the patents.

How is it that R&D inputs tend to increase more than proportionately along with firm size, but patented inventions tend to increase less than proportionately along with firm size? One answer to this apparent paradox is offered by Scherer (1983a), who again used the U.S. Federal Trade Commission's Line of Business Data to examine the relationship between R&D and patents, this time for 124 separate industries. He found evidence of increasing returns to scale for R&D in producing patented inventions in only 15.3 percent of the industries, but decreasing returns in one-quarter of the industries. Scherer's results would seem to indicate that diminishing returns for R&D exist in generating patents. That is, while large firms may exhibit greater R&D effort, decreasing returns to R&D result in the number of patented inventions increasing with firm size, but only at a decreasing rate. Scherer (1983a, 115–116), however, warned that "this evidence on patent output–R&D input relationships could have either of two rather different interpretations: that the largest firms in an industry generate fewer patentable inventions per dollar of R&D than their smaller counterparts, or that they choose to patent fewer inventions of a possibly proportionate or even disproportionate inventive output."

Because the innovation data we use in this book are aggregated to the industry level, the insights into the exact relationship between firm size and innovative output are constrained. Instead, the data are more conducive to yielding information about the relationship between market structure and innovative activity. In comparison to the number of studies investigating the relationship between firm size and technological change, those examining the market structure–technological change relationship are what Baldwin and Scott (1987, 89) term "minuscule" in number. The most comprehensive and insightful evidence has been made possible by utilizing the Federal Trade Commission's Line of Business Data, so we will concentrate on these studies.

Scherer (1983b) used the 1974 FTC Line of Business Survey to examine the relationship between R&D intensity and concentration. Using 236 manufacturing industry categories, which are defined at both the three- and four-digit SIC level, he found that company R&D expenditures divided by sales was positively related to the 1974 four-firm concentration ratio. Scherer (1983b, 225) concluded that "although one cannot be certain, it appears that the advantages a high market share confers in appropriating R&D benefits provide the most likely explanation of the observed R&D–concentration associations."

Scott (1984) also used the FTC Line of Business Survey Data and found the U-shaped relationship between market concentration and R&D that Scherer (1980) had earlier described. However, when he controlled for the fixed effects for two-digit SIC industries, no significant relationship could be found between concentration and R&D. These results are consistent with a series of studies by Levin et al. (1985, 1987), Levin and Reiss (1984), and Cohen et al. (1987). Using data from a survey of R&D executives in 130 industries, which were matched with FTC Line of Business industry groups, Cohen et al. (1987) and Levin et al. (1987) found little support for the contention that industrial concentration is a significant and systematic determinant of R&D effort.

Although these studies have produced somewhat ambiguous results, finding either a positive relationship between concentration and R&D or else no significant relationship between concentration and R&D, a negative relationship is usually not identified. Thus, there might exist some uncertainty about the exact nature of the relationship, but it appears unlikely that lower levels of concentration are associated with greater R&D effort.

While it has been hypothesized that firms in concentrated industries are better able to capture the rents accruing from an innovation, and therefore have a greater incentive to undertake innovative activity, there are other market structure variables that also influence the ease with which economic rents can be appropriated. For example, Comanor (1967) argued and found that, based on a measure of minimum efficient scale, there is less R&D effort (average number of research personnel divided by total employment) in industries with very low scale economies. However, he also found that in industries with a high minimum efficient scale, R&D effort was also relatively low. Comanor interpreted his results to suggest that where entry barriers are relatively low,[6] there is little incentive to innovate, since the entry subsequent to an innovation would quickly erode any economic rents. At the same time, in industries with high entry barriers, the absence of potential entry may reduce the incentive to innovate.

Comanor (1964, 1967) also argues that the extent to which products can be differentiated induces innovative activity by creating product niches. According to Comanor (1967, 646), "Product differentiation, it is well known, has the effect of insulating submarkets and creating entry barriers. While research expenditures may serve many functions, an important one is to foster and promote a rapid rate of new product introduction, which then serves to facilitate the achievement of differentiation."

3.3 Market Structure and Innovation Activity

Jaffee (1986), Scherer (1982a), and Mansfield (1981), among others, have assumed that innovative output is determined by innovation-inducing inputs in the previous period. Winter (1984) has argued that knowledge is perhaps the most important input into the production of innovations. A stable relationship between the investment by firms in R&D and the production of new economically useful knowledge has generally been assumed to exist in the literature. While new knowledge cannot be directly observed, some of its consequences are recognized. New knowledge leads to patents, innovations, and increasing productivity (Pakes and Griliches 1980; Pakes 1985; Griliches 1986). Economically useful knowledge in any industry may come from more than one source. R&D represents knowledge that is available only to the firm that produced it, but a second source of knowledge is drawn from firms in the same industry (Jaffe 1986; Iwai 1984a; Ziegler 1985). Finally, a third source is public knowledge. One source of similar knowledge comes from government and nonprofit enterprises (Winter 1984). The firm also draws upon the external knowledge environment inherent in the prior education and experience of its personnel.

We test the hypothesis that innovation activity is determined by factors creating knowledge, the ease of appropriability, and by firm size, through estimating the following model:

$$TIE = \beta_0 + \beta_1 RD + \beta_2 K/O + \beta_3 CR + \beta_4 UNION + \beta_5 AD/S$$
$$+ \beta_6 PILF + \beta_7 SKILL + \mu, \qquad (3.1)$$

where the dependent variable, TIE, is the innovation rate or number of innovations introduced in the four-digit SIC industry in 1982, divided by industry employment (thousands). As mentioned in chapter 2, where a complete explanation of the innovation data base can be found, the average period of time between the invention and the innovation was 4.3 years. Because 1982 innovations typically resulted from an invention in 1977, firms were most likely responding to market structure characteristics prior to 1978.[7]

Innovative intensity is assumed to result from three different sources of knowledge: 1977 company R&D expenditures/sales (RDC), government-supported R&D expenditures, which combine with RDC to comprise total R&D expenditures/ₐales (RDT), and the extent of skilled labor in the industry (SKILL). As virtually every empirical study relating innovative output to R&D input has found, we expect innovation activity to respond positively to R&D. The extent of skilled labor (defined as professional and kindred workers, plus managers and administrators, plus craftsmen and kindred workers) as a percentage of total employment reflects human capital and is expected to be positively related to innovative activity. Four different surrogates for appropriability included in the model have appeared in numerous previous empirical studies. These are the 1977 capital–output ratio (K/O), defined as gross assets divided by value-of-shipments; the 1977 four-firm concentration ratio (CR); the advertising intensity (AD/S), which is defined as advertising expenditures divided by 1977 value-of-shipments; and the mean percentage of employees in the industry belonging to a union between 1973 and 1975 (UNION). More recently, several models have been developed arguing that unions capture rents from intangible capital investments, and, in particular, those accruing from innovation-producing R&D (Connolly, Hirsch, and Hirschey 1986; Hirsch and Link 1986). To the extent to which unions are successful in such rent-seeking activities, the ease of appropriability by the innovative firm is clearly reduced. Therefore, a negative relationship between UNION and TIE is expected.

The measure of firm size is PILF, defined as the percentage of an industry that is accounted for by firms with more than 500 employees in 1977. The Schumpeterian Hypothesis implies that PILF will be positively related to innovative activity. Finally, μ is stochastic disturbance. All variable sources are listed in appendix A.

By substituting the large-firm innovation rate (LIE) and small-firm innovation rate (SIE) into equation (3.1), the hypothesis by Winter

(1984) that two technological regimes exist can be examined. According to Winter (1984, 267), "An entrepreneurial regime is one that is favorable to innovative entry and unfavorable to innovative activity by established firms; a routinized regime is one in which the conditions are the other way around." To the extent to which innovations by small and large firms emanate from different technological regimes, a difference in the parameters in the SIE and LIE equations would offer support for Winter's hypothesis that large- and small-firm innovations are promoted under different economic and technological conditions.[8] For example, Winter argues that the greater the extent of human capital in an industry, the greater will be the innovative advantage of small firms relative to large firms.[9]

Using the total innovation rate in 1982 as the dependent variable, the cross-section regressions for 247 four-digit SIC manufacturing industries are shown in table 3.1. While equation 1 uses the measure of company expenditures on R&D, equation 2 uses total expenditures on R&D. Not surprisingly, RDC in equation 1 is found to exert a positive influence on innovative activity. There is one major result that does not lend support to the hypothesis that innovative activity is promoted by imperfect competition. The negative coefficient of CR suggests that lower, and not higher, levels of concentration tend to be associated with increased innovation activity.

There is also one result that is consistent with the hypothesis that innovative activity is positively related to firm size. The positive coefficient of PILF indicates that the greater the proportion of an industry consisting of firms with more than 500 employees, the greater the innovation activity. Of the other variables representing the ease of appropriability, only UNION is negatively associated with the total number of innovations, providing support for the Hirsch and Link (1986) hypothesis. One result should be noted in equation 1. The negative and statistically significant coefficient of K/O does provide evidence that, as hypothesized by Comanor (1967), innovative activity tends to be reduced in highly capital-intensive industries.

In our 1988b paper we estimate a model similar to that in table 3.1 but with a considerably different specification. Rather than estimating the total innovation rates as the dependent variable, we estimated the total number of innovations. Because the specification was derived from a production-function model, the log of both sides of the equation was taken. However, the results that emerged were virtually identical to those presented in table 3.1. The only difference is that

Table 3.1
Regressions of total innovation rates (*t*-statistics listed in parentheses)[a]

	1	2
RDC	0.1773	—
	(8.2448)**	
RDT	—	0.0738
		(3.9412)**
K/O	−0.2981	−0.2147
	(−1.6903)*	(−1.1389)
CR	−0.0052	−0.0048
	(−3.1534)**	(−2.6754)**
UNION	−0.0032	−0.0054
	(−2.0617)**	(−3.3056)**
AD/S	23.8900	23.8440
	(1.4136)	(1.2847)
PILF	0.2372	0.4140
	(1.6155)	(2.6008)**
SKILL	0.3735	0.6132
	(1.2803)	(1.8236)*
Intercept	0.2072	0.2123
	(1.7489)*	(1.5968)
Sample size	247	247
R^2	0.358	0.225
F	19.012**	9.931**

Note: *Significant at the 90 percent level of confidence, two-tailed test. **Significant at the 95 percent level of confidence, two-tailed test.
a. The dependent variable is the total number of innovations divided by industry employment.

K/O is significant in equation 1 of table 3.1, whereas it was not significant when the double-log form was used and the log of the total number of innovations was estimated rather than the innovation rate. Thus, the results appear to be quite robust with respect to the specification of the regression equation.

Table 3.2 shows the results for analogous regressions where the large-firm innovation rate (LIE) and small-firm innovation rate (SIE) are the dependent variables. CR, K/O, AD/S, and perhaps PILF have disparate relationships with small- and large-firm innovation activity. While CR is negatively related to the innovative activity of large firms, it apparently has no effect on that of small firms. By constrast, there is at least some evidence suggesting that the small-firm innovation rate

Table 3.2
Regressions of large-and small-firm innovation rates (*t*-statistics listed in parentheses)[a]

Equation	RDT	RDC	CR	K/O	UNION	AD/S	PILF	SKILL	Intercept	R²	F
1	0.0445	—	-0.0045	-0.0548	0.0031	27.6970	0.3066	0.5207	0.1249	0.145	5.783**
(LIE)	(2.6455)**		(-2.7801)**	(-0.3232)	(-2.0991)**	(1.6605)*	(2.1432)**	(1.7231)*	(1.0450)		
2	0.1557	—	-0.0043	-0.6716	-0.0097	-12.1640	1.1570	1.2595	-0.0211	0.186	7.786**
(SIE)	(3.4534)**		(-1.0085)	(-1.4808)	(-2.4470)**	(-0.2725)	(3.0219)**	(1.5573)**	(-0.0659)		
3	—	0.1296	-0.0043	-0.1007	-0.0013	27.6810	0.1626	0.2696	0.1372	0.253	11.574**
(LIE)		(6.5331)**	(-3.1919)**	(-0.6384)	(-0.9345)**	(1.7759)*	(1.2011)	(1.0020)	(1.2554)		
4	—	0.3666	-0.0051	-0.8279	-0.0050	-12.0530	0.7961	0.7877	-0.0368	0.287	13.741**
(SIE)		(6.8967)**	(-1.2514)	(-1.9584)*	(-1.3223)	(-0.2885)	(2.1937)**	(1.0920)	(-0.1256)		

Note: *Statistically significant at the 90 percent level of confidence, two-tailed test. **Statistically significant at the 95 percent level of confidence, two-tailed test.
a. The dependent variables are the number of large-firm innovations divided by large-firm employment (LIE), and the number of small-firm innovations divided by small-firm employment (SIE).

is negatively related to capital intensity, but there is no relationship between K/O and LIE. Although AD/S is positively associated with large-firm innovation, it is apparently not related to SIE. In the first two equations, PILF is positively and significantly related to both LIE and SIE. However, when the company R&D measure is used in equations 3 and 4, PILF is found to be strongly related to small-firm innovation activity and not related to large-firm innovation activity. This suggests that, ceteris paribus, the greater the extent to which an industry is composed of large firms, the greater will be the innovative activity, but that increased innovative activity will tend to emanate more from the small firms than from the large firms. Perhaps this indicates that, in industries composed predominantly of large firms, the existing small firms must resort to a strategy of innovation in order to remain viable. This is consistent with the findings of Caves and Pugel (1980) that smaller firms in an industry tend to perform better if they use different strategies than those followed by the larger firms.[10]

3.4 Innovation and Firm Size

While the model and analysis in the previous section address the relationship between market structure and innovation, the essential question raised by the other central hypothesis, "Which firm size is more innovative?", is left unanswered. By directly comparing the large-firm innovation rate with the small-firm innovation rate, the relationship between innovation and firm size is addressed in this section. A regression model is presented estimating DIE, defined as the difference between the large-firm innovation rate (LIE) and the small-firm innovation rate (SIE), DIE = LIE-SIE, where the innovation rate is defined, as before, as the number of innovations per employee (thousands) in a four-digit SIC industry.

That the average innovation rate of small firms was considerably higher than that of large firms in 1982, as explained in chapter 2, does not imply that the answer to the question, "Which firm size is more innovative?" is unequivocally "the small firm." Rather, table 3.3, which shows the forty industries with the greatest differences between the large- and small-firm innovation rates, implies that the correct answer is: "It depends on the particular industry." For example, in the tire industry, the large-firm innovation rate exceeded the small-firm innovation rate by 8.46, or by about 8 innovations per 1,000 em-

Table 3.3
The industries with the largest differences between the large- and small-firm
innovation rates[a]

Industry	LIE	SIE	DIE[b]
Tires and inner tubes	8.4615	0.0000	8.4615
Agricultural chemicals	2.2642	0.0000	2.2642
General industrial machinery	2.2041	0.3939	1.8101
Food products machinery	2.0109	0.6704	1.3405
Ammunition, except for small arms	1.2281	0.0000	1.2281
Cottonseed oil mills	1.1111	0.0000	1.1111
Cheese, natural and processed	1.1258	0.0862	1.0396
Wet corn milling	1.0000	0.0000	1.0000
Storage batteries	0.9649	0.0000	0.9649
Converted paper products	0.9848	0.0617	0.9231
Truck and bus bodies	0.7643	0.0000	0.7643
Paper industries machinery	0.8696	0.1053	0.7643
Metal office furniture	1.1628	0.4000	0.7628
Woodworking machinery	0.7500	0.0000	0.7500
Building paper and board mills	0.6452	0.0000	0.6154
Pens and mechanical pencils	0.6154	0.0000	0.6154
Flat glass	0.5882	0.0000	0.5882
Raw cane sugar	0.5455	0.0000	0.5455
Industrial furnaces and ovens	1.6667	1.1250	0.5417
Primary metal products	1.3793	0.9375	0.4418
Scales and balances, except laboratory	0.8511	8.7500	−7.8989
Electronic computing equipment	0.9570	8.2246	−7.2676
Process control instruments	1.8785	9.0291	−7.1507
Synthetic rubber	0.0000	6.6667	−6.6667
Fluid meters and counting devices	0.4380	4.5455	−4.1075
Engineering and scientific instruments	1.5751	5.5333	−3.9582
Measuring and controlling devices	0.1442	3.9130	−3.7688
Gum and wood chemicals	0.2500	3.7500	−3.5000
Primary copper	0.0000	3.3333	−3.3333
Industrial controls	0.3538	3.5385	−3.1847
Surface active agents	0.5405	3.4483	−2.9077
Power-driven hand tools	0.5512	3.0435	−2.4923
Instruments to measure electricity	0.5534	2.9560	−2.4026
Surgical and medical instruments	0.9524	3.0769	−2.1245
Plastics materials and resins	0.5894	2.3810	−1.7916

Table 3.3
(continued)

Industry	LIE	SIE	DIE[b]
Transformers	0.1344	1.8033	−1.6689
Electric lamps	0.0000	1.5789	−1.5789
Industrial trucks and tractors	0.6701	2.1277	−1.4576
Measuring and dispensing pumps	0.0000	1.4286	−1.4286
Environmental controls	0.6452	2.0408	−1.3957

a. The twenty industries where the large-firm innovation rate (LIE) most greatly exceeds the small-firm innovation rate (SIE), and the twenty industries where the small-firm innovation rate most greatly exceeds the large-firm innovation rate. The innovation rate is measured as the number of innovations divided by total employment.
b. DIE = LIE − SIE.

ployees. The large difference in the tire industry is explained by the extremely high innovation rate in the large firms, 8.46, and the extremely low innovation rate in the small firms, 0.00.

The types of industries where the LIE most exceeds the SIE appear to the different from the types of industries where the SIE most exceeds the LIE. Of the twenty industries where the SIE exceeds the LIE, shown in table 3.3, seven are within the two-digit SIC sector 38 (instruments and related products). Similarly, five other industries are within sector 35 (nonelectrical machinery), four are within sector 28 (chemicals and chemical products), and three are within sector 36 (electric and electronic equipment). In fact, only one of the twenty industries lies outside these four two-digit sectors. This suggests that the industries where small firms have the innovative advantage are of a different type than the industries where large firms have the innovative advantage.

To examine the extent to which consistent patterns of the relative innovative advantage between large- and small-firm innovation rates exist within broad two-digit sectors, table 3.4 shows the number and percentage of industries where the LIE exceeds the SIE, where the SIE exceeds the LIE, and where the SIE and the LIE are equal. For example, of the forty-seven four-digit industries in the two-digit food sector, the LIE exceeds the SIE in twenty industries, the SIE exceeds the LIE in thirteen industries, and in fourteen industries the LIE and the SIE are identical, presumably zero. In some sectors, large firms contri-

Table 3.4
The number of industries where large-firm innovation rate (LIE) exceeds small-firm innovation rate (SIE) for two-digit SIC sectors (percentages in parentheses)[a]

Sector	Number of industries where LIE > SIE	Number of industries where SIE > LIE	Number of industries where LIE = SIE
Food	20 (42.55)	13 (27.66)	14 (29.79)
Tobacco	1 (25.00)	0 (0.00)	3 (75.00)
Textiles	2 (6.67)	4 (13.33)	24 (80.00)
Apparel	3 (9.09)	3 (9.09)	27 (81.82)
Lumber	3 (17.65)	1 (5.88)	13 (76.47)
Furniture	4 (30.77)	5 (38.46)	4 (30.77)
Paper	10 (58.82)	4 (23.53)	3 (17.65)
Printing	5 (29.41)	4 (23.53)	8 (47.06)
Chemicals	8 (28.57)	15 (53.57)	5 (17.86)
Petroleum	1 (20.00)	2 (40.00)	2 (40.00)
Rubber	3 (50.00)	1 (16.67)	2 (33.33)
Leather	1 (9.09)	3 (27.27)	7 (63.64)
Stone, clay, and glass	4 (14.81)	8 (29.63)	15 (55.56)
Primary metals	7 (26.92)	8 (30.77)	11 (42.31)
Fabricated metal products	11 (30.56)	15 (41.67)	10 (27.78)
Machinery (nonelectrical)	12 (27.27)	29 (65.91)	3 (6.82)
Electrical equipment	9 (24.32)	22 (59.46)	6 (16.22)
Transportation equipment	9 (52.94)	6 (35.29)	2 (11.76)
Instruments	2 (15.38)	10 (76.92)	1 (7.69)
Miscellaneous manufacturing	7 (35.00)	3 (15.00)	10 (50.00)
Total	122 (27.23)	156 (34.82)	170 (37.95)

a. Large-firm innovation rate (LIE) is defined as the number of innovations by large firms divided by total employment in large firms. Small-firm innovation rate (SIE) is defined as the number of innovations by small firms divided by total employment in small firms.

bute more innovation activity than do small firms; in other sectors, the pattern is reversed.

Although in 156 (or slightly more than one-third) of the industries the small firms were apparently more innovative than their larger counterparts, and in 122 (or slightly more than one-quarter) of the industries the large firms were more innovative, it would be erroneous to conclude that the small firm is more innovative than the large firm. Rather, as tables 3.3 and 3.4 show, the answer to the general debate regarding which firm size is the most conducive to innovation is along the lines of Scherer's (1980, 418) conclusion that, "No single firm size is uniquely conductive to technological progress. There is room for firms of all sizes."

A modified hypothesis from that presented in the previous section is that the large firms tend to have the relative innovative advantage in concentrated markets and markets imposing more significant structural barriers, but the small firms tend to have the innovative advantage in markets more closely resembling the competitive model. While the fundamental question addressed in the previous section was 'What market structure conditions are conducive to innovative activity?" here the relevant question is "Which market conditions promote the relative innovative advantages of large and small firms?"

To test the hypothesis that the difference between the large- and small-firm innovation rates is attributable to the extent of imperfect competition in the market, we estimate the following model:

$$DIE = \beta_0 + \beta_1 K/O + \beta_2 AD/S + \beta_3 CR + \beta_4 UNION + \beta_5 GR \\ + \beta_6 PILF + \beta_7 SKILL + \beta_8 TIE + \mu. \tag{3.2}$$

A substitute variable is also used to measure product differentiation (ADC/S), where ADC/S = AD/S × D, and D is a dummy variable taking on the value of one in consumer industries that are also convenience goods and zero otherwise. This follows the procedure used by Porter (1976) and Pugel (1978), who argue that product differentiation plays a more significant role only in these industries.

Several studies, including Pavitt and Wald (1971), suggest that the opportunity for small-firm innovation tends to be greatest when the industry is in the early stages of the product life cycle. The introduction and growth stages of the life cycle are defined by Vernon (1966) as the absence of a standardized product concept in the market. Because product design is subject to rapid change and evolution, innovative opportunities for small firms are presumably greatest during the early life-cycle stages and least in the mature and declining stages. To measure the stage of the industry life cycle, we include as an explanatory variably the real growth rate between 1972 and 1977, divided by five (GR). Since an industry tends to rely on the highest component of skilled labor during the early stages of the life cycle, and the least amount of skilled labor after the product has become standardized in the mature and declining phases, SKILL is expected to be negatively related to DIE. Similarly, since industries in the early life-cycle stages tend to be the most innovative, and small firms are presumably relatively more innovative during the early life-cycle stages, high levels of TIE are expected to be conducive to small-firm relative to large-firm innovation, implying a negative relationship between TIE and DIE.

Although 247 four-digit SIC industries were compatible for estimating the above model, a large number of industries experienced no innovation. In these industries the difference between the large- and small-firm innovation rates is, of course, zero. Hence, the sole determinant of DIE in these industries is the lack of innovation. That is, when considering what determines the differences in innovation rates between large and small firms, it may be appropriate only to examine industries where a difference can possibly exist—industries with at least some innovation activity. Thus, the above model is estimated for two different samples: (1) highly innovative industries, which includes the highest fourth of industries that had at least some innovative activity; and (2) innovative industries, which includes those industries that had some innovative activity.

Using DIE, the 1982 difference between the large- and small-firm innovation rates, as the dependent variable, the cross-section regressions were estimated for the two different samples of innovative intensity and are shown in table 3.5. Equation 1 includes the highly innovative industries. The positive and statistically significant coefficient of K/O indicates that, ceteris paribus, large firms tend to have the relative innovative advantage over their smaller counterparts in the more capital-intensive industries. Conversely, the smaller firms tend to be relatively more innovative in the less capital-intensive industries. This lends support to a slightly reinterpreted Galbraithian view: *Where* capital intensity plays an important role in the industry, innovation tends to be greater in large firms than in small firms.

The coefficient of AD/S is positive, although not statistically significant. The coefficient of CR is also positive, suggesting that the larger firms tend to have the relative innovative advantage in the highly concentrated industries, and that the smaller firms tend to have the relative innovative advantage in the less concentrated industries.

The positive, although not statistically significant, coefficient of UNION suggests that large firms frequently have the innovative advantage in industries that are highly unionized, while small firms more often have the innovative advantage in industries that are relatively nonunionized. The coefficient of GR is very weak, implying that, among the highly innovative industries, the growth rate has a similar effect on large- and small-firm innovation rates. Because the coefficient of PILF is negative, it appears that the more an industry is composed of large firms, the greater the relative innovative advantage of small firms over their larger counterparts. Perhaps this reflects the use of a strategy of innovation by small firms to remain viable in industries dominated by large firms.

The statistical insignificance of SKILL is somewhat surprising; the explanation may lie in the fact that virtually all of the industries in the highly innovative industry sample are skilled-labor-intensive. The mean value of SKILL is considerably higher in the highly innovative industries, 0.129, than in the low-innovative industries, 0.073. Since all of the highly innovative industries tend also to be high in skilled-labor intensity, the lack of variation in SKILL may explain its statistical insignificance in equation 1.

Finally, the negative and statistically significant coefficient of TIE implies that, even among the highly innovative industries, the relative innovative advantage of the small firms increases as the total innovation rate of the industry also increases. That is, the relative innovative advantage of small firms over large firms is most pronounced in the industries that are the most innovative.[11]

In equation 2, the highly innovative industry sample is again used, but ADC/S is substituted for AD/S. The results remain virtually unchanged. It appears, therefore, that advertising intensity is a barrier to small-firm innovation across manufacturing in the highly innovative industries and not just in the consumer goods industries.

The same model is estimated using the sample of innovative industries—where there was at least some innovative activity—in equations 3 and 4. The major difference between equations 1 and 3, and equations 2 and 4, is that the innovative industry sample contains a number of industries that are low-innovative. Thus, in equations 3 and 4, neither the coefficients of K/O, CR, nor UNION are statistically significant. It is apparent that, while capital intensity may have a differential effect on large- and small-firm innovation rates in the highly innovative industries, it has a similar effect in innovative industries overall. In equations 1 and 2, the coefficient of K/O is 5.972 and 5.371, respectively; in equations 3 and 4, the coefficient decreases to 0.684 and 0.651. Similarly, the coefficients of AD/S and ADC/S are only about half as large in equations 3 and 4 as they are in equations 1 and 2. When a broader spectrum of skilled-labor industries is considered in equations 3 and 4, SKILL is found to have a greater effect on the differential between large-firm and small-firm innovation rates. The smaller firms tend to have the relative innovative advantage in the industries utilizing a fairly high component of skilled labor, whereas the large firms tend to have the relative innovative advantage in the industries utilizing less skilled labor.

Both of the samples shown in table 3.5 consider the question of what explains the differential between large- and small-firm innovation rates from a slightly different perspective. We view the sample including only the highly innovative industries as being the most appropriate and the most relevant. Explaining the differences, or lack of differences, in innovation rates in industries with only modest innovative activity seems both less relevant and somewhat misleading. The major source of the small differences between the large- and small-firm innovation rates in low-innovative industries is simply the lack of innovation. That is, a low value of DIE in a very innovative industry presumably means something very different than a low value of DIE in an industry with little innovative activity.

Based on the results in table 3.5, the differences between the innovation rates of large and small firms, particularly in highly innovative industries, can generally be explained by (1) the degree of capital intensity, (2) the extent to which an industry is concentrated and is comprised of small firms, and (3) the total innovative intensity of the industry. In particular, the relative innovative advantage of large firms tends to be promoted in industries that are capital-intensive, advertising-intensive, concentrated, and highly unionized. By contrast, in industries that are highly innovative and composed predominantly of large firms, the relative innovative advantage is held by the small firms.

Table 3.5
Estimates of model of the difference in large- and small-firm innovation rates (DIE)[a]

Independent variable	Highly innovative industries (1)	Highly innovative industries (2)	Innovative industries (3)	Innovative industries (4)
Intercept	1.737	2.093	0.780	0.748
	(1.009)	(1.329)	(2.161)**	(2.107)**
K/O	5.972	5.371	0.684	0.651
	(1.766)*	(1.612)	(1.091)	(0.977)
AD/S	169.970	—	61.614	—
	(1.442)		(1.212)	
ADC/S	—	148.620	—	74.630
		(1.183)		(1.279)
CR	0.029	0.031	-0.004	-0.003
	(1.390)	(1.476)	(0.667)	(0.600)
UNION	0.023	0.023	-0.001	-0.001
	(1.353)	(1.380)	(0.167)	(0.167)
GR	4.196	3.329	1.565	1.556
	(0.906)	(0.727)	(1.073)	(1.068)
PILF	-6.601	-6.776	-0.797	-0.893
	(2.693)**	(2.691)**	(1.400)	(1.518)
SKILL	2.123	1.658	-2.934	-2.883
	(0.405)	(0.315)	(1.455)	(1.428)
TIE	-1.789	-1.753	-1.021	-1.007
	(4.374)**	(4.265)**	(5.579)**	(5.564)**
Sample size	42	42	172	172
R^2	0.524	0.515	0.295	0.296
F	4.538**	4.371**	8.527**	8.556**

a. The dependent variable is the industry difference between large- and small-firm innovation rates (DIE); t-statistics are listed in parentheses.
Note: *Statistically significant at the 90 percent level of confidence, two-tailed test. **Statistically significant at the 95 percent level of confidence, two-tailed test.

3.5 Conclusion

The results in this chapter strongly suggest that the innovative activity of small firms makes an important contribution distinct from that of large firms. This conclusion is based on the new and more direct measure of innovative activity used here to test the two essential hypotheses that have emerged in the literature—that innovation activity is promoted by large firms and in markets characterized by imperfect competition. While previous studies have found a somewhat ambiguous relationship between concentration and various measures of technical change, our results are unequivocal: Industry innovative activity tends to decrease as the level of concentration rises.

Equally important, there is considerable support of Winter's (1984) notion that two technological regimes exist. What Winter named the entrepreneurial regime can be characterized as those market conditions found to be conducive to small-firm innovative activity; the routinized regime can be characterized by those market conditions that promote the innovative activity of large firms. We find that these two technological regimes are not only distinct, but that they are the product of the market structure environment. Industries that are capital-intensive, concentrated, highly unionized, and produce differentiated goods tend to be more characterized by the routinized regime. By contrast, highly innovative industries, where the use of skilled labor is relatively important and where large firms comprise a large share of the market, are characterized by the entrepreneurial regime.

Theory should perhaps develop further how firms of varied size may have disparate innovative responses to different economic environments, rather than focusing on which firm size is uniquely endowed to best promote technological progress. Similarly, public policies undertaken to spur innovative activity should perhaps also consider that small-firm innovation is a significant and distinct entity from large-firm innovation and thus may respond to a different set of incentives.

4   The Presence of Small Firms

4.1   Introduction

This chapter provides two contributions. First, we present a model leading to the hypothesis that the presence of small firms in any given industry emanates from four distinct sources: (1) the exogenous stock of entrepreneurial talent, (2) a stochastic element of managerial and entrepreneurial talent, (3) economies of scale and capital requirements, and (4) the entrepreneurial strategy deployed by small firms. Second, we test this hypothesis utilizing a cross-section of manufacturing industries, spanning the entire spectrum of firm sizes. This is facilitated by using the data newly released by the U.S. Small Business Administration and described in chapter 2.

In the second section of this chatper we examine the extent of small firms in manufacturing industries. We find that, in fact, considerable variation of small-firm presence exists across manufacturing. Thus, in the third section, we combine three strands of literature to develop a model explaining the inter-industry variation in the presence of small firms. This model is then estimated and the hypotheses tested in the fourth section. We find that the existence of scale economies, high capital requirements, product differentiation, R&D intensity, and the reliance upon innovative strategy by small enterprises explain a considerable proportion of the variation in the presence of small firms.

4.2   Small Firms across Manufacturing Industries

The distribution of employment sizes of firms in manufacturing for 1982 is shown in table 4.1. Of all manufacturing firms, 94.2 percent had fewer than 100 employees, and 98.9 percent had fewer than 500 employees. The share of sales and employment accounted for by

Table 4.1
The presence of small firms in manufacturing, 1982

| | Employment size of firms | | | | | | | | | | | |
	1–4	5–9	10–19	20–49	50–99	100–249	250–499	500–999	1,000–4,999	5,000–9,999	10,000 and over	Total
Number of firms	137,601	82,574	60,531	52,383	21,179	13,220	4,494	1,941	1,610	243	347	376,123
Average sales ($thousands)	141	388	821	1,857	4,115	9,181	22,272	44,624	155,985	610,995	3,211,832	6,206
Share of total sales (percentage)	0.8	1.4	2.1	4.1	3.7	5.1	4.2	3.5	10.6	7.0	57.5	100.0
Cumulative share of sales (percentage)	0.8	2.2	4.3	8.4	12.1	17.2	21.4	24.9	35.5	42.5	100.0	100.0
Average employment	2	6	13	29	66	145	335	665	2,007	6,792	39,234	74
Share of total employment (percentage)	1.2	1.9	2.8	5.5	5.0	6.9	5.4	4.6	11.6	5.9	49.0	100.0
Cumulative share of total employment	1.2	3.2	6.0	11.6	16.5	23.5	28.9	33.5	45.1	51.0	100.0	100.0
Firm sales per employee ($thousands)	57	60	63	63	63	63	67	67	76	89	80	75

Source: U.S. Small Business Administration, USEEM file.

these small firms is clearly important. While firms with fewer than 500 employees accounted for 21.4 percent of all sales and 28.9 percent of all employment in manufacturing, firms with fewer than 100 employees accounted for 12.1 percent of sales and 16.5 percent of employment.

The presence of small firms also varies considerably across manufacturing industries. The industries with the greatest presence of small firms, defined as enterprises employing fewer than 100, are listed in table 4.2. For example, the fur goods industry had the largest presence of small firms, accounting for 94.03 percent of total sales. The last column shows that the 667 small firms comprised 99.40 percent of all the firms in the industry. Despite the strong presence of small firms, the industry average sales per employee of $82,672 was considerably higher than the average in manufacturing of $75,000.

Industries with a relatively high presence of small firms tend to be concentrated in several sectors of manufacturing. For example, eight of the forty industries listed in table 4.2 are included in the two-digit SIC 23 sector, apparel. Similarly, four industries are included in lumber (SIC 24), printing (SIC 27), and the miscellaneous manufacturing products (SIC 39) sectors. An additional three industries are included in the nonelectrical machinery (SIC 35) and the fabricated metal products (SIC 34) sectors. Thus, half of the forty industries with the greatest presence of small firms are included in just four of the twenty two-digit SIC sectors.

By contrast, the industries with the least presence of small firms are shown in table 4.3. Small firms are least present in the cigarette industry, where they account for just 0.03 percent of all sales. Since nine of the fifteen firms in the industry are classified as small, the folly of measuring the presence of any particular firm-size classification by the number of enterprises within the class is clear: Despite comprising 60 percent of the total number of firms, small firms obviously do not play a significant role in the cigarette industry. Only two industries, cigarettes and beet sugar, have a small-firm presence of less than 0.10 percent. There are thirteen industries with a presence of small firms of between 0.10 percent and 1.00 percent. Nearly half of the industries in table 4.3 have a small-firm presence of between 1.00 percent and 2.00 percent. Thus in only a handful of industries is there just a negligible presence of small firms.

Table 4.2
The industries with the largest presence of small firms[a]

Industry	Small-firm presence[b] (%)	Sales per employee ($)	Number of small firms[c]
Fur goods	94.03	82,672	667 (99.40)
Cut stone and stone products	88.48	30,211	1,091 (99.00)
Logging	87.79	40,289	5,137 (99.55)
Wood pallets and skids	86.33	32,835	1,226 (98.95)
Commercial printing	85.29	34,280	521 (99.43)
Typesetting	84.30	23,267	2,333 (98.69)
Special product sawmills	84.11	45,818	417 (98.82)
Concrete block and brick	84.09	53,076	1,130 (97.50)
Jewelers' materials	82.23	61,147	639 (98.01)
Machinery, except electrical	79.23	32,190	22,358 (99.14)
Plating and polishing	79.04	26,646	3,154 (97.74)
Paving mixtures and blocks	77.76	92,644	436 (95.40)
Apparel and accessories	77.18	31,549	284 (96.27)
Machine embroideries	77.11	28,617	255 (98.84)
Architectural metalwork	75.45	54,107	1,848 (98.61)
Special dies, tools, jigs	73.37	35,177	6,811 (98.11)
Millinery	72.35	29,011	140 (95.24)
Screw-machine products	71.40	38,255	1,706 (95.95)
Nailed wood boxes	71.08	34,703	452 (95.36)
Buttons	69.54	28,568	129 (94.85)

Industry			
Bookbinding and related work	68.30	22,722	936 (95.51)
Structural wood members	68.15	49,699	595 (97.22)
Industrial patterns	67.88	33,095	1,013 (99.31)
Wood partitions and fixtures	67.65	37,637	1,797 (97.72)
Signs and advertising displays	66.25	34,229	3,747 (98.04)
Presses and molded pulp goods	66.13	39,005	40 (93.02)
Leather goods	66.10	30,525	782 (97.75)
Fertilizers, mixing only	65.49	127,494	290 (97.64)
Leather and sheep-lined clothing	64.52	37,230	282 (93.07)
Lithographic services	64.20	33,693	255 (98.84)
Artificial flowers	63.83	40,162	285 (95.64)
Tire cord and fabric	63.77	69,771	14 (87.50)
Pleating and stitching	63.72	25,525	650 (95.17)
Processed textile waste	63.62	44,417	120 (90.91)
Apparel belts	63.21	34,403	284 (92.51)
Photoengraving	63.08	31,553	397 (95.20)
Petroleum and coal products	62.89	69,431	46 (97.87)
Women's and misses' outwear	62.52	49,712	2,614 (90.80)
Space vehicles' equipment	62.28	52,530	18 (94.74)
Household furniture	61.54	35,208	426 (96.60)

a. A small firm is measured as a firm with fewer than 100 employees.
b. Small-firm presence is defined as the proportion of total industry sales accounted for by small firms.
c. The percentage of all firms in the industry that are small is listed in parentheses.

Table 4.3
The industries with the least presence of small firms[a]

Industry	Small-firm presence[b] (%)	Sales per employee ($)	Number of small firms[c]
Cigarettes	0.03	60,750	9 (60.00)
Beet sugar	0.04	43,000	2 (16.67)
Motor vehicles	0.19	55,833	459 (91.62)
Aircraft	0.21	39,666	131 (83.44)
Space propulsion units	0.44	79,222	5 (55.56)
Household laundry equipment	0.47	52,456	24 (85.71)
Glass containers	0.48	65,978	41 (63.08)
Malt beverages	0.57	58,280	24 (48.00)
Primary aluminum	0.57	125,473	21 (77.78)
Tobacco stemming and redrying	0.58	204,017	9 (64.29)
Chewing gum	0.69	34,565	5 (55.56)
Alkalies and chlorine	0.76	81,680	37 (78.72)
Blast furnace and steel mills	0.85	67,776	417 (83.40)
Cane sugar refining	0.88	148,287	15 (65.22)
Carbon black	0.89	84,797	6 (75.00)
Tires and inner tubes	0.92	249,225	76 (72.38)
Wet corn milling	1.00	96,970	19 (86.36)
Papermills	1.01	59,663	151 (68.64)
Cement, hydraulic	1.12	152,473	43 (58.11)
Cellulosic manmade fibers	1.13	55,097	49 (90.74)

Industry			
Transformers	1.14	36,313	304 (84.21)
Pulpmills	1.15	74,200	72 (81.82)
Calculating machines	1.24	55,016	44 (84.62)
Soybean oil mills	1.28	90,992	30 (85.71)
Chewing and smoking tobacco	1.35	34,096	19 (79.17)
Electronic computing equipment	1.35	52,154	776 (83.71)
Gypsum products	1.44	62,833	58 (89.23)
Cereal breakfast foods	1.47	105,646	37 (88.10)
Metal cans	1.51	55,490	156 (78.79)
Internal combustion engines	1.54	48,799	142 (90.45)
Hard surface floor coverings	1.56	50,333	22 (88.00)
Aluminum rolling and drawing	1.67	62,473	31 (75.61)
Sewing machines	1.77	63,813	92 (92.00)
Men's footwear, except athletic	1.86	28,252	114 (66.28)
Petroleum refining	1.95	201,551	265 (82.55)
Motors and generators	2.00	37,814	302 (81.84)
Industrial organic chemicals	2.02	82,635	310 (91.72)
Pharmaceutical preparations	2.09	57,660	673 (88.20)
Paperboard mills	2.23	68,497	37 (48.68)
Aircraft engines and parts	2.27	38,488	136 (82.42)

a. A small firm is measured as a firm with fewer than 100 employees.
b. Small-firm presence is defined as the proportion of total industry sales accounted for by small firms.
c. The percentage of all firms in the industry that are small is listed in parentheses.

4.3   A Model of Small-Firm Presence

Three strands of literature shed light on the pattern of variation in small-firm presence across manufacturing industries observed in tables 4.1–4.3. The first strand is concerned with explaining the intra-industry distribution of firm size, or how firms of varying size can simultaneously exist in any given industry. The second strand implies that market structure, and scale economies along with capital requirements in particular, help shape the inter-industry variation in small-firm presence. In focusing on the relationship between firm size and entrepreneurial strategy, the third strand considers how smaller firms can deploy strategy to compensate for size-specific disadvantages. By integrating these three strands of literature, we will develop a model explaining the inter-industry variation in the presence of small firms.

Under the assumption that individual firms have identical U-shaped long-run average cost functions, Viner (1932), in his classic article, predicted that a unique size distribution—that is, a singular firm size—would occur in every industry. Kaldor (1934) similarly argued that a singular optimal firm size would result from the fixed input of entrepreneurial talent into the firm production function. Lucas (1978) has proposed a theory explaining why large and small firms can simultaneously exist in a given industry. He attributes the existence of an intra-industry size distribution of firms to the exogenous stock of entrepreneurial abilities of managerial agents. In his model, Lucas assumes that all individuals are identical as workers but are endowed with varying amounts of entrepreneurial ability. An entrepreneur is defined as someone who combines labor and captial inputs into output through some production process. The more efficiently the inputs are transformed into output, the better the entrepreneur. Given a distribution of entrepreneurial ability, each individual relates his expected profits from undertaking entrepreneurial activity to the competitive wage and decides whether to become an entrepreneur or to remain a worker. The resulting distribution of intra-industry firm size is therefore attributable to the given talent distribution of managers. However, while Lucas's model may explain the simultaneous existence of varying firm size within a given industry, his model does not explain why this intra-industry distribution should vary across different industries.[1] That is, according to Lucas's model, we would expect to see the same degree of small-firm presence in every industry.

Similarly, Oi (1983) presents a model where each firm possesses a single entrepreneur endowed with a fixed amount of calendar time. The entrepreneur must allocate his talent between two competing activities, organizing and coordinating production, and supervising workers. Oi assumes that the ability to organize and coordinate production varies across entrepreneurs. Those who are more efficient are able to supervise more workers, thus resulting in a size distribution of firms within a given industry. Like the model presented by Lucas, Oi's model accounts for intra-industry variation in firm size but not for variation across industries.

The second strand of literature implies that the firm-size distribution is determined by the nature of the long-run average cost function. The starting point is Modigliani's (1958) synthesis of models of Bain (1956) and Sylos-Labini (1962). Modigliani assumed that the cost of production roughly follows a J-shaped curve, where the average cost is constant beyond some level of output. This level of output, termed the minimum efficient scale of output (MES), is formally defined as the minimum level of output at which scale economies are exhausted. The greater the amount of output required to attain MES, the less hospitable in industry will be to small firms (Weiss 1976). In addition, the greater the differential between the average cost of production at MES and the average cost experienced by firms of suboptimal scale, the less conducive an industry will be to the presence of small firms (Caves et al. 1975).

A not unrelated factor influencing the viability of small firms is what Bain (1956) termed absolute capital requirements, or the amount of capital needed by a firm to exhaust scale economies. There are at least three factors that determine the absolute capital requirements in an industry: (1) the optimal capital–labor ratio for production of a given good, (2) the "lumpiness" of the units of capital input, and (3) the relative efficiency of large and small capital inputs (White 1984).

There are compelling reasons why a high absolute capital requirement will serve as an impediment to small firms. Larger firms can finance capital expenditures from internal earnings, issuance of equity, or debt. By contrast, small firms are limited in the extent of their internal earnings and the potential for issuing equity. Andrews and Eisemann (1984) found that the flotation costs for nonconvertible notes and debentures offered to the public through security dealers fell from 17.0 percent for issues of between $1 million and $2 million, to 6.2 percent for issues between $2 million and $5 million, and to 1.0 percent for issues exceeding $50 million. The authors note that when the interest expense is added to the flotation costs, the first-year total cost of raising funds can easily 30 percent for a small firm.

Not surprisingly, small enterprises more frequently turn to commercial banks for funding of capital projects. But, as Stoll (1984) notes, smaller firms typically face higher interest rates than do their larger counterparts. For example, a Federal Reserve Board study of loan rates charged by commercial banks on loans made between November 3 and 7, 1986[2] found that short-term loans at a fixed rate had an average rate of 11.2 percent for loans of less than $24,000. However, the rate fell steadily to a mean of 6.8 percent for loans exceeding $1 million. For loans with a floating rate, the differential was not quite as great. The smallest loans had an average rate of 9.7 percent, while the largest loans were for 7.5 percent. Very similar patterns were identified for long-term loans at both fixed and floating rates. Thus, the evidence clearly indicates that the interest rate falls as the size of the loan increases.

Venture capital, or the prepublic market for risk capital, is another potential source of funding capital expenditures for small firms. There are essentially three major attributes characterizing a venture capital investment. First, there is typically some potential equity participation for the venture capitalist. This may occur either through the direct purchase of stock or else through warrants, options, or convertible securities. Second, venture capital financing frequently is of a long-term nature, requiring between five and ten years for the investment to materialize into a profitable return. Third, the venture capitalists generally participate in directing the firm's activities. Rather than passively supplying the financial capital, they instead play an active role in applying their experience and skill in helping the firm develop (Office of Technology Assessment 1984).

The venture capital market is a blossoming phenomenon in the United States. While there was $600 million of net new private capital committed to venture capital firms in 1978, the amount of venture capital had increased to $4,500 million by 1986. The total pool of venture capital correspondingly increased from $3,500 million in 1978 to $24,000 million in 1986 (National Science Board 1987). However, 26 percent of the 1986 venture-backed initial public offerings was in computers and an additional 18.7 percent was in biotechnology, so that most of the venture capital funds are concentrated in just a handful of industries. Although the venture capital market has been growing at rapid rates in recent years, it still affects only a minuscule portion of all firms, large or small. Based on a study of 2,994 new firms, Dunkelberg and Cooper (forthcoming) found that only 1 percent of the firms had obtained funds from venture capital. As Gaston (1989) concludes, the biggest source of external risk capital fueling entrepreneurial start-ups and small business growth is from the "informal capital market." Informal risk capital is defined as equity and near-equity dollars invested by private individuals directly but informally in entrepreneurs without any formal intermediation.

There is also evidence that small firms have more difficulty obtaining capital and that they are more likely to be subject to liquidity constraints than are larger firms. For example, Evans and Jovanovic (1989) provided empirical evidence that new entrepreneurs typically face a binding liquidity constraint. As a result, small firms tend to have lower capital–labor ratios than would otherwise be optimal. This is consistent with the findings of Fazzari et al. (1987) that the likelihood of a firm experiencing a liquidity constraint decreases along with increasing firm size. In addition, Fazzari et al. find that small firms are more reliant on commercial banks and internal funds than are larger firms. While the large firms in their study issued 99 percent of all new equity shares and 92 percent of all new corporate bonds, they accounted for only 74 percent of total manufacturing assets. Because smaller firms are more dependent upon loans from commercial banks, they are more prone to experiencing a credit crunch, especially during recessions.

Therefore, as Stoll (1984) and others note, it is virtually impossible for small firms to avoid a cost of obtaining capital in excess of that faced by larger firms. The relative advantage of small firms, then, is in industries where there is little need to raise capital funds, or those industries in which MES and absolute capital requirements are small. By contrast, the relative advantage of large firms is in industries where raising capital funds plays an important role, or those industries in which MES and absolute capital requirements are large.

The extent to which advertising plays an important role in an industry can also affect the viability of small firms. There are at least two hypotheses regarding the manner in which advertising expenditures create an unfavorable climate for small firms. First, the effect of advertising on firm revenues is subject to economies of scale that result from the increasing effectiveness of advertising message per unit of output.[3] Second, to the extent that scale economies exist in either production or advertising, the need to obtain funds for advertising will increase the capital requirements beyond what is needed for physical plant and equipment.[4]

The third strand of literature suggests that smaller firms can deploy certain strategies to compensate for size-specific cost disadvantages. For example, Mills and Schumann (1985) and Mills (1984) presented models where the existence of available technologies and entrepreneurial strategies afford a trade-off between static efficiency and flexibility.[5] The notion of flexibility in the operation of the firm seems to have been first introduced into the economics literature by Stigler (1939). He defined flexibility as those attributes of a production technology that accommodate greater output variation. In particular, Stigler argued that flexibility varies inversely with the curvature of total costs. The flatter the average total cost curve, the more slowly will marginal cost rise, and the greater will be the firm's reliance on flexible production.

Mills and Schumann's theory associates greater flexibility with smaller firm size, since smaller enterprises tend to achieve greater flexibility through a greater reliance on variable factors of production. This implies that flexible technologies have lower capital requirements than do inflexible technologies. Since flexibility apparently varies inversely with firm size, the results of Mills and Schumann's paper suggest that flexible production is a strategy that small firms can employ to remain viable in a relatively capital-intensive industry. Thus, small firms in capital-intensive industries presumably survive by adopting a strategy of flexible production and absorbing a relatively large share of market output fluctuations.[6]

The above line of reasoning is limited to those aspects of flexibility that have to do with the ability of firms to adjust to fluctuations in demand for their output. However, fluctuations in demand represent only one aspect of the environment of firms that calls for a strategy of flexibility. Adjustments may occur in the firm's product mix due to technological change. In addition, technological change may affect the production system in the form of new machinery and production methods (Carlsson 1989b). This aspect of flexibility is related to the planning or envelope curve of the industry, in that it reflects a menu of choices with respect to investment in plant and machinery.

An important step in this direction was taken by Marschak and Nelson (1962). They defined flexibility more broadly than did Stigler. They suggested that a more flexible plant requires less additional cost to move to the next position. Even more important, Marschak and Nelson stressed the applicability of the concept of flexibility beyond the choice of plant, focusing especially on the conduct of R&D, as it relates to future products, processes, and plants.[7]

Strategic flexibility therefore refers to the ability of firms "to reposition themselves in a market, change their game plans, or dismantle their current strategies when the customers they serve are no longer as attractive as they once were" (Harrigan 1985, 1). Smaller firms, because of their simpler organizational structure, may be better able to pursue a strategy of flexibility than their larger counterparts. Examining seventy-three manufacturing industries, Caves and Pugel (1980) found that smaller firms using strategies requiring proportionally lower levels of advertising outlays or capital intensity than their larger counterparts tended to earn higher profit rates.[8] Conversely, large firms tended to perform relatively better when they engaged in foreign direct investment. Similarly, Brock (1981) suggests that small firms can offset a comparative disadvantage vis-à-vis their larger rivals by pursuing a strategy of innovation. This is consistent with the findings of Mansfield (1962) that small firms that innovate tend to grow twice as fast as large firms that do not innovate.

4.4 Empirical Results

Based on the literature and model presented in the previous section, the level of small-firm presence in any given industry is hypothesized to emanate from four distinct sources: (1) the exogenous distribution of managerial talent within a given industry (based on Lucas 1978), (2) the stochastic element of managerial and entrepreneurial talent, (3) scale economies and absolute capital requirement, and (4) the innovative strategy implemented by small firms. As explained in the previous section, the first source should be constant across industries. To test the hypothesis that the presence of firms is attributable to the remaining three types of factors, we estimate a regression model where the dependent variable is the 1982 share of four-digit SIC industry sales accounted for by firms with 100 employees. In order to test the sensitivity of the model to varying measures of a small firm, we also provide an alternative definition of a small firm, including firms with fewer than 500 employees. Other small-firm definitions as well as other years (1976, 1978 and 1980) are used to measure the dependent variable, but they are only referred to and not explicitly reported here in order to keep the presentation of results manageable.

The challenge presented in measuring the extent of scale economies has been discussed in some detail in Scherer (1980) and Caves et al. (1975). As a proxy measure for MES we adopt the Comanor-Wilson (1967) approach, where MES is measured as the mean size of the largest plants accounting for one-half of the industry value-of-shipments. To transform the MES measure into the share of the market required to exhaust scale economies, MES is divided by 1977 industry value-of-shipments (MES/S). The amount of capital required to produce the MES output (KREQ) is measured as gross industry assets divided by value-of-shipments, multiplied by MES. In addition, the 1977 captial–labor ratio is included as an explanatory variable, since, as White (1982) points out, higher capital–labor ratios tend to be associated with greater scale economies.[9] This is partially because capital equipment tends to be "lumpy" in nature. Also, by enabling firms to take advantage of increased specialization and greater rates of utilization, the use of larger machines tends to reduce costs per unit of output. As was discussed in the previous section, there is persuasive evidence that smaller firms have a comparative disadvantage in raising funds to finance capital investment. Thus, the more capital-intensive the basic production process of an industry, the less conducive that industry will be to the presence of small firms.

Because of the inherently high costs required, industries in which R&D and advertising play an important role may not be particularly conducive to the presence of small firms. Thus, the small-firm presence is expected to be negatively related to 1977 company R&D/sales (RDC), and advertising/sales (AD/S), as defined and measured in chatper 3. The ratio of large-firm innovative activity to small-firm innovative activity (LI/SI) is included as an explanatory variable to measure the extent to which the relatvie innovative strategies of large and small firms differ. While innovative activity is perhaps the most significant strategic instrument available to small firms in compensating for size-related cost disadvantages, it also serves a dual function in a manner resembling an instrumental variable: Where small-firm innovative activity is relatively high, other significant but unmeasurable types of small-firm strategy are also likely to be present. Since small-firm strategy is hypothesized to be a mechanism for compensating for scale disadvantages, we expect that LI/SI should be negatively related to the presence of small firms. In addition, an alternative measure of the relative innovative activity between large and small firms, the large-firm innovation rate divided by the small-firm innovation rate (LIE/SIE), is also used. These innovation measures were explained in detail in chapter 2.

Because the dependent variable can vary only between 0 and 100 by definition, ordinary least squares estimation would produce inefficient variances of the estimated coefficients. Following the procedure recommended by Judge et al. (1980), we correct for this inefficiency by transforming the dependent variable from SFP to ln (SFP/100-SFP). While equations 1–3 in table 4.4 estimate the model using the presence of firms with fewer than 100 employees as the dependent variable, the last two equations use the presence of firms with fewer than 500 employees as the dependent variable. There are three main results from table 4.4. First, small firms apparently do not thrive in industries that are capital-intensive, measured either in terms of the capital–labor ratio or the absolute amount of capital required to attain the MES level of output, and where there are relatively large economies of scale, as measured by MES/S. This is not a particularly surprising result, since these three measures have been found to be important determinants of the extent of market concentration (Scherer 1980).

The second main result from table 4.4. is that small firms are evidently adversely affected by the need to devote resources to advertising and R&D. The coefficients of both RDC and AD/S are negative, indicating that the presence of small firms is relatively low in industries with high advertising and R&D intensities. The third result is that the ratio of innovative activity between large and small firms is negative, implying that the greater the extent to which small firms are more innovative than their larger counterparts, ceteris paribus, the greater will be their presence. Thus, while small firms are at a disadvantage in industries where scale economies play an important role, they can compensate for their size-inherent disadvantages by pursuing a strategy of innovation. Although not included in table 4.4, these results prove to be remarkably robust, even when four other measures of what constitutes a small firm (fewer than 250, 50, 20 and

Table 4.4
Regression results for the presence of small firms (*t*-statistics listed in parentheses)

	Small-firm measure				
	Fewer than 100 employees			Fewer than 500 employees	
	1	2	3	4	5
LIE/SIE	—	-0.2009 (-1.7158)*	—	—	—
LI/SI	-0.1281 (-4.5382)**	—	-0.1186 (-4.2297)**	-0.1261 (-4.3623)**	-0.1141 (-3.9540)**
RDC	-0.1486 (-2.2653)**	-0.1688 (-2.4387)**	-0.1347 (-2.0510)**	-0.1668 (-2.4823)**	-0.1491 (-2.2070)**
AD/S	-294.1200 (-5.0070)**	-254.2300 (-4.0976)**	-298.3200 (-5.0513)**	-266.2600 (-4.4246)**	-271.6200 (-4.4710)**
MES/S	-0.0390 (-1.7399)*	-0.0430 (-1.8322)*	-0.0359 (-1.5952)	-0.0513 (-2.2355)**	-0.0473 (-2.0468)**
K/L	-0.0084 (-2.1620)**	-0.0084 (-2.0777)**	—	-0.1066 (-2.6900)**	—
KREQ[a]	-1.4235 (-3.4097)**	-1.8732 (-4.4961)**	-1.7442 (-4.4430)**	-1.3222 (-3.0915)**	-1.7310 (-4.2865)**
Intercept	-0.3239 (-2.3190)**	0.6163 (3.9524)**	-0.4637 (-3.7231)**	0.6264 (4.3773)**	0.4482 (3.4982)**
R^2	0.283	0.242	0.272	0.279	0.2622
F	20.150**	16.320**	22.971**	19.822**	21.896**

Note: *Statistically significant for the 90 percent level of confidence, two-tailed test. **Statistically significant for the 95 percent level of confidence, two-tailed test.
a. The coefficient of KREQ has been multiplied by 10,000 for presentation purposes.

10 employees) are substituted for the dependent variable as well as when the model is estimated for three alternative years (1976, 1978, and 1980).

4.5 Conclusion

This chapter shows that the presence of small firms in U.S. manufacturing is not trivial. Further, there is apparently considerable variation in the small-firm presence across manufacturing industries. While some industries are dominated by small firms, in others small firms are noticeably absent. Combining three strands in the literature, our model suggests that the presence of small firms can be attributed to four factors: the exogenous stock of entrepreneurial talent, the stochastic element of managerial and entrepreneurial ability, scale economies and capital requirements, and the entrepreneurial strategy deployed by small firms. Testing the hypothesis that the last three factors account for the observed variation in the small-firm presence across manufacturing industries, we find that the presence of small firms is generally negatively related to the extent of scale economies, but that implementing a strategy of innovation can at least somewhat compensate for the size-related disadvantages confronting small firms.

Therefore, the results presented here suggest that there is at least some evidence confirming the long-standing hypothesis in industrial organization (see, for example, Phillips 1956) that the size distribution of firms is determined by characteristics of technology. In particular, we find that industries that are R&D-intensive, high in capital intensity, and in which advertising plays an important role tend to promote a firm-size distribution comprised predominately of larger enterprises. However, the extent to which small firms pursue an innovation strategy can at least somewhat offset the size-related disadvantages facing small enterprises.

5   Entry, Market Structure, and Innovation

5.1 Introduction

The literature on entry has expanded in several directions in recent years. Building upon the seminal work of Bain (1956) and Sylos-Labini (1962), Caves and Porter (1977) incorporated exit, mobility, and diversification into a general theory of net entry, and Baumol and Willig (1981) argued that large fixed costs do not constitute a barrier to entry. Despite such an evolution regarding the role of entry, most of the literature has focused on the entry of relatively large firms or else has not distinguished between different firm sizes. That is, the determinants of small-firm entry have not been examined as a distinct phenomenon from those of large firms. That the debate in industrial organization has tended to focus particularly on what exactly constitutes a barrier to the entry of large firms is somewat surprising since, as Scherer (1980, 248) observes, "Measured by the sheer number of entities making the decision to enter, most new entry involves relatively small firms." However, there is little reason to assume that small-firm entry is an exact replica of that of larger rivals. This chapter attempts to fill this gap in the literature and to examine the extent and determinants of small-firm entry in manufacturing industries.

There are three contributions in this chapter. First, we examine the pattern of small-firm entry, as distinct from entry by all firms or by large firms, over manufacturing industries. Second, while most of the empirical studies have been restricted to examining market structure characteristics in explaining entry, we are able to include measures of small-firm strategy, and in particular the small-firm innovation rate, as a determinant of small-firm entry. This enables us to test the hypothesis posited by Nelson and Winter (1978) and Gort and

Klepper (1982) that entry is greater in industries experiencing a high degree of innovative activity. Finally, we are able to compare the results based on traditional net entry measures with a new measure of gross entry weighted by the number of employees in entering firms, or what we term "births."

In the second section of this chapter we examine the extent of small-firm entry across manufacturing industries. Using the new measure of births, we find, in fact, that considerable variation in small-firm births exists in manufacturing. Thus, in the third section, we draw upon the existing literature to develop a model explaining the determinants of industry births. Using different measures of firm sizes, the relationship between birth rates, market structure, and innovative activity is examined in the fourth section. In the fifth section the results from the birth data and from using aggregated industry data in previous studies are compared for small firms by applying the more traditional measured of net entry. Finally, in the last section, a summary and conclusion from the empirical results are provided. Lagged growth rates and a strategy of innovative activity by small firms generally promote births. However, advertising clearly serves to deter firms from entering. There is also evidence that small-firm entry behavior differs from that of large firms. For example, while small firms are deterred from entering concentrated markets, large-firm births are apparently greater in industries that are concentrated. Similarly, the evidence suggests that small firms but not large firms are deterred from entering a high R&D environment.

5.2   Entry as Measured by Industry Births

The most common measure of entry used in studies attempting to empirically identify the determinants of entry has been the change in the number of firms in an industry over a given period.[1] This measure suffers from three significant deficiencies that, although widely acknowledged, have not all been overcome in any one study. First, the change in the number of firms does not account for enterprises that exited the industry over the relevant period, resulting in a measure of net entry rather than in the desired measure of gross entry.[2] That is, given an amount of gross entry, the measure of net entry will increase as the number of exits from the industry decreases. Thus, it is quite conceivable that an industry could have a negative amount of net entry, if many firms actually entered the industry (i.e., if gross entry was positive), but only if even more firms exited from the industry. Because the pattern of industry exits varies across industries, the extent to which net entry deviates from actual gross entry will also vary from industry to industry.

Second, the traditional entry measure is weighted by the number of firms, or in several cases plants, but not by either the sales or employment of the entrants.[3] However, the implicit assumption that each unit of entry is homogenous with respect to size is obviously erroneous. In 1982, 590 U.S. manufacturing firms with employment exceeding 5,000 accounted for 64.5 percent of sales, while 354,268 firms with fewer than 100 employees accounted for only 12 percent of sales.[4] Although most entry is by small firms, the entry by a single large firm can more than offset (in terms of sales) the entry of hundreds of small firms. Thus, inter-industry comparisons based on numbers of firms obscure differences due to the different sizes of entering firms.

Finally, the data constraints have not enabled any study to examine the entry behavior for various firm-size classes across manufacturing industries. As Gorecki (1975) observed, studies attempting to explain entry patterns have treated entrants as if they were all the same size. That is, the behavior of entry at a relatively small scale has not been examined independently of that at a larger scale. The SBDB data, which were described in detail in chapter 2, make it possible to empirically examine entry by using an alternative measure, births, which is defined as the number of employees in entering firms. Not only is this a gross measure of entry, but because the birth data are in terms of employees, it is weighted by the magnitude of the entry.

The method by which Dun and Bradstreet record the birth of a new establishment was explained in chapter 2. Further explanations can be found in Phillips and Kirchhoff (1989). When a new establishment appears in a four-digit SIC industry, the amount of the new employment is recorded in the data base as "births." The bias created when treating all entrants as homogeneous with respect to firm size becomes clear when comparing the births of small firms (fewer than 500 employees) with those of large firms. Between 1976 and 1984, there were 2.214 million new jobs created by small-firm births and 1.418 million by large-firm births in U.S. manufacturing. During this period, there were 174,961 entrants that were small firms but only 978 that were large firms. Thus, large firms accounted for only 0.5 percent of the entry in terms of the numbers of firms, but 39.0 percent of the resulting employment or births. The traditional measure, based on the net change in the number of all firms in an industry over a specific time period, will therefore tend to understate the extent of entry when the new firms are relatively large and overstate it when they are relatively small.

The bias created when using the traditional measure of net change in the number of firms within a given period as a proxy for gross entry is shown in table 5.1. Because the traditional net entry measure is typically derived from changes in the number of establishments, in table 5.1 we use the SBDB data to compare gross and net measures of plant entry between 1980 and 1986, classified according to firm size and for major sectors of the U.S. economy. Gross entry, then, refers to the number of new establishments created during this period, and exits are defined as the number of establishments disappearing. In addition, the gross entry rate, which has commonly been used in empirical studies to adjust the extent of net entry for industry size, is defined as the number of entrants divided by the number of establishments in 1980. The exit rate is similarly defined as the number of exits divided by the number of establishments in 1980.

Since there was a total of 4.479 million establishments in the United States in 1980 and 4.965 million in 1986, net entry is defined as the difference, 486,000. This measure of net entry obscures the fact that there were actually 2.513 million new entrants, while 2.027 million establishments exited. Comparing the extent of net entry, or net entry rates, among the manufacturing, service, and finance sectors, one would conclude that there was relatively little entry of new establishments in manufacturing. In fact, establishments entering subsequent to 1980 represented a little less than one-half of all the establishments in manufacturing in existence in 1986. Because of the equally high rate of exit from manufacturing, there was only a slight *net* increase in the number of plants, but their ownership changed considerably, that is, there was substantial *gross* entry.

It should also be noted from table 5.1 that the entry patterns for smaller establishments (fewer than 500 employees) do not merely mirror those for larger establishments. For example, in the manufacturing sector the gross entry rate was greater for small establishments than for large ones, while the exit rate of large establishments exceeded that of their smaller counterparts. Thus, the net entry rate was actually negative for large establishments while it was positive for small ones. By 1986, there were about 9 percent more small-firm

Table 5.1
Entry and exit for establishments, by size of firm (thousands), 1980–1986[a]

	Aggregate			Manufacturing			Services			Finance		
	Small	Large	Total	Small	Large	Total	Small	Large	Total	Small	Large	Total
1980	4,093	386	4,479	379	69	448	856	67	924	301	37	338
1986	4,485	480	4,965	413	68	480	1,052	92	1,144	350	62	412
Gross entry	2,274	239	2,513	177	29	205	589	52	641	198	36	234
Exit	−1,881	−146	−2,027	−143	−30	−173	−392	−28	−421	−150	−11	−160
Net entry	393	93	486	33	−1	32	196	24	220	49	25	74
Gross entry rate	0.555	0.619	0.561	0.467	0.420	0.458	0.688	0.776	0.694	0.658	0.973	0.692
Exit rate	0.460	0.378	0.452	0.377	0.435	0.386	0.458	0.418	0.456	0.498	0.297	0.473
Net entry rate	0.096	0.241	0.108	0.087	−0.014	0.071	0.229	0.358	0.238	0.163	0.676	0.219

Source: U.S. Small Business Administration, Small Business Data Base.
a. The entry (exit) rate is defined as number of entrants divided by the number of establishments in 1980. The net entry rate is defined as the net change (entries minus exits) in the number of establishments between 1980 and 1986, divided by the number of establishments in 1980. A small firm is defined as an enterprise with fewer than 500 employees. A large firm is defined as an enterprise with at least 500 employees.

Table 5.2
Industry births (number of employees), the small-firm birth share (percentage), and net entry for high- and low-birth industries

Industry	Births	Small-firm birth share	Net entry 1978–1980	(Rank)
High-birth industries				
Radio and TV communication equipment	152,524	0.1220	90	(47)
Miscellaneous plastic products	149,065	0.4672	687	(4)
Motor vehicle parts and accessories	120,334	0.1260	235	(17)
Electronic computing equipment	118,833	0.1964	224	(21)
Electronic components	92,107	0.3312	284	(12)
Machinery, except electrical	77,612	0.7501	1,904	(2)
Commercial printing, lithographic	70,074	0.7616	3,579	(1)
Oilfield machinery	68,880	0.1653	154	(27)
Petroleum refining	65,306	0.1178	43	(92)
Newspapers	55,034	0.3820	193	(22)
Semiconductors and related devices	51,377	0.2788	51	(80)
Radio and TV receiving sets	49,279	0.1019	−2	(292)
Motor vehicles and car bodies	46,240	0.0727	40	(97)
Fabricated platework (boiler shops)	44,225	0.2552	191	(23)
Blast furnaces and steel mills	42,706	0.1616	5	(236)
Low-birth industries				
Blended and prepared flour	590	0.5548	−4	(324)
Paddings and upholstery filling	584	0.6197	−11	(368)

Cigars	540	0.7151	−8	(356)
Tobacco stemming and redrying	529	0.3354	−2	(296)
Processed textile waste	511	0.8996	−17	(386)
Schiffli machine embroideries	505	0.9805	0	(270)
Ordnance and accessories	463	0.4539	−1	(279)
Malt	419	0.2313	−2	(299)
Presses and molded pulp goods	283	0.4368	−5	(329)
Primary lead	210	0.1154	−3	(311)
Chewing and smoking tobacco	142	0.3067	−5	(234)
Millinery	112	0.8803	−24	(404)
Space propulsion units and parts	100	0.5856	−4	(317)
Chewing gum	90	1.0000	0	(277)
Electrotyping and stenotyping	16	1.0000	−12	(370)

manufacturing establishments but 1.4 percent fewer large-firm establishments. By comparison, the net entry rates were greater for the large than for the small establishments in both the service and finance sectors. thus, it is clear that just as net entry is not a reliable measure of gross entry, small-firm entry is not an exact replica of large-firm entry.

The manufacturing industries that had the highest and the lowest number of births between 1976 and 1982 are listed in table 5.2. The second column shows the share of those births accounted for by small firms, and the third column shows the number of net entrants, or the change in the number of firms, between 1978 and 1980. There is not a particularly close correspondence between the net entry and the birth measures. For example, while there were 3,579 net entrants in commercial printing (lithographic) but only 90 in the radio and TV communication equipment industries, births in the latter industry were more than twice as great as in the former.

The second column shows that the small-firm share of industry births varies considerably across markets, both for high- and low-birth industries. Just as small firms accounted for 75 percent of the births in nonelectrical machinery, but only 7 percent in motor vehicles and car bodies, they accounted for all of the births in electrotyping and stenotyping, but only 12 percent in primary lead.

5.3 Determinants of Entry

It is clear from the previous section that both entry in general as well as small-firm entry, as measured by births, varies greatly across manufacturing industries. What explains small-firm entry into manufacturing industries, and whether the determinants of small-firm entry are different from those for large-firm entry, has not been clearly distinguished in either the theoretical or empirical literature on entry. However, both a theoretical and empirical literature have evolved identifying the determinants of entry of firms of all sizes.

The starting point for the analysis of entry barriers is taken from the approach introduced by Bain (1956), Sylos-Labini (1962), and Modigliani (1958). The existence of entry barriers essentially depends upon two conditions: (1) the presence of structural conditions, such as economies of scale, absolute cost advantages, and product differentiation, and (2) the conduct of the incumbent firms in exploiting these conditions in the presence of potential and actual entry. Bain

(1956, 43) argued that entry would be impeded from three main sources—scale economies, the cost advantages established firms have over new entrants, and product differentiation. If there are no or only minimal entry barriers, entry can occur on a small scale, so that the effect of each additional entrant can be sufficiently unnoticeable and price is only negligibly influenced. In such cases, Bain (1956, 21–22) argued, existing firms will tend not to adjust prices in order to deter entry, but rather will maintain prices in excess of the level required to impede entry, so that short-run profits will be maximized. Of course, such levels of profits are not sustainable and are, ultimately, eroded by the ensuing entry.

However, Bain (1956) predicted a different situation in industries with substantial entry barriers. Here a potential entrant faces a choice—either enter at a level of scale that is suboptimal, where the level of output is less than that needed to attain MES, or else enter at a level of output that is at least sufficient to attain the MES level. The advantage of the first option is that the existing firms are less likely to engage in some retaliatory conduct in the event of suboptimal scale entry. The disadvantage of the second option is that prices are likely to decrease, since increased output of the new entrant will drive down the market price. Both Bain and Sylos-Labini argued that the existing firms would not alter their output levels in the presence of large-scale entry, but rather would end up reducing their prices. Either choice concerning the scale of output has negative implications for the entrant. If MES requires a substantial share of the market, a new entrant faces either a suboptimal plant and consequently higher unit costs, or prices below those existing prior to entry, and therefore profits below the level enjoyed by the established firms (Bain 1956, 53–55). Of course, as Scherer (1980, 246) points out, this conclusion holds only to the extent that the existing firms do not choose to reduce output when confronted by new entry.

The second type of barrier that Bain identified exists because the entrenched firms enjoy a cost advantage over potential entrants. Examples include ownership of technologies that, perhaps due to patents or mineral reserves, cannot be replicated at the same cost to the potential entrant as that experienced by existing firms.

The third type of barrier to entry is advertising. Bain argued that product differentiation can erect entry barriers in three ways. First, high prevailing levels of advertising create additional costs for new entrants that exist at all levels of output. Second, as mentioned in the previous chapter, the effect of advertising on firm revenues may be subject to economies of scale that result from the increasing effectiveness of the advertising message per unit of output. (However, there is at least some evidence questioning the existence of such scale economies [Boyer 1974; Simon 1970].) Third, if economies of scale exist in either production or advertising, the need to obtain funds for advertising will increase the capital requirements beyond what is needed for physical plant and equipment. While Bain focused on the higher promotional expenditures and/or price discounts that entrants must offer to induce switching by consumers who have a strong preference for an existing firm's product, Schmalensee (1978) offered an alternative way in which advertising poses an impediment to entry. There are substantial economies in advertising and other promotional methods, so that the introduction of a new product in a market where brand loyalty plays an important role requires a considerable lump sum of advertising expenditures. The proliferation of products by a single existing producer will deter entrants because any remaining product niches do not offer sufficient demand to enable new firms to justify the requisite expenditures on advertising. In fact, Schmalensee (1978) has demonstrated that a strategy of product proliferation in a market in which product differentiation is an important characteristic is more effective in deterring entry than is pursuing a strategy of limit pricing.

Following Bain (1956) and Sylos-Labini (1962), Gaskins (1971), Kamien and Schwartz (1971), and Matthews and Mirman (1983) also argued that pricing policies can serve as a deterrent. Similarly, various authors have suggested that patent policy (Gilbert and Newbery 1982), contract setting (Aghion and Bolton 1987), reputation (Milgrom and Roberts 1982), information (Fudenberg and Tirole 1986), and scale and capacity (Spence 1977; Dixit 1980) can serve to deter entry. Dixit (1987) and Milgrom and Roberts (1987) have similarly emphasized the importance of informational asymmetrics and first-mover advantage in rendering entry-deterring strategies profitable. However, as Smiley (1988) emphasizes, only a paucity of evidence exists that such policies are actually successfully implemented by firms.

In fact, the notion that structural conditions present entry barriers has become an issue shrouded in controversy. Stigler (1968), among others, was sharply critical of Bain's notion of entry barriers. By contrast, Stigler defined an entry barrier as additional costs that the entrant incurs, but that existing firms do not. Thus Stigler (1968, 67) rejected the argument that scale economies present a barrier to entry: "[I]f we define a barrier as differentially higher cost of new firms, there is no barrier and the firm size is governed by economies of scale and demand conditions." According to Stigler, industries in which substantial amounts of capital are required do not present a barrier to entry because the existing firms had to raise and presumably must continue to raise funds for capital investment, just as new entrants must finance the requisite capital. Stigler also applied this reasoning to the concept of advertising as a barrier to entry. Only if there are cost differentials other than those resulting from the quantity of advertising purchased does Stigler recognize that product differentiation can pose an entry barrier.

Following Stigler's earlier arguments, Schmalensee (1981) and Baumol and Willig (1981) similarly challenged the notion that scale economies and/or high capital requirements in an industry constitute an entry barrier. Baumol and Willig argued that, in fact, fixed costs and therefore large capital requirements and scale economies do not constitute a barrier to entry. Entry is impeded only in the presence of sunk costs, which are defined as costs that cannot be eliminated, even by the complete cessation of production. While capital that is not sunk can be shifted to producing other goods and therefore has a positive opportunity cost, sunk capital cannot be applied toward any alternative use and has no positive opportunity cost. Baumol and Willig (1981, 408) follow Stigler's earlier interpretation of barriers to entry by defining an entry barrier as "anything that requires an expenditure by a new entrant into an industry, but that imposes no equivalent cost upon an incumbent." Thus, while Bain considered capital requirements and cost advantages to constitute a barrier to entry, Baumol and Willig do not. This is partly because, like von Weizsäcker (1979), they consider an entry barrier to exist not only if an incumbent enjoys a cost advantage over an entrant, but also "if that advantage produces a welfare loss" (Baumol and Willig 1981, 408).

The notion that capital intensity does not constitute an entry barrier was attacked by Stiglitz (1987), who argued that even a very small amount of sunk costs serves to erect an entry barrier. According to Stiglitz's argument, if the fixed captial costs contain even an arbitrarily small component of sunk costs, capital will serve as a barrier to entry.

However, the debate in the literature may be more relevant to the entry of relatively large firms more than for small firms. As Scherer (1980, 243–244) observes, in general, "new entrants or existing fringe firms add output on such a small scale relative to total market volume that they can reasonably assume their influence on price to be negligible." To such small firms the possitively sloped cost of raising capital discussed in chapter 4 means that entering industries where large amounts of capital are required is more difficult than entering those industries that are less capital-intensive. That is, even if there is no barrier to entry in the Baumol-Willig sense of an accompanying welfare loss, the difficulty or cost of entry for small firms is certainly inversely related to the extent to which large amounts of capital, advertising, and R&D are required to survive. The recent work by Fazzari et al. (1987) discussed in the previous chapter documents that small firms face considerably greater difficulties and costs in obtaining capital funds than do their larger counterparts.

Considerably less controversial determinants of entry are the pre-entry profits and growth of the industry. Given a level of entry barriers and other market structure characteristics, the greater the industry profitability, the higher the incentive and profit potential for new entrants. Growth is hypothesized to be a catalyst for new entrants, since the existing firms may not be able to expand rapidly enough to meet increases in demand. In addition, it has been argued that incumbents are less likely to engage in retaliatory strategies in rapidly growing markets (Bhagwati 1970).

While the theoretical controversy regarding scale economies, capital intensity, and advertising as entry barriers has only intensified in the last decade, a considerable amount of empirical evidence has been accumulated. In fact, empirical tests have generally found a negative relationship between entry and capital requirements (Orr 1974; Gorecki 1975; Khemani and Shapiro 1986), although Highfield and Smiley (1987) found no such relationship. MES was found to be a barrier to entry, while past profit rates were found to be only a weak determinant of entry by Orr (1974) and Duetsch (1984). However, Khemani and Shapiro (1986) found past profits to be a strong determinant of entry.[5]

There is also some evidence relating R&D intensity and advertising influence with entry patterns. Orr (1974) found both advertising and R&D to constitude a barrier to entry, while Khemani and Shapiro (1986) found that R&D intensity has no effect on entry but that advertising deterred entry. Neither Duetsch (1984) nor Highfield and Smiley (1987) found advertising intensity to be a barrier to entry.

Two contradictory hypotheses have emerged in the literature regarding the relationship between market concentration and entry. On the one hand is the argument that the incumbent firms' ability to retaliate against entering firms depends upon the speed with which the entrants are detected. Thus, Khemani and Shapiro (1986) hypothesize that incumbent firms in concentrated industries should be able to detect entry more easily than in unconcentrated industries. Concentration is "designed to proxy the ability of incumbents to effect various entry deterring and retaliatory strategies" (1986, p. 1245). Alternatively, Simon and Bonini (1958) and Weiss (1976, 1979) suggest that, in fact, market concentration may actually be conducive to the viability of firms at suboptimal scale, ceteris paribus. Because market concentration is statistically associated with higher profits (Weiss 1974), firms at a level of output less than the MES level may be more likely to survive since prices are elevated above long-run average cost. Thus, more entry may occur in concentrated markets, for a given level of entry barriers and industry growth, since suboptimal scale firms have a greater opportunity of surviving. In fact, both Orr (1974) and Khemani and Shapiro (1986) found concentration to be negatively related to entry, while Duetsch (1984) found no relationship to exist. However, based on the two opposite hypotheses discussed above, it may be that, after controlling for entry barriers, smaller firms have a greater tendency to enter concentrated markets, since they are less likely to suffer the wrath of some retaliatory action by the incumbents, and since the elevated price would offer an otherwise difficult opportunity.

While much of the debate in the literature has focused on entry deterrence, there have been recent discussions on strategies that can be implemented to compensate for barriers to entry and entry-deterring strategies by existing firms (Yip 1982). For example, the existence of a high technological opportunity class has been hypothesized to induce entry,[6] but only Highfield and Smiley have found evidence supporting this. Both Nelson and Winter (1978) and Gort and Klepper (1982) have argued that a high level of innovative activity should be conducive to a high rate of entry. According to Gort and Klepper (1982, 631), "[W]ith the commercial introduction of a new prodcut by its first producer (though in rare instances there is a concurrent introduction of the product by more than one producer)" follows "a sharp increase in the rate of entry of new competitors into the industry." Since this entry occurs in the first stage of the product life cycle (Audretsch 1987), most of this entry will be by small firms. As the amount of innovative activity falls, Gort and Klepper argue, the rate of entry will tend to decrease until there is negative net entry in the final stages of the life cycle. Thus, even in a relatively unprofitable industry, substantial entry may follow a product innovation. For example, if someone had an idea for a business aircraft made of carbon composite materials and powered by a new type of fan engine, the fact that existing manufacturers of all-metal, jet-engined planes were losing money and experiencing sales declines *might* be regarded as *positive* factors in an entry decision.[7]

5.4   Birth Rates, Market Structure, and Innovative Activity

From the discussion of the literature in the previous section it should be clear that the major hypotheses concerning the determinants of entry behavior are (1) high growth and profit rates induce entry; (2) structural barriers impede entry; and (3) while a high-technology environment may serve as a barrier to entry, the extent to which small firms (new entrants in general) are able to innovate should promote entry. To test these hypotheses, we estimate the following regression model:

$$BR = \beta_1 GR + \beta_2 PCM + \beta_3 K/L + \beta_4 CRSFP + \beta_5 AD/S$$
$$+ \beta_6 SKILL + \beta_7 CR + \beta_8 TI + \beta_9 SIE + \mu, \tag{5.1}$$

where the dependent variable is the 1976–1982 birth rate, defined as the employment contributed by new firms during this period divided by the mean of industry employment in 1976 and 1982. This measure of employment-weighted gross entry is scaled by industry employment to adjust the birth measure for industry size. That is, in comparing industry entry within a cross-section context, it is important not to attribute a certain industry with a relatively high amount of entry activity merely because it is a large industry and contains a lot of firms (and a high level of employment). This is analogous to the procedure used by Orr (1974), Duetsch (1975), Highfield and Smiley (1984), and others in adjusting their measures of net entry, or net changes in the number of firms in an industry, by the total number of firms or sales in that industry. To compare the birth rates between large and small firms, the birth rates are alternatively calculated for firms with fewer than 100 employees, fewer than 500 employees, and with at least 500 employees.

GR refers to the average annual industry real growth rate between 1972 and 1977. PCM is defined as the 1977 industry price–cost margin. While, as previously discussed, empirical studies have generally identified a positive relationship between net entry and lagged profits, it should be noted that Storey and Jones (1987) found that profitability does not exert a strong influence on the formation of new firms. They hypothesized that since most small and new firms are in local and not national markets, the profitability of the industry at the national level may be less important than are variations in price–cost margins across different regions.

K/L is the 1977 capital–labor ratio and AD/S is advertising intensity, measured as advertising expenditures divided by value-of-shipments, 1977. Caves et al. (1975) argue that not only is capital intensity an important measure of scale economies, but the extent to which smaller firms experience a cost disadvantage relative to their larger counterparts plays an important role in encouraging or discouraging potential entrants. They introduced a measure of the cost disadvantage ratio of small firms, which they define as the average value-added per worker in plants supplying approximately the bottom half of industry value-added, as a percentage of the average value-added per worker in establishments supplying the top half. If the cost disadvantage ratio falls over time, firms might respond by entering. Conversely, increases in the cost disadvantage ratio may retard the rate of entry. Thus, changes in the cost disadvantage ratio may have a greater influence on entry than does a static level. We therefore use a slightly different measure, the relative change in small-firm productivity (CRSFP), which is measured as the small-firm change in sales per employee between 1976 and 1982, divided by the industry average change in sales per employee over the same period. Thus, a value of CRSFP exceeding one suggests that the productivity change of small firms over this period has been greater than that of large firms, while a value of CRSFP less than one implies that the productivity change of small firms has been less than that of their larger counterparts. Since this measure should reflect the change in the inherent cost disadvantage faced by small firms, we expect a positive relationship to emerge between CRSFP and the small-firm birth rate. That is, the greater the increase in small-firm efficiency relative to that of large firms, the greater should be small-firm entry, ceteris paribus.[8]

To measure the technological environment, total innovation activity (TI), which was discussed in detail in chapter 2, is included as an explanatory variable. Because of the somewhat ambiguous results that have emerged in the net entry studies, we also include a measure of the extent to which the industry relies upon skilled labor (SKILL). CR, defined as the four-firm concentration ratio in 1977, is expected to have a negative influence on birth rates.

Finally, SIE is defined as the small-firm innovation rate, measured as the number of innovations in the industry contributed by firms with fewer than 500 employees, divided by small-firm employment. Since small-firm innovation strategy is hypothesized to be a mechanism for compensating for inherent size disadvantages, SIE is expected to be positively related to the small-firm birth rate.

Table 5.3 shows the regression results, based on 238 four-digit SIC manufacturing industries, for the 1976–1982 birth rates of firms with fewer than 100 employees, fewer than 500 employees, at least 500 employees (large firms), and all firms. Several striking contrasts appear between the entry behavior of large and small firms, as well as between the results for the birth data and what has been found in the literature using the traditional measure of net changes in the number of firms.

First, lagged industry growth is apparently a greater inducement to entry than is lagged profits. This generally conforms to the results found for net entry. Further, this tendency seems to hold across all firm sizes. Second, in contrast to what has typically been found in net entry studies, advertising intensity appears to present a greater barrier to births than does capital intensity. Again, this result is consistent for both large and small firms. However, small-firm births are clearly inhibited in concentrated industries, but large-firm births tend to be greater. That large firms have a relative advantage in entering concentrated markets and small firms in unconcentrated markets perhaps explains some of the inconsistencies found for concentration when all firm sizes are combined in one cross-section regression model. For example, Orr (1974) and Khemani and Shapiro (1986) both found that high levels of concentration tend to deter entry in Canadian manufacturing industries, but this was not supported by either Duetsch (1975, 1984) or Highfield and Smiley (1987). In addition, the finding that small-firm births tend to be deterred in concentrated in-

Table 5.3
Regressions estimating birth rates for varying firm size[a]

	Firm-size class (employees)			
	1–99	1–499	500 +	All
K/L	-0.5834	0.5074	-0.5915	-0.0841
	(-0.3292)	(0.1733)	(-0.0491)	(-0.0062)
AD/S	-3.2139	-6.8340	-26.7510	-33.5850
	(-1.7014)*	(-2.1954)**	(-2.0901)**	(-2.3165)**
CR	-6.4952	-7.3256	39.3840	32.0580
	(-4.5447)**	(-3.1184)**	(4.0775)**	(2.9301)**
GR	9.4398	2.4831	10.9500	134.3300
	(2.0678)**	(3.1954)**	(3.5343)**	(3.8277)**
PCM	0.0010	-0.0514	0.5699	0.5185
	(0.0029)	(-0.0932)	(0.2512)	(0.2018)
SKILL	-0.1569	-0.2464	-0.0602	0.3066
	(-4.0218)**	(-3.8297)**	(-0.2275)	(1.0231)
TI	-3.0016	-5.7180	-12.2890	-18.0070
	(-2.6861)**	(-3.1135)**	(-1.6275)	(-2.1052)**
SIE	49.8861	10.7290	40.1280	50.8570
	(1.5890)	(2.0766)**	(1.8890)*	(2.1134)**
CRSFP	-91.6500	74.3970	27.0090	34.4480
	(-1.2836)	(0.4882)	(0.4311)	(0.4854)
Intercept	37.5170	29.6310	-13.7850	15.8460
	(1.5355)	(0.7075)	(-0.0801)	(0.0812)

Table 5.3
(continued)

	Firm-size class (employees)			
	1–99	1–499	500 +	All
Sample size	238	238	238	238
R^2	0.269*	0.220	0.146	0.129
F	9.337*	7.158**	4.345**	3.745**

Note: *Significant at the 90 percent level of confidence, two-tailed test. **Significant at the 95 percent level of confidence, two-tailed test.

a. t-statistics are listed in parentheses. The dependent variable has been multiplied by 1,000.

Table 5.4
Regressions estimating the ratio of small-firm births to total births[a]

	Measure of small firm (employees)	
	1–99	1–499
K/L	−4.8990	−8.5643
	(−0.8234)	(−1.1401)
AD/S	6.0695	9.3046
	(0.9570)	(1.1652)
CR	−28.7020	−41.6020
	(−5.9817)**	(−6.9034)**
GR	−15.3700	−32.6120
	(−1.0028)	(−1.6872)*
PCM	−0.7574	(0.9880)
	(0.6773)	(0.6980)
SKILL	−0.5215	−0.6420
	(−3.9829)**	(−3.8900)**
TI	−7.1023	−11.4660
	(−1.8931)*	(−2.4338)**
SIE	16.8870	24.0080
	(0.1602)	(0.1811)
CRSFP	−54.2670	19.2830
	(−2.2638)**	(0.4933)
Intercept	18.2950	24.4350
	(2.2302)**	(2.2744)**
Sample size	238	238
R^2	0.326	0.349
F	12.230**	13.558**

Note: *Significant at the 90 percent level of confidence, two-tailed test. **Significant at the 95 percent level of confidence, two-tailed test.
a. t-statistics are listed in parentheses. The dependent variables are the respective measures of small-firm births divided by births for the entire industry.

dustries is consistent with the conclusions of three different studies (Scherer 1973; Weiss 1976; and Pratten 1971) that the industry share of shipments accounted for by plants at suboptimal scale is negatively related to the degree of market concentration.

Finally, the technological environment apparently has disparate influences on small- and large-firm births. Both SKILL and TI are negative and statistically significant for small-firm births but not for large-firm births. This supports the hypothesis that industries in which innovative activity plays an important role are more accessible to large than to small firms. However, the positive coefficient of SIE for both small- and large-firm births suggests that industries in which small firms are able to contribute a relatively high share of the innovations are accessible to firms of all sizes. This provides at least some evidence supporting the Gort–Klepper (1982) hypothesis that innovative activity by new firms is conducive to entry.

To examine more precisely the differential behavior associated with large- and small-firm births, table 5.4 substitutes the ratio of small-firm births to total industry births as the dependent variable. The results generally confirm the tendencies observed in table 5.3. Relative to large firms, small-firm births are deterred in industries that are highly concentrated, use a high component of human capital, and have a high amount of innovative activity. In addition, when including slightly larger small firms in the second equation, the lagged industry growth rate is found to induce more large-firm births than small-firm births.

5.5   A Comparison with Net Entry Measures

The SBDB data also make it possible to construct the traditional net entry measures for different firm-size classes. This enables us not only to compare the traditonal measure of net entry with the measure of births or employment-weighted gross entry, which we introduced in the previous sections of this chapter, but also to determine if the behavior of small-firm net entry is consistent with the results in the literature found for the net entry of all firms. Thus, we use the same basic model as in the previous section, but substitute the 1978–1980 small-firm net entry rate for the dependent variable. The small-firm net entry rate is defined as the change in the number of firms with fewer than 500 employees between 1978 and 1980, divided by the average total number of firms in the industry in 1978 and 1980. It should be noted that unlike many other empirical entry studies, the SBDB data enable us to measure changes in the numbers of firms (enterprises) and not just new subsidiaries, branches, or plants (establishments) of existing firms.

Because all other empirical studies of net entry use a measure of R&D intensity instead of the measure of total innovative activity (TI), which we used in the previous section, we present regression results substituting the 1977 total R&D/sales (RDT) for TI. However, when TI is included in the model instead of RDT, the results are qualitatively unchanged.

Using the 1978–1980 small-firm net entry rate as the dependent variable, the regression model was estimated for 247 four-digit SIC industries and the results are shown in table 5.5. Equation 1 shows that, as for the birth rate, lagged growth significantly induces small-firm entry. However, in contrast to the results using the birth data, the positive and statistically significant coefficient of PCM suggests that small firms are induced to enter those industries that have been more profitable, even after controlling for other major influences. As was found for birth rates, capital intensity apparently does not represent a substantial entry barrier for firms with fewer than 500 employees. While advertising intensity similarly has no significant effect on small-firm net entry, it was found to significantly deter small-firm births. Just as TI was found to deter small-firm births, RDT is negatively related to small-firm net entry. However, it is quite plausible that this statistical correlation is more attributable to the fact that in some industries government R&D represents a substantial amount of the total R&D, and government R&D funds generally goes to larger firms. In addition, the shakeout of small firms from defense contracting in the early 1970s may have had lagged effects on entry, which are captured in our data. However, substituting company R&D for total R&D yields the same results in table 5.5.

SKILL has no influence on small-firm net entry, although it was found to be negatively related to the small-firm birth rate. Just as the level of market concentration was found in the previous section to exert a negative effect on small-firm births, the negative and significant coefficient of CR reinforces the conclusion that small firms are deterred from entering highly concentrated industries. Finally, the positive and statistically significant coefficient of SIE implies that innovation is a viable strategy used by small firms to enter an industry.

Table 5.5
Regression results for models for small-firm entry (t-ratios listed in parentheses)[a]

Variable	Equation			
	(1)	(2)	(3)	(4)
Intercept	-1.630	-6.597	-6.460	-0.185
	(-0.505)	(-1.759)*	(-1.734)*	(-0.042)
GR	39.654	39.588	41.047	41.803
	(3.096)**	(3.126)**	(3.258)**	(3.361)**
PCM	0.015	0.017	0.017	0.016
	(1.699)*	(1.962)**	(1.971)**	(1.854)*
K/L	-0.035	-0.043	-0.031	-0.043
	(-0.820)	(-1.005)	(-0.735)	(-1.003)
AD/S	0.484	1.898	1.320	-1.397
	(0.095)	(0.375)	(0.262)	(-0.275)
RDT	-1.031	-1.042	-1.067	-1.133
	(-1.784)*	(-1.822)*	(-1.874)*	(-2.019)**
SKILL	7.113	10.170	7.745	-0.088
	(0.333)	(0.481)	(0.368)	(-0.004)
CR	-0.075	-0.101	-0.101	-0.121
	(-1.959)*	(-2.576)**	(-2.592)**	(-3.108)**
SIE	1.453	1.605	1.544	1.497
	(1.953)*	(2.175)**	(2.105)**	(2.067)**
UNION	—	1.088	0.098	0.085
		(2.523)**	(2.271)**	(1.991)**

CRSFP	—	—	0.505 (2.071)**	0.527 (2.191)**
SFP7	—	—	—	−0.070 (−2.694)**
R^2	0.120	0.143	0.159	0.184
F	4.068**	4.405**	4.448**	4.811**

Note: *Statistically significant at the 90 percent level of confidence, two-tailed test. **Statistically significant at the 95 percent level of confidence, two-tailed test.

a. The small-firm entry rate is measured as the net change in the number of firms with fewer than 500 employees between 1978 and 1980, divided by the average of the total number of firms in 1978 and 1980. The dependent variable has been multiplied by 100 and the coefficient of AD/S has been divided by 100.

This is consistent with the findings based on the birth data in the previous section.

Equations 2, 3, and 4 include three additional variables that also might be expected to influence net entry behavior. The percentage of employees in an industry that belong to a union in 1975 (UNION) is included in equation 2. Because unionization has been found to exert a positive influence upon wage rates, it could be expected that small firms, which typically can avoid becoming unionized by virtue of their size, would be induced to enter industries in which their larger counterparts have relatively high wages. While the positive and significant coefficient of UNION supports this hypothesis, this result may also reflect the fact that unionized workers were well protected from rapid inflation by wage escalators during the 1970s, creating unique opportunities for small firms to enter. These conditions might not be replicated in the 1980s.

In equation 3 the positive and significant coefficient of CRSFP suggests that the greater the increase in small-firm productivity, relative to that of large firms, the greater the rate of net small-firm entry. This variable was not found to have a significant effect in the previous section when the birth data were used. Finally, in equation 4, the small-firm share of industry sales (SFP7) is included to examine whether small firms tend to enter those industries in which they already dominate the industry or industries with only a low small-firm presence. The negative coefficient indicates that, in fact, after controlling for other influences, small firms generally do not enter those industries in which there is already a considerable presence of small firms.

5.6 Conclusion

There are perhaps two puzzling results emerging in this chapter. The first is that firms are apparently not deterred from entering industries that are capital-intensive. Capital intensity failed to have a significant effect on either the traditional measure of net entry or the new measure of births. Since this result holds for small firms as well as for large firms, it raises the questions, "Why do firms enter an industry at a scale of output that presumably is suboptimal?" and "How can such firms, subsequent to entry, possibly hope to survive?"

The answers to these questions may, in fact, be related to the second puzzling result. While the innovative activity of small firms is found to promote the entry of firms of all sizes, the extent of both total innovative activity and R&D intensity is found to inhibit entry. This suggests that the relationship between innovation and entry is complex. Apparently entry is promoted in a technological environment conducive to small-firm innovative activity. However, given a level of small-firm innovative activity, the greater the total amount of innovation in the industry, the less the technological environment facilitates entry. These two distinct technological environments may not be so different from what Winter (1984) hypothesized as comprising the entrepreneurial regime and the routinized regime. That is, innovative activity may provide the vehicle for entry in the entrepreneurial regime but not in the routinized regime.

This might also provide at least some explanation as to why firms are not deterred from entering capital-intensive industries. The expected result from innovation is growth, enabling the firm to attain the MES level of output. That all entering firms, in fact, do not successfully innovate (and ultimately fail) plays an important role in intra-industry dynamics—the topic of chapter 7.

6

Flexible Technology and the Size Distribution of Firms

6.1 Introduction

The starting point for this chapter is the observed shift in the firm-size distribution in the group of industries comprising the engineering or metalworking industries. Using the SBDB and Bureau of the Census data, we find that both the mean employment size of firms (enterprises) and plants (establishments) has decreased, resulting in a considerable increase in the share of sales accounted for by small firms between 1976 and 1986. Of course, as Scherer (1980, 99) warns, both substitution of capital for labor along with increases in productivity will tend to bring about smaller plant and firm sizes in terms of employment, but not in terms of sales. However, the view throughout this book, as well as elsewhere in much of the literature (see, for example, Bolton Report 1971), is that the distinguishing feature of size, at least where small firms are concerned, is the employment criterion. Thus, a shift in the size distribution toward firms and plants with fewer employees would be significant, even if there were no concomitant change in the size distribution of firms toward enterprises and establishments with fewer sales. It is also important to recognize that any such observed shift in the size distribution of firms does not distinguish between larger firms becoming smaller, or the number of smaller enterprises in existence simply increasing.

In fact, shifts in the size distribution of firms have been observed in other industries over various time periods. For example, Sands (1961) identified an apparent increase in plant size between 1904 and 1947. On a somewhat related issue, Scherer (1980) measured an increase in MES between 1958 and 1970 in the steel, cement, brewing, paint, refrigerator, and battery industries, while there was a modest decrease in bearings, shoes, and weaving. Blair (1948) argued that plant and firm size have generally increased sinced the Industrial Revolution. He pointed out that plants with more than 1,000 employees increased their employment share in U.S. manufacturing by 9 percent between 1914 and 1937. However, Blair (1948, 154) argued that due to particular innovations and fundamental shifts in technology, the trend toward increasing size had been replaced by the opposite trend toward smaller size: "[B]ecause of the greater machinability of light metals, the simplicity and low cost of producing plastics and plywood, and the reduced obsolescence and greater productivity of machinery resulting from the use of alloys, it may be expected that the increased substitution of these new materials will reduce the amount of capital required per unit of product and thereby tend to result in the establishment of new, smaller, and more efficient plants."

Following in this tradition, the purpose of this chapter is to try to shed some light on the shift in the firm-size distribution in the metalworking industries by suggesting that the adoption of new technologies and production methods have accounted for at least some of this shift. Throughout most of this century, the industrial technology in these markets favored mass production, or the application of special-purpose machines to produce standardized products. However, more recently manufacturing technology "has been revolutionized by the cost reduction of small-scale production relative to large-scale and the degree of flexibility offered by the technology" (Carlsson 1984, 91). In this chapter we examine the effect that adoption of numerically controlled (NC) machines and robots has had on the size distribution of firms and, in particular, on the share of sales accounted for by small firms.

In the second section we examine the emergence of flexible-production technology along with the evolution of small firms in the engineering or metalworking sector. Compared with other manufacturing industries, the engineering industries have the most intensive use of machine tools. After developing the model in the third section, we test the hypothesis that the change in the share of sales accounted for by small firms is positively related to the application of NC machines and robots. Finally, in the last section a conclusion and summary are provided. Based on two different measures of small firms and three distinct time periods, we find that the implementation of certain flexible technologies, such as NC machine tools and programmable robots, has tended to promote an increased small-firm share of sales. Thus, we conclude that there is at least some evidence supporting the hypothesis that certain flexible technologies have contributed to the shift in the size distribution toward a greater presence of small firms.

6.2   The Emergence of Flexible Technologies and Small Firms

Machine tools have played an important role in manufacturing ever since the Industrial Revolution. Until the end of the last century, a major limitation of their applicability was an inadequate source of power. However, with the development of the electric motor in 1892 as a power source for individual machine tools, and with the widespread electrification throughout U.S. manufacturing at the turn of the century, this problem was alleviated. By the end of the 1920s, a major new technology had been introduced in the machine tool industry—the transfer machine or station-type machine. Transfer machines consist of a number of smaller machines or work stations, each used for a separate operation such as drilling or milling, organized to work together in such a fashion that a workpiece is automatically put in place at one work station and then transferred automatically to the next work station. Transfer machines were at the core of the increased reliance on mass production that emerged following the Second World War. The first large-scale application of automation was at the Ford engine plant in Brook Park, Ohio. Ford tied together several large transfer machines into a continuous system of automatic assembly machines. This system became known as "Detroit automation." While the development of automation continued into the early 1970s, the most important aspect of technological progress in the last thirty years appeared in an entirely different direction—the development of numerical controls.

With the advent of numerical controls in the late 1940s, the potential emerged for reversing the 150-year technological trend in machine tools favoring large-scale production. The original developments in numerical controls started around 1949, when the U.S. Air Force began to use machine tools in the aircraft industry that could produce highly complex parts that were not only more accurate than those produced by conventional methods, but also less expensive. Using the financial support from the government, John Parsons and the Servomechanisms Laboratory at MIT developed prototypes by 1951. The first commercial NC machines were displayed in 1955 at the National Machine Tool Builders Association show (Romeo 1975).

NC machines occupy an intermediate position between transfer machines and conventional hand-operated machines. Since the 1970s, there has been an increased emphasis on manufacturing larger and faster NC machines, thereby enhancing their competitiveness vis-à-vis transfer machines. A computerized system consisting of several NC machines, a programmable robotic material-handling system, a tool-changing system, and a central control system comprises a flexible manufacturing system. A flexible manufacturing system serves the same purpose as a conventional automated production system, except that it can be more easily reprogrammed and made compatible with computer-aided design (CAD) and computer-aided manufacturing (CAM), rendering the overall system of production substantially more flexible than transfer machines. Subsequently the cost of small-volume production of complex parts has been reduced much more than that of large-volume production of standardized products. Such systems represent an enormous advantage for small-batch production (Carlsson 1984, 1989b).

That the implementation of NC machines and robots enhances the flexibility of production is generally uncontested. And, given the long tradition in industrial organization of considering technology to be one of the main determinants of market structure (see Scherer 1980, ch. 4), it is not surprising to think that this new technology might have had some impact on the size distribution of firms. What is less certain, however, is the exact nature of this impact. Just as there are several reasons for thinking that flexible manufacturing technology may reduce scale economies, thereby enhancing the viability of smaller plants and firms, there are also counter-arguments suggesting that this new technology may help larger firms more than their smaller counterparts.

One of the reasons why the implementation of flexible technology may shift the firm-size distribution toward larger firms is the higher price for comparable machinery. Gerwin (1983) notes that a NC machine typically costs more than conventional machinery that performs the same function. Based on a 1983 in-depth survey of forty small engineering firms in southeast England, Dodgson (1985) found that the mean cost of a NC machine tool was £80,979 (roughly $140,000). Since this represented 4.1 percent of the mean firm sales and 21.8 percent of the average net book value of plant and machinery in 1982 of the firms included in the sample, investment in NC machines requires a substantial financial commitment. In an even more recent survey comparing the application of NC machine tools in small, medium, and large firms, Burnes (1988) found that the prices varied between £20,000 (roughly $35,000) and £500,000 (roughly $875,000), with most of the machines costing between £50,000 (roughly $87,500) and £150,000 (roughly $260,000).

Perhaps the relatively high cost of NC machines explains both their slow rate of diffusion as well as the bias in diffusion rates toward large firms. Although the major technological inventions for NC machines occurred during the end of the 1950s, they were not commercially applied until the late 1960s (Nabseth and Ray 1974). By the end of the 1960s, the production of NC machine tools accounted for about one-fifth of the U.S. production of all machine tools. In fact, this share declined in the early 1970s and did not exceed 20 percent until the end of the decade. As Carlsson (1990) notes, the extensive diffusion of NC machine tools did not really begin until 1975, when the minicomputer began to be used as the basis for the numerical control unit, thus enabling computer numerical control (CNC) to be used.

There is substantial evidence that the diffusion rate of NC machine tools has varied between large and small firms. Romeo (1975) examined a sample of 152 firms from ten manufacturing industries and found that the rate of adoption by 1970 was positively related to firm size. In the same year, a study by Globerman (1975) used a survey of ninety Canadian firms to confirm the earlier findings by Mansfield et al. (1971) that the probability of a firm adopting NC machine technology is positively related to size. Romeo offered three reasons why the diffusion rate was observed to be higher for larger than for smaller firms. First, because more equipment is depreciated and needs to be replaced in the larger firms, they are presented with more opportunities for introducing new equipment. Second, the scope of production, in terms of product lines, tends to be greater in large than in small firms. Thus, large firms are more likely to be producing some good, or set of goods, that are particularly conducive to application of the new technology. Finally, the financial resources available to large firms exceed those at the disposal of small firms, enabling the larger firms to more easily finance a new capital investment and survive should that risky investment fail.

Despite this evidence that the diffusion rate of large firms exceeded that of small firms in the adoption of NC machines in the 1960s, there is substantial evidence that such machines were available and widely used by small firms in the late 1970s and early 1980s. For example, Northcott and Rogers (1984) found that of 1,200 factories with at least twenty employees in the United Kingdom, 23 percent used CNC machine tools in 1983, and they predicted that this would rise to 30 percent in 1985. Most significantly, they found that the share of large firms that had adopted CNC technology was 31 percent and declined only slightly with decreasing firm size, so that 22 percent of the firms with between 200 and 499 employees and 21 percent with between 20 and 199 employees used CNC machines. Similar results were found in a 1982 survey, which identified that one-fourth of all adopters of CNC machines had fewer than 50 employees (Dodgson 1985).

A massive 1985 survey of 6,000 firms in the Netherlands revealed similar results. Koning and Poutsma (1988) found that about 55 percent of the plants with at least 200 employees had adopted CNC machines, while about 40 percent of the plants with between 50 and 199 employees used this new technology. Thus, considerable evidence exists that by the early 1980s the use of CNC machines had clearly spread to small firms as well as to large firms.

There is at least some indication that smaller firms employ different strategies in implementing CNC machines than do their larger counterparts. For example, using the same survey for the Netherlands described above, Poutsma and Zwaard (1989) found that the operator, rather than a supervisor, is much more likely to program a CNC machine in smaller than in larger firms and when the batches are of a smaller lot. Similarly, the machines were more frequently programmed directly at the location of the machine for small firms, but more likely either somewhere else on the shop floor or elsewhere in the plant for larger firms. Dodgson (1985) also found that the percentage of cost savings tended to be greater for the smaller than for the larger firms that had adopted CNC technology.

However, it should clearly be noted that while there has been considerable diffusion of CNC machine tools among smaller firms, this is less the case for robots, computer-aided design (CAD) and computer-aided manufacturing (CAM), flexible manufacturing cells, and certainly not the case for so-called flexible manufacturing systems (FMS), and the most recently introduced fully automated factory (FAF). That is, while NC and CNC were the first forms of flexible machinery, the continued evolution of new flexible technologies has brought a host of various other flexible production techniques. It should be emphasized that reference to "flexible technology" may include any of the various forms of flexible production, whereas any specific type, such as a stand-alone NC machine tool, is clearly distinct from, say, a flexible manufacturing system (FMS).

An industrial robot is typically composed of three components. The first is a mechanical system of grippers or some other special-purpose device, such as a welding or painting mechanism. The second element is a "servo-system," which precisely controls and positions the "arms" of the robot. Finally, a computer control system is required to coordinate and direct the robot (International Trade Administration 1985). Industrial robots are primarily used for material handling and machine loading, as well as for specific process functions such as spot and arc welding, spraying, finishing, and assembly.

Computer-aided design involves an interactive computer terminal that designs product models as well as performs modifications and tests. In particular, CAD is used in computer graphics and simulation models. Computer-aided manufacturing systems typically involve applying CAD to control the actual manufacturing process. CAM enables the integration of systems comprised of machine tools, robots, and other process machinery used in manufacturing (Beatty and Gordon 1988). The mean cost of a CAD/CAM system fell from $400,000 in 1980 to $250,000 in 1985. However, using a microcomputer, smaller stand-alone CAD/CAM work stations cost as little as $10,000 in 1982 (International Trade Administration 1985).

What has been termed a "flexible manufacturing cell" (FMC) involves the integration of a system of several machine tools and pallet-changing equipment, such as an industrial robot. Since a FMC is usually a fixed process where the separate parts flow sequentially between operations, it is generally oriented toward manufacturing low-volume batches comprised of multiple parts.

A flexible manufacturing system typically consists of multiple work stations, an automated material-handling system, and a supervision system through computer control. In addition, a FMS may often rely on CAM technology as well as automatic tool changing, in-process inspection, parts washing, and automated storage and retrieval systems. An important distinction between FMC from FMS is that FMS is controlled by a central computer, but FMC is not. Thus, an advantage of FMS is that only minimal operator attention is required.

Numerous researchers, such as Shepherd (1982), have argued that the advent of NC machine tools may have decreased the MES in at least some industries. At the close of his comprehensive survey,

Dodgson (1985, 98) concluded that, "The ability to produce quality goods quickly and at competitive prices is enhanced when CNC machines are used with a skilled workforce capable of performing a wide range of tasks. With declining mass markets, engineering firms became increasingly forced to cater for smaller and more specialized market niches. Once identified, the ability to adapt production effort to these smaller markets quickly has enormous benefits." *The Engineer* (1984, 26) also noted how the adoption of NC machinery may have promoted the viability of smaller firms: "It is generally acknowledged that one NC lathe can displace four conventional machines; or one NC machinery center, three conventional. First cost may be multiplied by three, but the number of operators significantly reduced."

However, while the main hypothesis in this chapter is that implementation of several of the earliest flexible technologies—NC machines and robots—has promoted the viability of small firms, some of the most recent technological developments, such as the FMS, may actually reverse this trend. The first FMS in the world was installed in the United States in 1970. Subsequently there were forty-six additional FMS plants in operation in the United States by 1985. These plants were mostly in the farm machinery, automobile, aircraft, and locomotive industries. As a major U.S. government study concludes, the main reason for their relatively slow rate of diffusion is that, "The FMS typically requires substantial initial outlays, the justification of which is often difficult" (International Trade Administration 1985, viii). Not surprisingly, Tombak and De Meyer (1988) concluded from a 1985 survey of U.S. and European firms that U.S. adopters of FMS were 2.67 times larger than nonadopters. Similarly, they found that the European adopters were 1.92 times larger than nonadopters.

While it seems likely that FMS will continue to be adopted almost exclusively by large firms, there is at least some evidence that implementation of FMS can reduce employee size of firms. In a detailed study of FMS in sixty Japanese firms, which included almost all of the Japanese firms that had adopted FMS, Jaikumar (1986) found that holding constant the number of parts produced per system, the mean number of operators fell from 601 with the conventional system to 129 with the FMS. Similarly, the required number of machine tools was reduced from 253 with the conventional system to 133 using FMS. This is consistent with the conclusion of Merrifield (1987, 6) that even flexible manfacturing systems will ultimately "accelerate both the decentralization and the proliferation of thousands of new small businesses throughout the country."

Jaikumar also pointed out that FMS plants required about one-thrid less floor space, and about one-half fewer CNC machines. In this sense, FMS can actually be viewed as a substitute for the older and considerably simpler NC technology.

This discussion of the evolution of flexible technologies should serve to point out that even if the adoption of NC machine tools shifted the size distribution toward a greater presence of small firms, such a shift should not be in any way considered permanent. The diffusion of more advanced technologies, such as FMS or the fully automated factory of the future, is just as likely to result in shifts in the size distribution toward larger firms. However, it does seem clear, as Blair (1948) pointed out over forty years ago, that the size distribution of firms is subject to considerable influence from the prevailing technology. The hypothesis that at least certain types of flexible technologies have contributed to a shift in the firm-size distribution is summarized by Dosi (1988, 1155): "As an historical example, I suggest we are currently observing, at least in the industrial countries, a process of change in the size distribution of plants and firms that is significantly influenced by the new flexibility–scale trade-offs associated with electronic production technologies. . . . [I]n mass-production industries the higher flexibility of the new forms of automation is likely to allow the efficient survival of relatively smaller firms (as compared to the past)."

In fact, small firms have accounted for an increased share of sales over time in the engineering industries—nonelectrical machinery, electrical machinery, transportation equipment, and instruments—where the application of mass production technology was historically the norm and large-scale firms tended to dominate the industry.[1] As shown in table 6.1, firms with fewer than 100 employees in the engineering industries included in our sample accounted for 15.6 percent of total sales in 1976. This was just slightly above the average for all U.S. manufacturing industries of 14.9 percent. The share of sales accounted for by small firms in the engineering industries subsequently increased and accounted for 22.5 percent of total sales in 1986. The increase in the presence of firms with fewer than 500 employees during this time period was even more dramatic, rising from a share of 30.1 percent of sales in 1976 to 39.7 percent of sales in 1986.

Table 6.1
Mean share of total sales accounted for by small firms in the engineering
industries (standard deviations listed in parentheses)[a]

Small-firm measure	1976 (percentages)	1982	1984	1986
Fewer than 100	15.6	17.2	21.4	22.5
employees	(12.7)	(13.2)	(20.2)	(20.8)
Few than 500	30.1	30.2	36.8	39.7
employees	(21.7)	(19.4)	(30.6)	(33.0)

a. See appendix C for a list of the industries included.

Of course, this increased importance of small firms in the engineering
industries during the last decade cannot necessarily be attributed to
the diffusion of flexible technologies. A more formal statistical test is
performed in the next section.

6.3   Technology and Shifts in the Firm-Size Distribution

In chapter 3 we identified specific characteristics of technology and
knowledge that determine the size distribution of firms. We found
that the small-firm share of industry sales (SFP) in any given period
t is determined by factors representing the states of technology (T)
and knowledge (K), along with the extent of what could be termed
structural barriers to entry (BE), so that

$$SFP_t = f(T_t, K_t, BE_t). \tag{6.1}$$

Using the standard linear assumption for tractibility led to a cross-
section regression model

$$SFP_1 = \beta_0 + \beta_1 T_1 + \beta_2 K_1 + \beta_3 BE_1 + \mu_1. \tag{6.2}$$

An implication is that an industry firm-size distribution would remain constant over time as long as these basic underlying determinants remain invariant. That is, the small-firm presence (SEP) would
not be expected to change unless there was a change in T_1, K_1, or BE_1.
In such a case, the change in the industry firm-size distribution, or in
our case the SFP, between periods 1 and 2 is given by

$$SFP_2 - SFP_1 = \beta_0 + \beta_1 (T_2 - T_1) + \beta_2 (K_2 - K_1)$$
$$+ \beta_3 (BE_2 - BE_1) + \mu_2 - \mu_1. \tag{6.3}$$

Although the original inventions for NC machines and programmable robots were generally made several decades ago, as was mentioned in the previous section, the diffusion has only generally taken place within the last decade. Thus, if the technological states T_1 and T_2 are represented by the application of NC machines and programmable robots for the years 1976 and 1986, T_1 would virtually be zero, since their use was still trivial in the United States in 1976 (Carlsson 1984).[2]

To empirically test the hypothesis that the implementation of certain flexible-production technology has tended to promote small firms relative to large firms, we estimate

$$SFC = \beta_0 + \beta_1 SPR + \beta_2 SNC + \beta_3 SMP + \beta_4 SST$$
$$+ \beta_5 SAA + \beta_6 RD/S + \beta_7 NPEMPL + \beta_8 K/L + \mu, \quad (6.4)$$

where SFC is defined as the change over time in the share of sales accounted for by small firms or $SFC = SFP_2 - SFP_1$. To test for robustness of results, three different time periods are used, 1982–1986, 1976–1984, and 1976–1986. Comparing the results for these three different time periods enables us to find out whether the model varies substantially over different phases of the business cycle.[3] Similarly, two distinct measures of a small firm are used—firms with fewer than 500 employees, and firms with fewer than 100 employees. Since there is no widely accepted definition of the size boundary for small firms, using these two measures also provides a test of robustness.

The first five explanatory variables are specific measures of technologies used in the production process. SPR represents the share (percentage) of the total number of machines accounted for by programmable robots in 1983. Using programmable robots rather than mechanical devices to connect various machines to each other enhances the flexibility of NC machine tools.

The share (percentage) of the total number of machines accounted for by NC machine tools is represented by SNC. As described in the previous section, the application of NC machine tools is conducive to flexible production, and therefore batch production and short production runs. It is hypothesized that the application of NC machine tools should contribute to the shift in the size distribution toward small firms, and therefore a positive relationship between SNC and SFC is expected.

The share (percentage) of the total number of machines accounted for by mechanical presses in 1983 is represented by SMP. Mechanical presses were the most prevalent type of machine used in the engineering industries, accounting for an average of 6.65 percent of all machines used. Since mechanical presses tend to be used more predominantly for mass production, β_3 is expected to be negative. SST represents the share (percentage) of the total number of machines accounted for by transfer or station-type machines in 1983. The transfer machine represents the most rigid use of mass production technology. Since transfer machines are related to the extent of mass production, SST is expected to exert a negative effect on the change in the share of sales accounted for by small firms.

SAA represents the share (percentage) of the total number of machines in the industry accounted for by automatic assembly machines in 1983. The greater the extent to which a production process relies upon a highly mechanized production of commodity-like goods, the greater will be the share of total machines accounted for by assembly machines. Since SAA reflects a mass production technology, it should be negatively related to SFC.

It should be recognized that these five different types of machine tools cannot at all be considered homogeneous. That is, one automatic assembly machine is not the equivalent of one programmable robot or one mechanical press. Rather, these are very heterogeneous measures that cannot be readily compared to determine which type of machine tool is most prevalent in any given industry. The usefulness of these measures is only in comparing the application of any given type of machine tool across different industries.

To represent changes in knowledge in the industry, the 1982 R&D/ sales ratio (RD/S) and a measure of skilled labor (NPEMPL), defined as the share of total employment accounted for by nonproduction employees in 1982, are included as explanatory variables. The 1982 measure of R&D intensity is based on National Science Foundation two- and three-digit SIC estimates, and are then repeated across common four-digit SIC industries. These two variables may affect the size distribution of firms differently. While industries in which the evolution of knowledge has been more dependent upon R&D have not been hospitable to small firms, as discussed and found in chapter 4, Winter (1984) has argued that smaller firms are more likely to prosper in industries in which the evolution of knowledge emanates more from skilled labor and high levels of human capital. In the third chapter we found support for Winter's hypothesis that small-firm innovation emanates from a different technological regime than

Table 6.2
Correlation matrix for production process variables

	SNC	SPR	SST	SAA	SMP
SNC	1.00	–	–	–	–
SPR	0.27	1.00	–	–	–
SST	−0.04	0.11	1.00	–	–
SAA	−0.38	0.25	−0.01	1.00	–
SMP	−0.59	−0.16	−0.10	0.37	1.00

Source: See appendix A.

does large-firm innovation. In particular, we found that in industries where skilled labor plays a relatively important role, small firms tend to have the innovative advantage. In such industries, the evolution of knowledge is more likely to be the product of high levels of human capital, resulting in a firm-size distribution more favorable to small firms.

In chapter 4 we found that the presence of small firms is impeded in industries that are high in capital intensity. In such industries the barriers to entry and expansion facing small firms may be too great to afford anything other than a nominal role for small firms. To control for such structural barriers, we include the capital–labor ratio (K/L) as an explanatory variable. K/L is expected to exert a negative effect on the change in the share of sales accounted for by small firms over any given period of time, since a high level of capital intensity represents industries in which there could exist substantial barriers to small-firm entry and expansion.

It should be recognized that while SAA, SMP, and SST are types of technology generally associated with mass production, they are not at all interchangeable measures. That is, as table 6.2 shows, the correlation between SAA and SST is virtually zero, while that between SMP and SST is actually negative (−0.10).[4] These measures clearly represent distinct types of technologies associated with mass production that are not necessarily used in conjunction with each other. For example, mechanical presses are typically used in metal-forming industries, while transfer machines tend to be used in metal-cutting industries. Similarly, although they both measure the extent of flexible production, SNC and SPR should not be considered substitute measures of the same phenomenon. As the low correlation of 0.27

between SNC and SPR indicates, NC machine tools and programmable robots are clearly two very distinct types of technology that have not been applied consistently across the engineering industries.

Another important qualification of these technology measure is that they do not exhaust all types of machinery applied. That is $\sum_{i=1}^{5}$ $S_i + S_0 = 1$, where S_i represents each of the five types of machinery discussed above and S_0 represents all other types of machinery. Thus all five measures can be included in the regression model without the problems of a singular matrix.

6.4 Empirical Results

Using ninety-eight four-digit SIC engineering industries (SIC sectors 34–38), the regression model was estimated. The dependent variable is defined as the change in the share of sales accounted for by firms with fewer than 500 employees between 1982 and 1986 (SF58286). The results are shown in table 6.3.[5] Some, but not all, of the production process variables are significantly related to the change in the small-firm presence over this period. As expected, the relative presence of small firms has tended to increase in industries with a relatively extensive application of NC machine tools (SNC) and programmable robots (SPR). Small firms have been less successful in industries in which transfer machines play an important role, as indicated by the negative (but insignificant) coefficient of SST. Neither of the coefficients of the other two measures of mass production technology, SAA and SMP, is statistically significant, suggesting that the relative presence of small firms has remained stable in industries where these technologies are important. The coefficient is also negative but not significant for capital intensity (K/L).

While skilled labor (NPEMPL), is found to be positively related to the increased presence of small firms, the coefficient of RD/S is not statistically significant. This provides at least some evidence that the type of knowledge emanating from high levels of human capital is more conducive to small firms than to large ones. Not only is this consistent with the findings in chapter 3, but it supports the hypothesis of Winter (1984) that new and small firms have a relative advantage in industries in which skilled labor makes a key contribution to additions in the knowledge base. The F-ratio is the greatest in equation 4, where only two of the measures of mass production tech-

Table 6.3
Regression results for change in share of sales accounted for by small firms, 1982–1986 (t-ratios listed in parentheses)[a]

	(1) OLS	(2) OLS	(3) OLS	(4) OLS	(5) LOGIT
SPR	0.7016 (1.7629)*	0.6686 (1.7791)*	0.6880 (1.7380)*	0.6726 (1.7993)*	0.0045 (1.4679)
SNC	0.5099 (1.5691)	0.5463 (1.8666)*	0.5659 (1.8294)*	0.5262 (1.8436)*	0.0038 (1.6832)*
SMP	-0.3881 (-0.5846)	-0.3520 (-0.5447)	—	-0.3566 (-0.5546)	-0.0029 (-0.5593)
SST	-0.4169 (-0.0539)	-0.2081 (-0.0272)	-2.1521 (-0.3025)	-0.3616 (-0.0476)	-0.0156 (-0.2506)
SAA	0.2575 (0.2639)	—	0.1401 (0.1472)	—	—
K/L	-0.1246 (-0.3941)	-0.1091 (-0.3531)	-0.1069 (-0.3410)	-0.1227 (-0.4024)	-0.0017 (-0.6651)
RD/S	43.4250 (0.4203)	32.4520 (0.3449)	30.5450 (0.3850)	—	—
NPEMPL	0.3103 (2.7467)**	0.2968 (2.9578)**	0.2834 (2.7565)**	0.2878 (2.9854)**	0.0020 (2.5235)**
Intercept	-35.3400 (-1.4051)	-35.2040 (-1.4073)	-38.8290 (-1.5951)	-32.1540 (-1.3808)	-0.8744 (-4.5889)**
R^2	0.160	0.159	0.157	0.158	0.125
F	2.117**	2.435**	2.389**	2.849**	2.166**

Note: *Statistically significant at the 90 percent level of confidence, two-tailed test. **Statistically significant at the 90 percent level of confidence, two-tailed test.
a. A small firm is defined as an enterprise with fewer than 500 employees.

nology, SMP and SST, and one measure representing changes in knowledge, NPEMPL, are included in the model.

One statistical concern with the estimation is that the dependent variable, the difference between the share of sales accounted for by small firms in 1986 and 1982, is by definition bounded by 100 and −100. By first transforming the dependent variable to vary between zero and one,[6] we then correct for this potential inefficiency by using a logit transformation, where the transformed dependent variable (SFC*) is again transformed from SFC* to (SFC*/(1-SFC*)). As shown in equation 5, the logit transformation has virtually no effect on the results. In terms of coefficient signs and significance, the results yielded in equation 5 are quite similar to those in equation 4. The major difference is that the coefficient of SPR cannot be considered to be statistically significant in equation 5. In general, the results were identical regardless of whether the OLS or logit method of estimation was used for all of the equations in table 6.3.

It is possible that the inferences made from table 6.3 are sensitive to both the small-firm measure and the time period used. To provide a sensitivity analysis, both the small-firm measure and the time period vary in table 6.4.[7] The results of equation 2 in table 6.4 are similar to those of equation 4 in table 6.3, where the same model is used for the time period 1982–1986. For both time periods SNC, SPR, and NPEMPL are positively related, and SMP and SST negatively (and not statistically significant) related to the change in the relative small-firm presence.

An alternative measure of small firms (enterprises with fewer than 100 employees) is substituted and compared for both time periods in equations 3, 4, and 5. Although the results are generally the same as for the first measure of small firms, SNC appears to have had less of an impact on the relative increase in firms with fewer than 100 employees than on firms with between 100 and 499 employees. Not only are the t-ratios of the coefficient of SNC considerably smaller in equations 3, 4, and 5, but in equations 3 and 5 they cannot even be considered statistically significant. Similarly, the coefficent for SMP is significantly negative in equation 5, whereas it remains nonsignificant (although still negative) in equations 3 and 4. This provides at least some evidence that the implementation of transfer machines has not been responsible for the shift in the size distribution toward small firms. In general, however, the results appear to be remarkably

Regression results for change in sales for varying definition of small firms and over alternative periods (*t*-ratios listed in parentheses)

	Fewer than 500 employees		Fewer than 100 employees		
	(1) 1976–1984	(2) 1976–1986	(3) 1982–1986	(4) 1976–1984	(5) 1976–1986
SPR	0.0084	0.2917	1.3361	0.1208	1.4878
	(0.0213)	(0.7380)	(2.9835)**	(0.4914)	(3.2355)**
NC	0.5242	0.5442	0.1795	0.4525	−0.0060
	(1.7305)*	(1.8031)*	(0.5146)	(1.9847)**	(−0.0150)
SMP	−1.0726	−0.6071	−0.8120	−0.7562	−1.2671
	(−1.6036)	(−0.8928)	(−1.0543)	(−1.5704)	(−1.6723)*
SST	1.5475	−4.8997	7.0196	9.3226	—
	(0.1954)	(−0.6093)	(0.7696)	(1.5345)	
SSA	—	—	—	—	1.6667
					(1.3895)
K/L	−0.0259	0.1084	−0.1682	−0.0496	−0.2853
	(−0.0881)	(0.3362)	(−0.4569)	(−0.2013)	(0.7325)
RD/S	−174.9000	—	−90.4940	−113.3000	−78.2030
	(−1.7960)*		(−0.8071)	(−1.5623)	(−0.6125)
NPEMPL	0.0603	0.1975	0.5280	—	0.5474
	(0.5807)	(1.9371)*	(4.4143)**		(3.9257)**
Intercept	0.4348	−12.0460	−13.6920	18.5440	−3.2655
	(0.1679)	(−0.4892)	(−0.4593)	(0.9834)	(−0.1051)
R^2	0.139	0.123	0.244	0.135	0.223
F	2.072**	2.126**	4.139**	2.374**	3.698**

Note: *Statistically significant at the 90 percent level of confidence, two-tailed test. **Statistically significant at the 95 percent level of confidence, two-tailed test.

robust with respect to the time period and the measure of small firms used.

The results from tables 6.3 and 6.4 indicate that the application of certain flexible technologies in the engineering industries is related to changes in the firm-size distribution. In particular, it appears that the implementation of programmable robots and NC machines has tended to be a catalyst for the shift in the size distribution toward small firms and away from large ones.

6.5   Flexible Technology and Changes in Establishment Size

An implication from the previous section is that if the share of sales accounted for by small firms is increasing in the engineering industries, the mean establishment (plant) size in these industries would be expected to be decreasing over a similar period. Similarly, if the relative shift in the size distribution toward small firms is related to the application of flexible technologies, the expected decline in establishment size would also be expected to be related to the implementation of flexible technologies. In this section we examine establishment size data from the *Census of Manufactures* to (1) identify whether a decrease in mean establishment size has acompanied the shift in the firm-size distribution toward an increased presence of small firms in the engineering industries, and (2) test whether any such shift in mean establishment size is related to the application of flexible technologies by using the model from the previous section.

The percentage changes in the mean establishment size, mean firm (enterprise) size, number of establishments, number of firms, and employment in the 106 engineering industries between 1972 and 1982 are generally consistent with the changes ove time in the firm-size distribution that we observed in table 6.1. Both the establishment and firm sizes are measured in terms of employees. In general, the trends in these variables strongly suggest that a structural change in the engineering industries has taken place. Not only did the mean establishment size of all 106 engineering industries decline by 12.7 percent, but the average plant size declined in 79 out of the 106 four-digit SIC engineering industries. While the mean establishment size declined by more than 50 percent in ten of these industries, the decrease was between 50 percent and 25 percent in twenty-five industries, and between 25 percent and zero percent in forty-four industries.

Table 6.5
Correlation matrix for 106 four-digit SIC industries

	Change between 1972 and 1982 in				
	Number of establishments	Number of companies	Establishment size	Company size	Gross output
Change in number of companies	0.971				
Change in establishment size	−0.248	−0.267			
Change in company size	−0.192	−0.263	0.940		
Change in gross output	0.525	0.448	0.537	0.589	
Change in value-added	0.521	0.448	0.555	0.594	0.938

Source: U.S. Department of Commerce, Bureau of the Census, *Census of Manufacturing*, 1972–1982, Washington, D.C., 1986. Taken from Carlsson (1989a, 24).

The mean firm size in the engineering industries declined by 13.4 percent between 1972 and 1982.Similarly, in seventy-eight industries the average firm size declined. The distribution of mean firm size changes across the engineering industries closely resembles that for the change in mean plant size described above. As table 6.5 shows, the correlation between the change in establishment size and company size was 0.94 (Carlsson 1989a).

A second striking aspect is that while the mean establishment and firm sizes have been decreasing in the engineering industries, there has generally been an increase in both the number of establishments and the number of companies. For the entire group of engineering industries, the number of establishments increased by 27.5 percent between 1972 and 1982. There was an increase in the number of establishments in 86 of the 106 four-digit SIC engineering industries. Similarly, the mean number of companies for the entire group of engineering industries increased by 28.6 percent. These trends are consistent with the shift in the firm-size distribution toward an increased presence of small firms (measured by share of sales) observed in table 6.1. The trend toward smaller establishments and firms cannot be attributed to a decrease in overall employment. Rather, employment increased by 11.3 percent for the entire group of engineering industries between 1972 and 1982. Similarly, all but 49 of the industries experienced at least some employment growth over the period (Carlsson 1989a).

In the previous section we found that the implementation of flexible technologies is positively related to the increase in the share of industry sales accounted for by small firms over time. To test the hypothesis that the changes in mean establishment size are related to the application of flexible technologies, we use the same model from the previous section. Using the percentage change in the mean establishment size between 1972 and 1982 as the dependent variable, the regression model was estimated for 68 four-digit SIC industries for which there were compatible data, and the results are shown in table 6.6. As the negative and statistically significant coefficients of SPR and SNC indicate, the mean establishment size has tended to decrease the most in those engineering industries in which there has been the greatest application of programmable robots and NC machines. The positive and statistically significant coefficient of SST suggests that the mean establishment size has tended to increase, or decrease the least, in those industries relying on transfer machines

Table 6.6
Regression results for change in mean establishment size, 1972–1982 (*t*-ratios listed in parentheses)

	(1)	(2)	(3)	(4)	(5)
SPR	−0.0823	−0.0729	−0.0831	−0.0811	−0.0858
	(−3.0271)**	(−2.1619)**	(−3.0848)**	(−2.4576)**	(−3.1611)**
SNC	−0.1164	−0.1232	−0.1214	−0.1252	−0.0966
	(−2.0115)**	(−1.8567)*	(−2.1630)**	(−1.8920)*	(−1.7908)*
SMP	−0.0450	−0.0441	−0.0445	−0.0457	—
	(−1.4590)	(−1.3251)	(−1.4541)	(−1.4034)	
SST	1.3368	1.1985	1.4311	1.4347	1.3791
	(1.8679)*	(1.7095)*	(2.1287)**	(2.1143)**	(2.0360)**
SAA	0.0372	0.0820	—	—	—
	(0.4061)	(0.9701)			
K/L	0.0277	0.0239	0.0303	0.0297	0.0279
	(0.8582)	(0.7133)	(0.9690)	(0.9215)	(0.8831)
RD/S	−9.0212	—	−10.6460	—	−5.8674
	(−0.9477)		(−1.2409)		(−0.7338)
NPEMPL	—	0.0058	—	0.0011	—
		(0.6062)		(0.1097)	
Intercept	6.5205	5.5986	6.6405	6.6134	3.4335
	(2.6249)**	(2.4579)**	(2.7110)**	(2.6647)**	(3.1931)**
R^2	0.201	0.194	0.199	0.193	0.171
F	2.161**	2.067**	2.528**	2.134**	2.565**

Note: *Statistically significant at the 90 percent level of confidence, two-tailed test. **Statistically significant at the 95 percent level of confidence, two-tailed test.

and mass production technology. Perhaps not surprisingly, the results from table 6.6 imply that the same factors that are related to the increased sales share of small firms are also related to the decrease in the mean establishment size.

6.6 Conclusion

In this chapter we have examined how the application of certain flexible technologies has affected the size distribution of firms and, in particular, the change in the presence of small firms. We find that the implementation of both programmable robots and NC machine tools is related to a shift in the size distribution toward small firms, as well as a decrease in the mean establishment size. Not surprisingly, measures of mass production technology, such as the share of the total number of machines accounted for by transfer machines, are positively related to the change in mean establishment size. These results proved to be quite robust using two different measures of what constitutes a small firm and three different time periods representing different stages of the business cycle.

One important qualification of the results is that the type of technology used in an industry may, in fact, by the result, and not just the determinant, of the firm-size distribution. This would suggest that the observed positive statistical relationship between the application of NC machine tools and the change in the small-firm presence could reflect the tendency for small firms, once established in an industry, to select certain flexible technologies and refrain from using mass production technologies. However, the simple correlation coefficient of -0.15 between the share of sales accounted for by small firms (less than 100 employees) in 1976 and the share of the total number of machines accounted for by NC machine tools in 1983 does not suggest that such machines tended to be used where small firms were particularly prevalent.[8] Rather, as the regression results indicate, in industries in which NC machines are extensively used, small firms have accounted for an increased share of subsequent sales in the markets. In Acs et al. (1988), the technology variables were included in a regression model estimating the share of sales accounted for by small firms in a single year. It was found that neither programmable robots nor NC machine tools are related to the presence of small firms. Thus, there is compelling evidence that the implementation of at least certain flexible technologies is not related to the extent to which small firms exist, but rather the extent to which the size distribution is shifting toward smaller firms. This would suggest that the relationship between the application of these flexible technologies and the shift in the firm-size distribution is a very recent phenomenon.

A second qualification of these results is that while the application of NC machinery may have promoted the viability of small firms, subsequent developments in flexible technologies, such as FMS and the FAF of the future, may have a very different impact on the size distribution of firms. Any such shift in the relative efficiency of large and small firms is certainly consistent with the 1948 observation by Blair that fundamental changes in technology often result in shifts in the firm-size distribution.

7   Intra-industry Dynamics

7.1 Introduction

Nearly thirty years ago, Mansfield (1962, 1023) made a plea for greater emphasis on intra-industry dynamics:

Because there have been so few econometric studies of the birth, growth and death of firms, we lack even crude answers to the following basic questions regarding the dynamic processes governing an industry's structure. What are the quantitative effects of various factors on the rates of entry and exit? How well can the growth of firms be represented by Gibrat's law of proportionate effect? What have been the effects of successful innovations on a firm's growth rate? What determines the amount of mobility within an industry's size structure?

Although some important studies have provided at least provisional answers to Mansfield's questions, particularly in the area of Gibrat's Law and the variations in firm growth rates, knowledge about the process by which industry structures evolve remains limited. Thus, Scherer (1980, 150) was moved nearly two decades later to comment, "A sophisticated explanation of how industry structures come to be what they are must blend the conventional, more or less static, determinants with dynamic considerations. . . . This is where future research on the determinants of market structure is most urgently needed." The purpose of this chapter is to examine some of the issues concerning intra-industry dynamics that have been raised by Simon and Bonini (1958), Mansfield, Scherer, and others. The SBDB and innovation data enable us to consider the movement of firms into, within, and out of a given industry over a certain time interval. In particular, we raise two questions: (1) Are the growth rates of large firms and small firms identical? and (2) What determines the extent of turbulence in an industry, or the amount of simultaneous expansion, contraction, entry, and exit by firms in the same market and firm-size class? The answers to these questions contribute to understanding the dynamic manner in which industries evolve.

In the second section of this chapter, the assumptions underlying Gibrat's Law are tested. The determinants of the extent of industry turbulence are identified in the third section. Not only do we find evidence that the amount of turbulence varies across different firm-size classes within an industry, as well as between industries, but that the determinants of small-firm turbulence differ considerably from those for the entire industry.

7.2 Gibrat's Law Reconsidered

While there are various interpretations of Gibrat's Law, the most common view is that firm growth is independent of firm size, or that the "probability of a given proportionate change in size during a specified period is the same for all firms in a given industry—regardless of their size at the beginning of the period" (Mansfield 1962, 1030–1031). There are, in fact, at least three renditions of Gibrat's Law. The first version postulates that the law holds for firms that exited the industry as well as for those remaining in existence. The second interpretation is that the law holds only for firms that survive over the period (Hart and Prais 1956). Thus, according to this interpretation, firms that have exited from the industry should not be included in a sample used to statistically test Gibrat's Law. The third main version is that the law applies only to firms that are large enough to exceed the MES level of output (Simon and Bonini 1958).

Based on four ten-year periods in the steel and petroleum industries, and two shorter intervals in the tire industry, Mansfield (1962) found that Gibrat's Law failed to hold in more than one-half of the cases, regardless of the version tested. Other empirical studies found varying results, depending upon the time period, size measure, and interpretation used (Hymer and Pashigian 1962; Singh and Whittington 1975; Mansfield 1962; and Kumar 1985). For example, Hart and Prais (1956) found that firm growth is roughly independent of the size of the firm—and therefore evidence that Gibrat's Law holds.

Three recent studies have considerably expanded the state of knowledge about the relationship between firm size and growth. Hall (1987) assembled a large panel data set from the COMPUSTAT files and identified a four percentage point difference in the annual growth rates between firms in the 25th and 75th percentiles. The smaller firms were found to grow faster than their larger counterparts. In addition, she found that the variance of growth rates is greater for small than for large firms. While Hall's sample was biased toward relatively large firms, Evans (1987a, 1987b) was able to use the SBDB data to test Gibrat's Law for the entire spectrum of firm sizes. In his 1987a paper, Evans selected 100 four-digit SIC industries from the SBDB and calculated individual firm growth rates between 1976 and 1980. In his 1987b study, Evans drew a sample of 27,046 firms from the SBDB and intentionally oversampled larger firms, but did not aggregate the firms according to industry, as in his other study. In both papers, Evans reaches the same conclusion. The firm growth rate is found to decrease with both firm size and firm age. In addition, in his 1987a paper, Evans finds, like Hall, that the variation of growth rates tends to decrease with rising firm size. Neither Hall's nor Evans's sample included firms that ultimately exited form the industry, although they both tried to analyze the effect of this sample bias. Similarly, like most of the other empirical studies mentioned (with the exception of Kumar 1985), they were not able to differentiate between internal growth and growth from merger.

Using the SBDB data aggregated at the industry level, we are able to construct employment growth rates for four firm-size classes directly incorporating firm exits. Specifically, the mean employment growth rate of firms in firm-size class i (EGR$_i$) between 1976 and 1980 is defined as

$$EGR_i = (EMPL80_i^* - EMPL76_i)/EMPL76_i, \tag{7.1}$$

where $EMPL76_i$ represents the employment in firm-size class i in 1967 and $EMPL80_i^*$ represents the 1980 employment of *firms that were in existence in 1976*. If no new firms entered the industry, and if no existing firms exited the industry between 1976 and 1980, then $EMPL80_i = EMPL80_i^*$, where $EMPL80_i$ is the actual employment level of firm-size class i in 1980. However, the greater the extent of entry in the firm-size class during this time period, the greater will be the differential between $EMPL80_i^*$ and $EMPL80_i$. It should be emphasized that firms exiting the industry are included in this measure of growth, since $EMPL80_i^*$ decreases by the amount of employment reduction due to firm exits.

In fact, there is no way to directly measure $EMPL80_i^*$ using the SBDB. However, using certain variables included in the SBDB,

EMPL80$_i^*$ can be indirectly measured. That is, the SBDB (USELM file) provides measures of expansion, contraction, and deaths, which can be used to estimate EMPL80$_i^*$. Expansion is defined as the number of jobs in a specific firm-size class that emanate from new positions generated by firms in existence during the initial period. By definition, expansion is bounded by zero, which would indicate that the firms in existence in that size class during the first year did not create any employment beyond that amount already in effect in the initial period. Contraction is defined as the number of jobs in a specific firm-size class that were eliminated by firms that were in existence during the entire period. Contraction is also bounded by zero, which would indicate that none of the firms in that size class that were in existence during the initial year decreased the number of jobs over the relevent period. Of course, if a firm exits from the industry, the loss of employment will not be included in the contraction measure. However, a separate variable, deaths, measures the amount of employment in the firm-size class that is lost due to firm exits. This measure is symmetrical to the birth measure introduced in chapter 5.

Using these various dynamic measures from the SBDB, EMPL80$_i^*$ can be calculated as

$$EMPL80_i^* = EMPL76_i + EXP_i - CONTR_i - DEATH_i, \qquad (7.2)$$

where EXP_i is the amount of employment expansion in firm-size class i between 1976 and 1980, $CONTR_i$ is the amount of employment contraction in firm-size class i between 1976 and 1980, and $DEATH_i$ is the amount of employment lost due to firm exits in firm-size class i between 1976 and 1980. Substituting into equation (7.1) yields

$$EGR_i = (EXP_i - CONTR_i - DEATH_i)/EMPL76_i. \qquad (7.3)$$

There are several important qualifications that must be made about these employment growth rates. First, the growth rates represent the mean growth for firms existing in the relevant size class in 1976. Most other studies have used the growth rates of individual firms rather than a mean for the aggregation of firms within a given size class. The advantage here is that the employment effect of the exiting firms can easily be incorporated into this measure of mean growth. Second, as was the case for Evans (1987a, 1987b), along with most other studies examining Gibrat's Law, the SBDB data do not differentiate between expansion due to internal growth and expansion due to merger. This, of course, is an important distinction that needs to be explicitly examined in further research. Third, while boundary crossings create problems when the USEEM file of the SBDB is used for static comparisons, this does not present a problem when the expansion and contraction measures from the USELM file are applied. That is, a firm's expansion or contraction is classified according to the size class based on the firm's employment in 1976, regardless of any subsequent upward or downward movements of the firm into adjoining size classes.

The mean employment growth rate between 1976 and 1980 was calculated for four distinct firm-size classes (based on 1976 firm size) in each four-digit SIC industry: (1) fewer than 50 employees (EGR_1), (2) between 50 and 99 employees (EGR_2), (3) between 100 and 499 employees (EGR_3), and (4) at least 500 employees (EGR_4). To determine whether the mean growth rates are independent of firm size, the hypothesis that the growth rate was identical for all four firm-size classes, H_0: $EGR_1 = EGR_2 = EGR_3 = EGR_4$, was subjected to a chi-square test. The results are shown in table 7.1. For example, the growth rates were found to be equal in twenty-three of the forty-two four-digit SIC industries within the food and beverage sector, while they were found to be unequal in the nineteen remaining industries. Overall, about 60 percent of the industries experienced growth rates not significantly unequal across the four firm-size classes, whereas in about 40 percent of the industries the growth rates were significantly different. However, this pattern varies considerably across sectors. Sectors with predominately equal growth rates across industry firm-size classes include transportation equipment, instruments, apparel, and fabricated metals. By contrast, unequal growth rates between industries prevailed in the petroleum, rubber and plastics, paper, and leather sectors.

These results differ somewhat from those of Hall (1987) and, in particular, Evans (1987)a, who found no support for Gibrat's Law in 89 percent of his industries. We find that the assumption underlying Gibrat's Law does not hold with about one-half the frequency that Evans did, although he used the same source of data as we do. The reason for this apparent discrepancy is that Evans's sample excluded firms that exited the industry, while we are able to include them in our sample. Evans did find a strong positive relationship between the likelihood of survival and firm size. He found this relationship to hold in 81 of the 100 industries he examined. Thus, as both Evans and Hall documented, smaller firms have higher growth rates, but they tend to exit with greater frequency. When we incorporate the impact of exits

Table 7.1
Results of chi-square test for equality of growth rates within manufacturing industries[a]

Sector	Number of industries	Number of industries with unequal growth rates	Number of industries with equal growth rates
Food and beverages	42	19 (45.23)	23 (54.77)
Textiles	27	12 (44.44)	15 (53.56)
Apparel	29	9 (31.03)	20 (68.97)
Lumber	13	5 (38.46)	8 (61.54)
Furniture	12	3 (25.00)	9 (75.00)
Paper	16	11 (68.75)	5 (31.25)
Printing	14	3 (21.43)	11 (78.57)
Chemicals	26	8 (30.77)	18 (69.23)
Petroleum	4	3 (75.00)	1 (25.00)
Rubber and plastics	5	3 (60.00)	2 (40.00)

Industry			
Leather	23	12 (52.17)	11 (47.83)
Primary metals	25	12 (48.00)	13 (52.00)
Fabricated metals	35	13 (37.14)	22 (62.86)
Machinery (nonelectrical)	45	20 (44.44)	25 (55.56)
Electrical equipment	37	16 (43.24)	21 (56.76)
Transportation equipment	12	0 (0.00)	12 (100.00)
Instruments	13	3 (23.08)	10 (76.92)
Miscellaneous	17	8 (47.06)	9 (52.94)
Total[b]	408	163 (39.95)	245 (60.05)

a. Percentages are indicated in parentheses.
b. Includes industries not shown in table.

in our mean growth rate, the higher growth rate of small firms is apparently offset by their greater propensity to exit, at least in some industries. Thus, incorporating the impact of exits tends to produce more support for the assumptions underlying Gibrat's Law than would otherwise be found.

7.3   Turbulence

Alfred Marshall (1920, 263) described the process of industry evolution by analogy, where one can observe "the young trees of the forest as they struggle upwards through the benumbing shade of their older rivals." Marshall's view of industry dynamics is not so different from the prevalent view held by most economists in industrial organization today, although this process has gone under the guise of various terms. Roughly speaking, the extent to which firms enter, grow, decline, and exit an industry has been termed "mobility," "turnover," "dynamic evolution," and "turbulence," depending upon the author. We adopt the term turbulence here to avoid confusion with the European meaning of "turnover," which is widely used to mean sales, and "mobility," which has most recently come to refer to the movement of firms between strategic groups within an industry (see, for example, Oster 1982). Instead, we draw upon the concept of turbulence (Beesley and Hamilton 1984; Gudgin 1978), which we define as the extent of movements of firms within as well as into and out of an industry.

   The extent of intra-industry firm movement is important for several reasons. For example, Simon and Bonini (1958, 616) argued that, "As a matter of fact, a measure of mobility . . . would appear to provide a better index of what we mean by 'equality of opportunity' than do the usual measures of concentration." Grossack (1965) similarly argued that a measure of intra-industry firm movements may provide important dynamic information than can supplement the strictly static measure of market concentration.

   The 1971 Bolton Committee in the United Kingdom argued that new firms in an industry would promote new products and ultimately shape the evolutionary path of the industry, as well as constrain any market power exercised by the entrenched firms:

We believe that the health of the economy requires the birth of new enterprises in substantial number and the growth of some to a position from which they are able to challenge and supplement the existing leaders of industry. . . . This "seedbed" function, therefore, appears to be a vital contribution of the small firm sector to the long-run health of the economy. We cannot assume that the ordinary working of market forces will necessarily preserve a small firm sector large enough to perform this function in the future. (Bolton Report 1971, 85)

Caves and Porter (1977, 241) argued that the theory of entry be extended to a more "general theory of mobility of firms among segments of an industry, thus encompassing exit and intergroup shifts as well as entry." While the traditional analysis suffers from neglecting structural restraints on the ability of firms to change their market share, the ease with which market share can be altered should be constrained by the "same type of structural forces that deter the firm from increasing its output from zero to positive (entry) as from small share to large share (mobility)" (Caves and Porter 1977, 250).

Despite the recognition that the process by which firms enter, grow, recede, and exit plays a crucial role in the evolution of industrial markets, there have been only a few empirical studies actually attempting to measure the extent of intra-industry firm movements. Most of these (Kaplan 1954; Collins and Preston 1961; Mermelstein 1969; and Bond 1975) have been oriented toward making intertemporal comparisons of the largest U.S. corporations. The conclusion of these studies was unequivocal: The rate of turnover, at least among the largest corporations, has been declining over a long period of time.[1] For example, Collins and Preston (1961, 100) found that, "[I]n spite of the stability of the usual concentration measure there has been a significant decline in equality of opportunity in the upper reaches of the U.S. economy since the turn of the century."

While there are no unambiguous criteria for judging the extent of turbulence (Scherer 1980, 55), there have been at least three important issues raised concerning the empirical methodology.[2] First, measures of intra-industry firm movements over a period as long as a decade obscure changes for shorter periods. For example, Boyle (1971) found that the coefficients for measures for paired years differ significantly from the ones for decades. Second, the preoccupation with changes among the 100 largest corporations has no unique economic significance. The revevant measure should include a wide specturm of firm sizes (Boyle and Sorenson 1971; Porter 1976). According to Boyle (1971, 165), virtually no studies "have paid sufficient attention to the admonition in recent years." Third, and perhaps most significant, is the criticism that the appropriate unit of observation for examining turbulence should be the industry and not the aggregation of the largest firms (Stigler 1956b; Kamerschen 1971). Stigler (1956b, 35), for example, warns, "The statistical universe of the 100 or 200 largest corporations is inappropriate to studies of monopoly and competition and we may hope that Kaplan will be the last study to fall prey to its dramatic irrelevance. For Kaplan's central idea—that the extent of instability in the relative fortunes of the leading firms is an informative symptom of competition—is important and deserves to be applied on a correct industry basis."

We use the dynamic SBDB measures introduced in the previous section to construct turbulence measures that most closely resemble the turbulence measure used by Beesley and Hamilton (1984). Specifically, we define turbulence as the absolute value of all employment additions and contractions within an industry (or firm-size class) between 1976 and 1980. That is, a given amount of market growth will dictate a corresponding amount of additional employment, presumably from both existing firms as well as from new entrants. However, to the extent that existing firms experience employment reductions as well as exit from the industry, the greater will be the overall amount of expansion and number of births and, subsequently, the overall amount of turbulence.

In order to standardize turbulence for industry size, the turbulence rate is defined as

$$TR = (EXP + CONTR + BIRTH + DEATH)/(EMPL76). \qquad (7.4)$$

As Beesley and Hamilton (1984) note, factors that have a symmetrical effect on entry and exit, or expansion and contraction, will have little impact on TR. There is also reason to suspect that the determinants of small-firm turbulence are considerably different from those for all firms. In fact, for the 247 manufacturing industries included in the sample, the small-firm turbulence rate exceeds the large-firm turbulence rate by 35 percent. Reasons for this difference between large- and small-firm turbulence are apparent from both the evolutionary model of industry dynamics proposed by Gort and Klepper (1982) as well as the Jovanovic (1982) learning-by-doing model. Gort and Klepper argue that industry dynamics, and entry in particular, are determined by the relationship between two sources of information about new product technology. These two sources of information are firms already in the market and firms outside the set, or on the fringe, of the major producers. The first information source is the product of experience and contains both transferable and nontransferable components. Gort and Klepper emphasize that the accumulated stock of nontransferable information is the product of learning by doing, which firms outside the industry, by definition, cannot possess. The greater the role the accumulated stock of nontransferable information plays, the greater will be the extent to which innovative activity emanates from the major producers already existing in the industry. Consequently, innovation as a vehicle for entry and/or expansion is less of a viable alternative for firms either outside of or on the fringe of the market.

By contrast, entry and growth by outside firms are encouraged when the second source of innovation-producing information is relatively more important. Arrow (1962), Mueller (1976), and Williamson (1975) have all pointed out that when such information created outside of the industry cannot be easily transferred to those firms existing within the industry, perhaps due to organizational factors, the holder of such knowledge must enter (or expand in) the industry in order to exploit the market value of his/her knowledge.

Jovanovic (1982) suggests that the learning process by entrepreneurs determines intra-industry dynamics. In particular, Jovanovic assumes that individuals are unsure about their ability to manage a business. While they may enter a market based on a vague sense of expected profitability, they discover their ability to manage in the given environment once their business is established. With the passage of time, they alter their behavior as they learn to disentangle their inherent ability from random business fluctuations. Those entrepreneurs who discover that their ability exceeds their expectations expand the scale of their business, while those discovering that they have less inherent talent than expected contract the scale of output or possibly exit from the industry. An implication of Jovanovic's model is that firms begin at a small scale and then, if merited by subsequent performance, expand. Pakes and Ericson (1987) build on Jovanovic's model by arguing that firms can actively accelerate the learning process by investing in R&D. Those firms that are successful grow, while those that are not successful either remain small or else exit the industry.

All of these models have a common theme. Firms are more likely to enter an industry, even at suboptimal scale, if the technology is such that there is a greater chance of new products coming from firms outside the entrenched major producers. If firms successfully learn and adopt, they grow into viably sized enterprises. If not, they stagnate and may ultimately exit. An implication is that turbulence should be positively related to the potential that new and fringe firms have for becoming successful and at the same time the extent to which those less successful firms are forced to decline and/or exit the market.

While Gort and Klepper's (1982) concepts do not lend themselves to precise measurement, it is not unreasonable to consider the small-firm innovation rate (SIE) as a proxy measure indicating the extent to which firms outside the major producers are able to innovate. Thus, when SIE is high relative to the overall innovation rate (TIE), the technological and knowledge conditions may dictate a market more conducive to entry and growth from new and fringe firms. Of course, new and fringe firms not able to innovate or otherwise learn and adopt may be forced to contract and ultimately exit. Thus, TR should be positively related to SIE but negatively related to TIE. The extent of skilled labor (SKILL) may also reflect the degree to which knowledge is crucial to innovation, and would therefore be expected to be positively related to TR in the same manner as SIE. Gort and Klepper (1982) found evidence suggesting that markets are most accessible to outside firms in the early stages of the life cycle, when the growth rate is high. Therefore, GR is expected to be positively related to turbulence.

One implication of the passive and active learning models by Jovanovic (1982) and Pakes and Ericson (1987) is not only that firms that do not learn and adopt must exit the industry, but that the greater the cost disadvantage incurred by firms not able to successfully learn and adopt, the more rapid will be their decline and departure. This implies that industries that are capital-intensive and where scale economies play an important role may be particularly subject to high rates of turbulence, at least among the small firms. The technology and information conditions may provide, in the terms used by Gort and Klepper (1982), outside and/or fringe firms with the opportunity for entry and growth through successful innovation. However, the typical small entrant in a high-MES industry is at a suboptimal scale and therefore must either successfully innovate (or find some similar strategy) or else depart from the industry. Thus, high-MES industries may be particularly subject to a high degree of turbulence among small firms hoping to discover the successful innovative strategy, many of which will be forced to exit. This suggests that TR, at least for small firms, is expected to be positively influenced by MES/S, K/L, and KREQ. In chapter 5, we found that advertising intensity, but not capital intensity, served to deter firms from entering industry. Therefore, AD/S may promote industry stability more than turbulence and is expected to be negatively related to TR.

Industry profitability (PCM) is expected to be negatively related to TR, since firms are more likely to survive in highly profitable industries. As Beesley and Hamilton (1984) point out, industry profitability may promote entry without a concomitant positive effect on exits and, in fact, may reduce the amount of industry exits, thereby reflecting less and not more turbulence. Berry (1974) and Beesley and Hamilton (1984) argue that turbulence for large firms, but not for small firms, may be higher in concentrated than in nonconcentrated markets, because "only large firms are able to encroach—via the setting up of dependent units—into areas already dominated by other large firms" (Beesley and Hamilton 1984, 227). Thus, TR is hypothesized to be positively related to CON, except in the case of small firms.

Table 7.2 shows the regression results for estimating the turbulence rates of all firms (equation 1), small firms (equation 2), as well as the small-firm turbulence rate divided by the turbulence rate for all firms (equation 3), and the small-firm turbulence rate divided by the large-firm turbulence rate (equation 4). The regressions were estimated using 247 four-digit SIC industries. A small firm is defined here as having fewer than 500 employees.[3]

There are four important results in table 7.2. First, as the positive coefficient of SIE in the first two equations indicates, the evidence supports the hypothesis that there is relatively more turbulence in markets where small firms are able to implement a strategy of product innovation, but relatively less turbulence in markets where they are not able to innovate. Further, as the negative coefficient of TIE suggests, holding the small-firm innovation rate constant, increases in the overall innovative activity of the industry lead to less, not more, turbulence. This is consistent with Gort and Klepper's (1982) notion that markets in which the knowledge accumulated from experience plays a crucial role in innovative activity will tend not to be accessible to new firms, while markets in which such knowledge is relatively less important in producing innovations will generate much more activity from outside and fringe firms. These results apply for small firms as well as all firms.

Table 7.2
Regression results for turbulence rates (*t*-statistics listed in parentheses)[a]

	(1) All firms	(2) Small firms	(3) Small firms/ all firms	(4) Small firms/ large firms
PCM	-0.0028	-0.0726	-3.8776	-4.1381
	(0.0073)	(2.0714)**	(0.4809)	(-0.3887)
GR	7.3606	1.6066	-0.3450	-1.4332
	(1.3533)	(3.2922)**	(-0.3074)	(-0.9498)
SIE	1.2997	0.1379	-0.0847	-0.0708
	(2.8471)**	(3.3672)**	(-0.8990)	(-0.5590)
TIE	-2.6193	-0.1277	0.2535	0.2677
	(-2.3489)**	(-1.2767)	(1.1020)	(0.8651)
SKILL	-2.2735	0.3114	1.6117	2.0173
	(-0.3365)	(0.5137)	(1.1563)	(1.0763)
AD/S	-4.0130	-0.3234	1.6370	2.3437
	(-1.7626)*	(-1.5830)	(3.4716)**	(3.7105)**
CON	8.7681	-0.1719	-1.8887	-2.8133
	(4.2011)**	(-0.9177)	(-0.4386)	(-0.4859)
K/L	-1.2750	-0.2700	2.7775	2.4669
	(-0.6229)	(-1.4703)	(0.6577)	(0.4344)
MES/S	-6.9018	-1.2359	0.0418	0.0547
	(-0.6766)	(-1.3503)	(1.9881)**	(1.9334)*
KREQ	-7.7122	4.6689	1.1294	1.2954
	(-0.5074)	(3.4235)**	(3.6014)**	(3.0719)**

Intercept	0.4847	1.7395	0.9071	0.8477
	(0.3441)	(13.7640)**	(3.1214)**	(2.1693)**
R^2	0.148	0.217	0.186	0.167
F	4.091**	6.546**	5.406**	4.727**

Note: *Statistically significant at the 90 percent level of confidence, two-tailed test. **Statistically significant at the 95 percent level of confidence, two-tailed test.

a. Small firms are defined as having fewer than 500 employees.

Second, as the positive coefficient of KREQ in equation 2 indicates, the extent of turbulence within smaller firm-size classes is positively related to capital intensity. However, as the negative (and statistically insignificant) coefficient of KREQ in equation 1 implies, capital intensity does not stimulate turbulence in general. The positive coefficients of KREQ, MES/S and K/L in equations 3 and 4 substantiate the hypothesis that while capital intensity may promote higher rates of turbulence among small firms, it does not among larger ones. This is consistent with the notion that at least under certain technological conditions, smaller firms may still enter markets with substantial scale economies and capital requirements, but those firms not able to successfully learn and adopt are quickly forced to decline and exit. The larger firms, which Evans (1987a, 1987b) found to be older and more experienced, have already survived some of this learning process, and thus experience lower rates of turbulence. The negative and statistically significant coefficient of AD/S in equation 1, along with the positive and statistically significant coefficients of AD/S in equations 3 and 4, also implies that advertising intensity is negatively related to the extent of turbulence, although its impact is stronger for large than for small firms.

Third, as the positive coefficient of CON in equation 1 suggests, there is actually more, not less, turbulence in concentrated markets. Further, as the negative (and nonsignificant) coefficient of CON in equation 2 implies, the turbulence rate among smaller firms may not be as strongly affected by market concentration as that of their larger counterparts. Finally, the negative coefficients of PCM and positive coefficients of GR in the first two equations are consistent with the hypothesis that turbulence rates are diminished in highly profitable industries, but stimulated in growing markets. As the statistically nonsignificant coefficients of PCM and GR in the last two equations suggest, PCM and GR apparently have similar effects on the turbulence rates of large and small firms.

7.4 Conclusion

Two important questions concerning intra-industry dynamics, or the process by which industries evolve, have been raised in this chapter: (1) Are growth rates the same for large and small firms? and (2) What determines the extent of turbulence, or firm movements into, within, and out of an industry, and do these determinants vary for large and small firms? By utilizing some of the SBDB variables, we are able to construct relatively novel measures of intra-industry dynamics in order to answer these questions. In fact, the answer to the first question appears to be yes, at least for nearly two-thirds of the industries, and when the impact of industry exits is incorporated in measures of mean growth. While this result is considerably different from the conclusions in recent studies by Evans (1987a, 1987b) and Hall (1987), as well as by Mansfield (1962), these differences can be reconciled by considering the way in which the various tests of Gibrat's Law have been implemented. When we incorporate the employment impact of exits in our mean growth rates for large and small firms, we find that the greater propensity for small firms to exit the industry offsets the higher growth rates of the surviving small firms, at least in many of the industries examined. Thus, our results can be reconciled with the findings of Evans, Hall, and Mansfield.

In addressing the second question, we find evidence supporting the hypothesis of Gort and Klepper (1982) that the source of knowledge that produces innovations plays a key role in intra-industry dynamics. If innovative activity is particularly dependent upon knowledge that can be accumulated only through experience in the industry, existing producers will have the innovative advantage, and new and fringe firms will not find the industry to be especially accessible. Because relatively few firms will attempt entry into such an industry, there will also be a correspondingly low number of exits, resulting in a low rate of turbulence. On the other hand, if the knowledge required to produce innovations emanates largely from outside of the industry, or outside the main producers in the industry, the market will be accessible to new and frings firms. However, just because the structure of knowledge and technology creates a market that is accessible does not imply that entrants and expanding fringe firms will automatically survive. Rather, the learning-by-doing theory suggests that only those firms that are able to successfully learn and adapt will grow and/or survive. Not only do the empirical results in this chapter support the hypothesis that there will be greater turbulence in industries in which small firms are able to implement a strategy of innovation, but that, unless the small firms are able to participate in the ongoing innovative activity, the turbulence rate will be relatively low. In addition, we find that the turbulence rate for small firms, but not for large firms, tends to be greater in capital-intensive industries. This is consistent with the hypothesis that in such industries the small firms that successfully innovate and otherwise adapt (or are just plain lucky) grow to become viable entities, while the less fortunate small firms quickly decline and exit from the market. Because the larger firms tend to have accumulated more experience, the extent of turbulence among large firms is considerably less in capital-intensive industries.

Thus, the results from this chapter confirm the key role that technology and the process of learning play in market processes. As panel data sets are assembled, more evidence will hopefully be accumulated about intra-industry dynamics and how market structures evolve.

8   Conclusions

8.1   Major Findings

In this book we have tapped two new data sources to systematically examine innovative activity and the role that small firms play in markets. In the third chapter a direct measure of innovative activity is used to address three questions: (1) What determines innovative activity at the industry level? (2) Do these determinants vary between large and small firms? and (3) Under which circumstances do large firms have the relative innovative advantage, and under which circumstances do small firms have the relative innovative advantage? The answers to these questions were somewhat surprising. Concerning the first question, we found that, contrary to much of the conventional wisdom, innovative activity is apparently hindered, not promoted, in concentrated markes. The evidence also suggests that there tends to be more innovative activity in industries consisting of larger and not smaller firms. However, in answering the second two questions we find that, in fact, small firms tend to have the innovative advantage in industries consisting of predominantly large firms. This is consistent with the notion that small firms play an important role in introducing new products even in industries dominated by large firms. In addition, we find that the innovative advantage of small firms is promoted in industries that are highly innovative and that utilize a high component of skilled labor. By contrast, the large-firm innovative advantage is apparently greater in industries that are capital-intensive, advertising-intensive, but nonconcentrated. Thus, the empirical results suggest that both large and small firms play an important role in the innovative process, although their functions may be somewhat different, and the environments promoting innovative activity in large firms differ from that for small firms.

There is a long tradition in industrial organization that, just as market structure conditions influence technological change, technological change also affects market structure. This is pursued in the fourth chapter, where we sought to explain why the size distribution of firms, and in particular the share of industry sales accounted for by small firms, varies across manufacturing industries. The presence of small firms is found to be greater in industries where scale economies and capital intensity, as well as advertising and R&D, do not play an important role. There is, however, evidence that, by pursuing a strategy of innovation, small firms can at least somewhat offset their size-inherent cost disadvantages.

Given the finding that capital-intensive industries are not particularly hospitable to small firms, one would think that small firms shy away from entering such markets. However, in chapter 5, using a new measure of employment-weighted gross entry, or births, we find that this is apparently not the case. Rather, while advertising intensity and high levels of market concentration are found to deter small-firm births, capital intensity has no apparent effect on the entry behavior of either large or small firms. The total innovative activity of an industry also serves to impede both large- and small-firm births. Yet the more small firms innovate, the higher are the birth rates of both large and small firms. Thus it would appear that a highly innovative environment is hostile not only to the presence of small firms, but also to the entry of firms of all sizes. However, the extent to which small firms are successful at implementing a strategy of innovation helps them to enter and become viable in the industry.

Although chapter 6 does not explicitly use the measures of innovative activity, the primary focus is the impact on the firm-size distribution once a new technology has been diffused throughout a group of industries and is accessible to firms of all sizes. In particular, we attempt to shed some light on whether the diffusion and implementation of numerically controlled machines and robots has been conducive to a greater presence of small firms. Several stylized facts emerge for the engineering industries. Not only has the mean firm and plant size dramatically fallen in these industries, but there has been a marked increase in the share of sales accounted for by small firms. Further, there is at least some evidence suggesting that this shift has been greater in industries in which there is a greater application of numerically controlled machine tools and robots. These results support the long-standing view in industrial organization that the size distribution of firms can be affected, in either direction, by technological change.

The seventh chapter examined the roles that innovation and firm size play in intra-industry dynamics, or the process by which market structures evolve. In particular, we focus on two dynamic aspects of market structure—the assumptions underlying Gibrat's Law, or the relative growth rates of large and small firms, and the extent of turbulence or firm movements within, into, and out of an industry. Most recently, several studies have shown that small firms tend to experience higher rates of growth than do large firms. However, when the impact of exits from the industry is incorporated in our measure of mean firm-size class growth rates, we find that, in fact, equal growth rates across firm-size classes tend to hold for the majority of industries. Apparently, smaller firms not only have higher growth rates but also a greater propensity to exit the industry. These two tendencies offset each other, at least in a number of industries.

The extent of turbulence in an industry was found to be inhibited by the overall amount of innovative acivity, but promoted by the extent to which small firms innovate. This supports the notion that when the knowledge obtained from actual experience in the industry is a crucial input in the innovation production function, fewer firms will attempt to enter the industry and subsequently fewer will fail, leading to relatively low rates of turbulence. However, when knowledge from outside the industry is a key input into the innovation production function, firms outside and on the fringe of the industry are more likely to enter. Of course, those firms that are unable to successfully learn and adopt will subsequently fail, so that the turbulence rate will be relatively high. Consistent with this is the finding that small-firm turbulence is actually greater in capital-intensive industries. As the failure of capital intensity to significantly deter firm births in chapter 5 indicated, small firms do enter capital-intensive industries, presumably at a suboptimal scale. Those firms that successfully innovate or otherwise learn to adapt will become viable. Presumably many of the remaining firms will recede and ultimately fail. Thus, small-firm turbulence is particularly high in capital-intensive industries, where firms must quickly learn or else face extinction.

8.2 Broader Implications

Small firms can be considered to make at least four important contributions to industrial markets. First, as is clear from chapter 3, they play an important role in the process of technological change. Small firms can make an important "entrepreneurial" contribution, in the sense that Schumpeter, and Nelson and Winter (1982) have defined entrepreneurship. Second, as was clear from chapter 7, small firms generate much of the turbulence that not only creates an additional dimension of competition not captured in the usual static measures of market structure, such as concentration, but also provide a mechanism for regeneration. As Scherer (1980, 150) points out, "[T]he fact that many industries remain atomistically structured despite the concentration-increasing forces associated with stochastic growth suggests that static and dynamic managerial diseconomies of large size and rapid growth must frequently retard the rise of firms to dominance." It is often argued that mergers, even horizontal ones between large competitors, make an important contribution because they shift resources from less efficient to more efficient managements. However, the existence of a dynamic small-firm sector within an industry can similarly produce this effect, but without the accompanying increases in market concentration. This is consistent with the observation of management consultant Tom Peters, who notes that in large firms, "attempts to induce flexibility are vain: the 'ravages of time' that beset large organizations are largely irreversible. The only hope is to create brand-new, autonomous units."[1]

A third contribution small firms can make, which is related to the first two, is international competitiveness in newly created product niches. While the impact of foreign trade has not been explored in this book, it is clear that U.S. firms no longer have the international comparative advantage in capital-intensive and even skill-intensive industries. However, industries in which information and high technology are decisive inputs still tend to be dominated by the United States.[2] As the 1989 *Economic Report of the President* (p. 237) observes, high-technology goods are accounting for an increased share of U.S. trade. The typical life cycle of many of these high-technology products is short. Organizational flexibility plays an important role in markets with such short life cycles. It may well be that the internationalization of many products, particularly in the high technology sector, has contributed an increased presence and viability of smaller firms. The flexibility in adapting to market conditions, as well as the speed with which small firms seem to be able to exploit new product-class niches, can help give the United States the comparative advantage in high technology, high-information markets. Perhaps not unrelated, the Reagan administration instituted "Export Now," a program targeted at promoting exports from small firms, in February 1988. In any case, this is a topic that needs to be explored in detail in future research.

The fourth role that small firms have played in recent years is in job generation.[3] Again, this is not a topic that has been included in this study, mainly because the concept of job generation has no tradition in industrial organization. Rather, we have focused on issues that have a more meaningful definition and tradition in the literature, such as shifts in the size distribution of firms. Still, it is certainly the predominant role that small firms have played in generating the bulk of new jobs in the United States that has caught the public eye and the attention of the media. According to the SBDB data we have used in this book, 1.3 million new jobs in manufacturing were in fact created by small firms between 1976 and 1986, while the number of large manufacturing jobs decreased by 100,000.

Specific policy prescriptions beyond the customary plea for better and improved data sources and continued research are clearly inappropriate in a book concerned with identifying statistical tendencies at a broad aggregated industry level. Still, it should be remarked that, despite the important contributions from small firms in industrial markets, some of which have been analyzed in great detail in this book, a conventional wisdom oblivious to these contributions persists in the realm of public policy. An irony may be that, just when technological change depends upon a vital small-firm sector, public policy seems to be moving from an implicit toward an explicit nurturing of larger enterprises at the expense of smaller firms. For example, in 1986 the Secretary of Commerce, Malcolm Baldridge, asserted, "We are simply living in a different world today. Because of larger markets, the cost of research and development, new product innovation, marketing, and so forth . . . it takes larger companies to compete successfully" (Baldridge 1986). Baldridge pointed out that the American share of the largest corporations in the world had fallen considerably between 1960 and 1984. He warned that programs promoting large scale enterprise must "not be stopped by those who are preoccupied with outdated notions about firm size."[4]

An example of this conventional wisdom surfaced in the Reagan administration's proposed changes in the antitrust laws, particularly in the areas of merger policy, collusion, and joint ventures and cooperative R&D arrangements.[5] The Reagan administration advocated eliminating the antitrust statutes and promoting horizontal mergers as a means of enhancing the international competitiveness of U.S. firms. It was argued that, "if our industries are going to survive there have to be additional consolidations to achieve needed economies of scale."[6] Despite the general euphoria that seemed to surround U.S. takeovers in the 1980s (see, for example, Jensen 1988), Scherer (1988a) questions whether takeovers actually increase corporate efficiency. In fact, the evidence does not support such an unequivocal acceptance of the view that mergers promote economic efficiency. And when the head of the Bureau of Economics at the Federal Trade Commission under the Reagan administration concludes that, "The election of Ronald Reagan brought in new antitrust enforcement authorities and a new approach to antitrust. . . . Enforcement and case law generally has given more weight to economic efficiency and pro-innovation policies" (Langenfeld and Scheffman 1988, 94), this surely does not recognize the tendency for product innovations to emanate from smaller firms in competitive environments rather than from giant corporations in concentrated markets.

It has similarly been proposed that the United States abandon the Sherman Antitrust Act, either fully or partially (parts of Sections 1 and 2).[7] While there is evidence that legalized cartels have reduced and not enhanced corporate efficiency in West Germany (Audretsch forthcoming) and Japan (Nakazawa and Weiss forthcoming), the point here is, once again, the tendency for conventional wisdom to assume that "bigger is better."

This conventional wisdom has at least as great a following among policy-makers in Europe. More than two decades ago, J.-J. Servan-Schreiber (1968) warned Europeans to beware "The American Challenge," in the form of the "dynamism, organization, innovation, and boldness that characterize the giant American corporations" (p. 153). Because giant corporations are needed to amass the requisite resources for innovation, Servan-Schreiber advocated "creation of large industrial units which are able both in size and management to compete with the American giants," (p. 159) through the selection by government of "fifty to one hundred firms which, once they are large enough, would be the most likely to become world leaders of modern technology in their fields" (p. 160). Ironically, with the European integration that is expected in 1992, Servan-Schreiber's policy prescriptions are now more than ever likely to be followed. The long-standing policy tradition in Europe of cartelization, encouraging mergers, and subsidizing large-scale enterprises (Geroski and Jacquemin 1985) is being reinforced rather than questioned as 1992 nears (Audretsch 1989). Even in West Germany, the most prosperous European nation, there is considerable envy of two U.S. economic achievements during the last decade—the expansion of employment and corresponding reduction in unemployment, and the continued dominance of American companies in high-technology markets.[8] However, while Europeans have become increasingly aware of the American success, there is little questioning of the conventional wisdom that the source of this success is the greater efficiencies enjoyed by the giant U.S. corporations.

In the United States, as in Europe, the consequences of government policies on small firms need to be considered. For example, Scherer (1988b, 8) argues that the tax law of 1986, which eliminated differential capital gains taxation, may inhibit small-venture innovation. Probably an even more consequential area of public policy is government procurement. Newly created small firms in high-technology industries typically have limited profits and capital to invest in R&D. One important role for the government is the inclusion of small firms in its procurement policies. In fact, Rothwell and Zegveld (1981) found that the government's procurement policy plays perhaps the most decisive role in promoting innovative activity. Similarly, a U.S. government study examined a sample of high-technology and fast growing companies and found that almost half received at least 50 percent of their revenues from the government during their first year in existence (U.S. Small Business Administration 1980).[9]

Despite the importance of government procurement to the innovative output and viability of small firms, the gap between the share of government R&D contracts allocated to large and small firms has been growing over time. In 1973, the federal government allocated $307 million (4.3 percent) in R&D contracts to firms with fewer than 1,000 employees and $6,789 million (95.7 percent) to firms with at least 25,000 employees. By 1984, the small firms had been awarded $652 million (3.4 percent) while the large firms received $18,787 million (96.6 percent) of the federal government's R&D expenditures (National Science Foundation 1986).

In order to help smaller firms, Congress passed the Small Business Innovation Development Act of 1982. The Act requires federal agencies with R&D budgets of at least $100 million to participate in Small Business Innovation Research (SBIR) by allocating up to 1.25 percent of their budgets to small firms. SBIR projects are funded in two phases. The first phase awards funds for feasibility studies, usually of less than $50,000. Successful projects enter a second phase lasting two years, with up to $500,000 in funding. Since its inception, over $1 billion in SBIR funding has been allocated. The average recipient of SBIR awards in a ten-year-old company with thirty-five employees. Of these participating firms, 24 percent had received subsequent outside funding, which amounted to twice the dollar amount of the SBIR awards (Price Waterhouse 1985).

As previously mentioned, it is not appropriate here to make specific policy recommendations. However, it is important to point out that the results from our empirical examinations do cast considerable doubt on the conventional wisdom about the sources of innovative activity and technical change embedded in much of public policy. More than anything, though, the results here suggest that those studying the organization of industry cannot afford to ignore that part of the firm-size spectrum that most enterprises actually inhabit. Small firms apparently play a key role in the process of technological change as well as in the dynamic process by which industries evolve.

Appendix A:
Data Sources and
Further Explanations

The innovation data, principally the number of total innovations (TI), large-firm innovations (LI), and small-firm innovations (SI), come from the U.S. Small Business Administration Innovation Data Base and are explained in further detail in Edwards and Gordon (1984).

The U.S. Department of Commerce, Bureau of the Census, *Annual Survey of Manufactures*, 1977, *Industry Profiles*, Washington, D.C.: U.S. Government Printing Office, issued 1981, is the source for the capital–labor ratio (K/L), four-firm concentration ratio (CR), annual growth rate (GR) (the 1972 survey was also used to calculate GR), value-of-shipments (S), and minimum efficient scale (MES).

The employment and sales data by firm size, small-firm presence (SFP), large-firm presence (LFP), medium-firm presence (MFP) births (BIRTH), deaths (DEATH), change in relative small-firm productivity (CRFSP), and the data on expansion and contraction are from the U.S. Small Business Administration, Office of Advocacy, Small Business Data Base. Since 1979, the U.S. Small Business Administration had maintained a major microdata base. The U.S. Enterprise and Establishment Microdata (USEEM) and (USELM) files are a biannual data base containing observations on employment, sales, organizational relationship, and location for nearly all U.S. firms (enterprises) and their component establishments (individual business locations). The data are derived from the DUNS Market Identifier (DMI) file leased from the Dun and Bradstreet Corporation. More detailed description of the data can be found in Boden and Phillips (1985).

The union participation rates (UNION) are from Freeman and Medoff (1979). The percentage of total employment that is unionized for three-digit SIC industries between 1973 and 1975 is reported. We repeat these three-dight SIC values at the four-digit level. The advertising–sales ratio was derived by using the value-of-shipments data described above, and advertising expenditures from the U.S. Bureau of Economic Analysis, *Input-Output Structure of the U.S. Economy, 1972*. The measure of skilled labor (SKILL) is from the U.S. Department of Commerce, Bureau of the Census, Census Population 1970, Subject Report PC (2)–7c, *Occupation by Industry*, Washington, D.C.: U.S. Government Printing Office, issued 1972.

Human capital (HK) is derived from the total employment data from the U.S. Department of Commerce, Bureau of the Census, Annual Survey of Manufactures, 1970, *Industry Profiles*, Washington, D.C. issued 1973. The average annual wage of individuals with less than eight years' education comes from U.S. Department of Commerce, Bureau of the Census, Current Population Reports, *Consumer Income* (Series P-60), Washington, D.C., October 4, 1971. The human capital, skilled labor, and product life cycle (PLC) variables were all constructed by the U.S. International Trade Commission and are reported in U.S. International Trade Commission, *Industrial Characteristics and Trade Performance Data Base*, Washington, D.C., 1975. The data base is also used and described in Ray (1981).

The total R&D (RDT) and company R&D (RDC) data are from the Bureau of Economics, U.S. Federal Trade Commission, *Statistical Report: Line of Business Report, 1977*, Washington, D.C., April 1985.

The machinery data used in chapter 5 were obtained from American Machinist, *13th American Machinist Inventory Market Potentials Report* (New York: McGraw-Hill, 1983). The data for this inventory were gathered by questionnaire from metalworking plants in the forty-eight contiguous states during the period February to June, 1983. Estimation of the number of machine tools and related equipment has been based on this survey. The universe of the inventory is the following industries:

SIC 25   Furniture and fixtures (metal only)

SIC 33   Primary metals (metalworking only)

SIC 34   Fabricated metal products

SIC 35   Machinery (except electrical)

SIC 36   Electrical machinery

SIC 37   Transportation equipment

SIC 38   Precision instruments

SIC 39   Miscellaneous metal products

The AM Inventory covers data in four categories:

1. Number of units of equipment by 173 types.
2. Age of equipment in four categories.
3. Distribution of equipment within twenty-four geographic areas.
4. Distribution of equipment into four plant-size groups.

The data were obtained for the three-digit SIC level (except construction and handling machinery, metalworking machinery, aircraft and parts, and motor vehicles and parts; these industries were divided into two groups each). Numerically controlled (NC) machine tools, programmable robots, station-type machines, automatic assembly machines, mechanical presses, and total machinery figures were calculated from the AM Inventory Market Potentials Report for SIC industries 34–38. For more information about this inventory and details of the research method, see the summary of the report published in *American Machinist*, vol. 127, No. 11 (November 1983), pp. 113–144. These data are explained in more detail in Acs, Audretsch, and Carlsson (1988).

Appendix B:
Definitions of Variables

Variable	Definition
TI	Total number of innovations, 1982
LI	Large-firm (>500 employees) innovations, 1982
SI	Small-firm (<500 employees) innovations, 1982
TIE	Total number of innovations divided by total employment (thousands)
LIE	Large-firm innovations divided by large-firm employment (thousands)
SIE	Small-firm innovations divided by small-firm employment (thousands)
SKILL	Percentage of employment consisting of professional and kindred workers, plus managers and administrators, plus craftsmen and kindred workers, 1970
GR	Mean annual industry employment percentage growth, 1972–1977
K/O	Capital–output ratio, defined as gross assets divided by value-of-shipments, 1977
AD	Advertising expenditures (thousands), 1972
PILF	Percentage of industry employment accounted for by firms with more than 500 employees, 1977
UNION	Percentage of employees belonging to a union, 1973–1975
RDT	Total R&D expenditures divided by sales, 1977
CRD	Company R&D expenditures divided by sales, 1977
K/L	Capital–labor ratio, defined as gross assets divided by total employment (thousands), 1977
MES/S	Minimum efficient scale level of output, defined as the mean size of the largest plants accounting for one-half of the industry value-of-shipments, divided by industry value-of-shipments
S	Value-of-shipments (millions), 1977
CR	Four-firm concentration ratio (percentage), 1977

Variable	Definition
PCM	Price–cost margin, 1977
SFP5	Share of total sales accounted for by firms with fewer than 100 employees, 1978
SFP7	Share of total sales accounted for by firms with fewer than 500 employees, 1978
BIRTH5	Number of new jobs created by new firms with fewer than 100 employees, divided by mean employment of that firm-size class (percentage)
BIRTH7	Number of new jobs created by new firms with fewer than 500 employees, divided by mean employment of that firm-size class (percentage)
DEATH7	Number of jobs lost in disappearing firms with fewer than 500 employees, divided by mean employment of that firm-size class (percentage)
EXP7	Expansion rate for firms with fewer than 500 employees, defined as the number of jobs emanting from new positions in existing firms, divided by employment in 1976
EXPL	Expansion rate for firms with at least 500 employees, defined as the number of jobs emanating from new positions in existing firms, divided by employment in 1976
CONTR7	Contraction rate for firms with fewer than 500 employees, defined as the number of jobs that were eliminated by existing firms, divided by employment in 1976
CONTRL	Contraction rate for firms with at least 500 employees, defined as the number of jobs that were eliminated existing firms, divided by employment in 1976
SFE5	Net entry rate for firms with fewer than 100 employees, defined as the change in the number of firms between 1978 and 1980, divided by the mean total number of firms in the industry, 1978 and 1980
SFE7	Net entry rate for firms with fewer than 500 employees, defined as the change in the number of firms between 1978 and 1980, divided by the mean total number of firms in the industry, 1978 and 1980
CRSFP5	Relative change in small-firm productivity for firms with fewer than 100 employees, defined as the small-firm change in sales per employee between 1976 and 1982, divided by the industry mean change in sales per employee over the same time period
CRSFP7	Relative change in small-firm productivity for firms with fewer than 500 employees, defined as the small-firm change in sales per employee between 1976 and 1982, divided by the industry mean change in sales per employee over the same time period
SAA	Share of total number of machines accounted for by automatic assembly machines (percentage), 1983

Variable	Definition
SPR	Share of total number of machines accounted for by programmable robots (percentage), 1983
SMP	Share of total number of machines accounted for by mechanical presses (percentage), 1983
SST	Share of toal number of machines accounted for by station-type (transfer) machines (percentage), 1983
SNC	Share of total number of machines accounted for by numerically controlled machine tools (percentage), 1983
RD/S	Total R&D expenditures divided by sales, 1982
NPEMPL	The share of total employment accounted for by nonproduction employees, 1982
SF18286	Change in share of sales (percentage) accounted for by firms with fewer than 100 employees, 1982–1986
SF17684	Change in share of sales (percentage) accounted for by firms with fewer than 100 employees, 1976–1984
SF17686	Change in share of sales (percentage) accounted for by firms with fewer than 100 employees, 1976–1986
SF28286	Change in share of sales (percentage) accounted for by firms with fewer than 500 employees, 1982–1986
SF27684	Change in share of sales (percentage) accounted for by firms with fewer than 500 employees, 1976–1984
SF27686	Change in share of sales (percentage) accounted for by firms with fewer than 500 employees, 1976–1986
TR	Turbulence rate, defined as expansion plus contraction plus births plus deaths, divided by 1976 employment

Appendix C: Industries Included in the Sample in Chapter 6

SIC code	Industry
3410	Metal cans and shipping containers
3420	Cutlery, hand tools, and hardware
3430	Plumbing and heating
3440	Fabricated structural metal products
3450	Screw-machine products
3462	Iron and steel forgings
3480	Ordnance and accessories, not elsewhere classified
3510	Engines and turbines
3520	Farm and garden machinery
3530	Construction machinery
3531	Construction machinery
3540	Machine tools
3541	Other metalworking machinery
3552	Special industry machinery and miscellaneous machinery
3560	General industrial machinery
3570	Office and computer machines
3580	Refrigeration and service machinery
3610	Electric distributing equipment
3620	Electrical industrial apparatus
3630	Household appliances
3640	Electrical lighting and wiring equipment
3650	Radio and television receiving equipment
3660	Communication equipment
3670	Electronic components and accessories
3690	Miscellaneous electrical equipment and supplies
3710	Motor vehicles and supplies
3720	Aircraft

SIC code	Industry
3721	Aircraft parts
3730	Ship and boat building and repairing
3743	Railroad equipment
3752	Miscellaneous transportation equipment
3760	Guided missiles and space vehicles
3811	Engineering and scientific instruments and measuring devices
3832	Optical instruments and lenses
3840	Medical instruments and supplies
3861	Photographic equipment and supplies
3873	Watches, clocks, and watchcases

Appendix D:
Distribution of
Innovations by Four-Digit
SIC Code

SIC code	Description	Innovations			
		Large firm	Small firm	Not allocable	Total
0161	Vegetables and melons	2	0		2
0173	Tree nuts	1	0		1
0179	Fruits and tree nuts, nec	1	0		1
1021	Copper ores	1	0		1
1031	Lead and zinc ores	6	0		6
1311	Crude petroleum and natural gas	56	1		57
1382	Oil and gas exploration services	10	0		10
1389	Oil and gas field service, nec	11	0		11
1422	Crushed and broken limestone	1	0		1
1452	Bentonite	0	1		1
1473	Fluorspar	17	0		17
1629	Heavy construction, nec	24	2		26
1761	Roofing and sheet metal work	0	1		1
2011	Meat packing plants	1	2		3
2013	Sausages and other prepared meats	0	3		3
2016	Poultry dressing plants	8	1		9
2017	Poultry and egg processing	1	2		3
2022	Cheese, natural and processed	17	1		18
2023	Condensed and evaporated milk	0	1		1
2026	Fluid milk	14	0		14
2032	Canned specialties	1	0		1
2033	Canned fruits and vegetables	4	1		5
2034	Dehydrated fruits and vegetables, soups	2	1		3

SIC code	Description	Innovations			
		Large firm	Small firm	Not allocable	Total
2035	Pickles, sauces, and salad dressings	1	1		2
2037	Frozen fruit and vegetables	4	1		5
2038	Frozen specialties	9	1		10
2041	Flour and other grain mill products	4	1		5
2043	Cereal breakfast foods	5	2		7
2045	Blended and prepared flour	0	2		2
2046	Wet corn milling	6	0		6
2047	Dog, cat, and other pet food	0	0	1	1
2048	Prepared feeds, nec	3	2		5
2051	Bread, cake, and related products	0	3		3
2052	Cookies and crackers	1	0		1
2061	Raw cane sugar	3	0		3
2062	Cane sugar refining	4	0		4
2066	Chocolate and cocoa products	1	0		1
2074	Cottonseed oil mills	2	0		2
2075	Soyabean oil mills	1	1		2
2079	Shortening and cooking oils	4	0		4
2082	Malt beverages	5	0		5
2085	Distilled liquor, except brandy	5	0		5
2086	Bottled and canned soft drinks	2	0		2
2087	Flavoring extracts and syrups, nec	4	24		28
2092	Fresh or frozen packaged fish	8	11		19
2098	Macaroni and spaghetti	0	1		1
2099	Food preparations, nec	5	12		17
2111	Cigarettes	9	0		9
2211	Weaving mills, cotton	1	0		1
2221	Weaving mills, synthetics	1	1		2
2231	Weaving and finishing mills, wool	1	1		2
2241	Narrow fabric mills	0	2		2
2258	Warp knit fabric mills	0	1		1
2295	Coated fabrics, not rubberized	0	2		2
2311	Men's and boys' suits and coats	3	1		4
2328	Men's and boys' work clothing	2	0		2
2381	Fabric dress and work gloves	0	1		1
2392	House furnishing, nec	0	2		2
2394	Canvas and related products	0	6		6

SIC code	Description	Innovations			
		Large firm	Small firm	Not allocable	Total
2399	Fabricated textile products, nec	4	0		4
2421	Sawmills and planing mills, general	1	0		1
2431	Millwork	4	0		4
2441	Nailed wood boxes	0	4		4
2499	Wood products, nec	1	1		2
2511	Wood household furniture	2	1		3
2514	Metal household furniture	0	5	1	6
2521	Wood office furniture	1	1		2
2522	Metal office furniture	25	3		28
2531	Public building and related furniture	1	4		5
2541	Wood partitions and fixtures	2	2		4
2542	Metal partitions and fixtures	5	10		15
2591	Drapery hardware and blinds and shades	2	0		2
2599	Furniture and fixtures, nec	0	7		7
2611	Pulp mills	1	0		1
2621	Paper mills, except building paper	10	0		10
2631	Paperboard mills	4	0		4
2641	Paper coating and glazing	4	2		6
2643	Bags, except textile bags	5	0		5
2645	Die-cut paper and board	2	0	1	3
2647	Sanitary paper products	0	2	1	3
2648	Stationery products	1	0		1
2649	Converted paper products, nec	13	1		14
2651	Folding paperboard boxes	1	2		3
2652	Set-up paperboard boxes	0	3		3
2653	Corrugated and solid fiber boxes	2	0		2
2654	Sanitary food containers	2	0		2
2661	Building paper and board mills	4	0		4
2711	Newspapers	5	0		5
2721	Periodicals	0	1		1
2731	Book publishing	3	0		3
2741	Miscellaneous publishing	0	1	1	2
2751	Commercial printing, letterpress	3	1		4
2752	Commercial printing, lithographic	0	4		4
2761	Manifold business forms	1	0		1

SIC code	Description	Innovations			
		Large firm	Small firm	Not allocable	Total
2771	Greeting card publishing	1	0		1
2782	Blank books and looseleaf binders	2	2		4
2812	Alkalies and chlorine	4	0		4
2813	Industrial gases	7	2		9
2816	Inorganic pigments	5	1		6
2819	Industrial inorganic chemicals, nec	32	8		40
2821	Plastics materials and resins	30	15		45
2822	Synthetic rubber	0	4		4
2831	Biological products	1	4		5
2833	Medicinals and botanicals	27	5		32
2834	Pharmaceutical preparations	120	13		133
2841	Soap and other detergents	7	4		11
2842	Polishes and sanitation goods	13	19	1	33
2843	Surface active agents	2	10		12
2844	Toilet preparations	41	18		59
2851	Paints and allied products	6	11		17
2861	Gum and wood chemicals	1	3		4
2865	Cyclic crudes and intermediates	1	1		2
2869	Industrial organic chemicals, nec	17	3	1	21
2879	Agricultural chemicals, nec	24	0		24
2891	Adhesives and sealants	7	11		18
2892	Explosives	1	0		1
2893	Printing ink	1	2		3
2895	Carbon black	1	0		1
2899	Chemical preparations, nec	11	7		18
2911	Petroleum refining	14	0		14
2952	Asphalt felts and coatings	0	2		2
2992	Lubricating oils and greases	0	8		8
3011	Tires and inner tubes	11	0		11
3041	Rubber and plastics hose and belting	2	0		2
3069	Fabricated rubber products, nec	5	4		9
3079	Miscellaneous plastics products	22	82	3	107
3142	House slippers	0	1		1
3143	Men's footwear, except athletic	1	0		1
3161	Luggage	0	1		1
3199	Leather goods, nec	0	3		3

SIC code	Description	Innovations			
		Large firm	Small firm	Not allocable	Total
3211	Flat glass	12	0		12
3221	Glass containers	6	0		6
3229	Pressed and blown glass, nec	11	2		13
3231	Products of purchased glass	2	4		6
3261	Vitreous plumbing fixtures	0	1		1
3264	Porcelain electrical supplies	5	1		6
3275	Gypsum products	1	0		1
3291	Abrasive products	0	3		3
3293	Gaskets, packing, and sealing devices	2	3		5
3295	Minerals, ground or treated	0	1		1
3296	Mineral wood	2	1		3
3299	Nonmetallic mineral products, nec	0	2		2
3312	Blast furnaces and steel mills	10	1		11
3315	Steel wire and related products	0	1		1
3316	Cold finishing of steel shapes	3	0		3
3317	Steel pipe and tubes	0	1		1
3321	Gray iron foundries	15	1		16
3325	Steel foundries, nec	13	1		14
3331	Primary copper	0	1		1
3334	Primary aluminium	5	0		5
3339	Primary nonferrous metals, nec	1	0		1
3351	Copper rolling and drawing	0	1		1
3357	Nonferrous wire drawing and insulating	0	3		3
3361	Aluminum foundries	1	2		3
3362	Brass, bronze, and copper foundries	0	0	1	1
3369	Nonferrous foundries, nec	1	0		1
3398	Metal heat treating	0	1		1
3399	Primary metal products, nec	8	3		11
3411	Metal cans	6	1		7
3421	Cutlery	4	0		4
3423	Hand and edge tools, nec	27	11	1	39
3425	Hand saws and saw blades	2	3		5
3429	Hardware, nec	8	16	1	25
3431	Metal sanitary ware	0	2		2
3432	Plumbing fitting and brass goods	10	6		16

SIC code	Description	Innovations			
		Large firm	Small firm	Not allocable	Total
3433	Heating equipment, except electric	8	14		22
3442	Metal doors, sash, and trim	1	7		8
3443	Fabricated plate work (boiler shops)	29	9		38
3444	Sheet metal work	1	5		6
3446	Architectural metal work	0	2		2
3448	Prefabricated metal buildings	9	5		14
3449	Miscellaneous metal work	0	1		1
3451	Screw-machine products	1	0		1
3452	Bolts, nuts, rivets, and washers	2	3		5
3462	Iron and steel forgings	6	1	1	8
3465	Automotive stampings	2	0		2
3469	Metal stampings, nec	2	10		12
3471	Plating and polishing	0	3		3
3479	Metal coating and allied services	0	3		3
3483	Ammunition, except for small arms, nec	21	0		21
3492	Valves and pipe fittings	20	33	1	54
3496	Miscellaneous fabricated wire products	4	2		6
3498	Fabricated pipe fittings	0	5		5
3499	Fabricated metal products, nec	12	17	6	35
3511	Turbines and turbine generator sets	7	2		9
3519	Internal combustion engines, nec	13	2		15
3523	Farm machinery and equipment	13	17		30
3524	Lawn and garden equipment	2	2		4
3531	Construction machinery	11	10		21
3532	Mining machinery	0	7		7
3533	Oil-field machinery	0	2		2
3534	Elevators and moving stairways	3	3		6
3535	Conveyors and conveying equipment	4	17	1	22
3536	Hoists, cranes, and monorails	1	9		10
3537	Industrial trucks and tractors	13	20		33
3541	Machine tools, metal-cutting types	18	7		25
3542	Machine tools, metal-forming types	1	4		5
3544	Special dies, tools, jigs, and fixtures	0	6	1	7
3545	Machine tool accessories	1	5		6
3546	Power-driven hand tools	14	7		21

SIC code	Description	Innovations			
		Large firm	Small firm	Not allocable	Total
3547	Rolling mill machinery	1	0		1
3549	Metalworking machinery, nec	3	3		6
3551	Food products machinery	37	12	1	50
3552	Textile machinery	11	13		24
3553	Woodworking machinery	3	0		3
3554	Paper industries machinery	6	1		7
3555	Printing trades machinery	6	13		19
3559	Special industry machinery, nec	43	21		64
3561	Pumps and pumping equipment	18	16		34
3562	Ball and roller bearings	0	4		4
3563	Air and gas compressors	2	5		7
3564	Blowers and fans	10	8		18
3566	Speed changers, drives, and gears	4	3		7
3567	Industrial furnaces and ovens	12	9		21
3568	Power transmission equipment, nec	4	7		11
3569	General industrial machinery, nec	54	13		67
3572	Typewriters	0	59		59
3573	Electronic computing equipment	158	227	10	395
3574	Calculating and accounting machines	9	1		10
3576	Scales and balances, except laboratory	4	21		25
3579	Office machines, nec	67	10		77
3585	Refrigeration and heating equipment	10	14	1	25
3586	Measuring and dispensing pumps	0	2		2
3589	Service industry machinery, nec	2	19		21
3592	Carburetors, pistons, rings, valves	1	0		1
3599	Machinery, except electrical, nec	5	12		17
3612	Transformers	5	11	4	20
3613	Switchgear and switchboard apparatus	15	6		21
3621	Motors and generators	39	10		49
3622	Industrial controls	15	46		61
3623	Welding apparatus, electric	2	4		6
3624	Carbon and graphite products	2	0		2
3629	Electrical industrial apparatus, nec	0	5		5
3631	Household cooking equipment	2	2		4
3632	Household refrigerators and freezers	0	1		1
3633	Household laundry equipment	1	0		1

SIC		Innovations			
code	Description	Large firm	Small firm	Not allocable	Total
3634	Electric housewares and fans	47	6		53
3635	Household vacuum cleaners	3	0		3
3636	Sewing machines	1	1		2
3641	Electric lamps	0	3		3
3643	Current-carrying wiring devices	2	3		5
3644	Noncurrent-carrying wiring devices	0	1		1
3645	Residential lighting fixtures	2	0		2
3651	Radio and TV receiving sets	35	4	1	40
3661	Telephone and telegraph apparatus	2	7	3	12
3662	Radio and TV communication equipment	83	72	2	157
3673	Electron tubes, transmitting	0	5		5
3674	Semiconductors and related devices	91	29	2	122
3675	Electronic capacitors	3	0	2	5
3676	Electronic resistors	0	3		3
3677	Electronic coils and transformers	0	3		3
3678	Electronic connectors	0	3		3
3679	Electronic components, nec	54	73	1	128
3691	Storage batteries	22	0		22
3692	Primary batteries, dry and wet	0	1		1
3693	X-ray apparatus and tubes	17	10		27
3694	Engine electrical equipment	3	0		3
3699	Electrical equipment and supplies, nec	3	7		10
3711	Motor vehicles and car bodies	29	1		30
3713	Truck and bus bodies	12	0		12
3714	Motor vehicle parts and accessories	22	6		28
3721	Aircraft	31	1		32
3724	Aircraft engines and engine parts	4	0		4
3728	Aircraft equipment, nec	9	3		12
3731	Ship building and repairing	5	0	2	7
3732	Boat building and repairing	2	0		2
3743	Railroad equipment	2	0		2
3751	Motorcycles, bicycles, and parts	2	0		2
3761	Guided missiles and space vehicles	14	0		14
3764	Space propulsion units and parts	1	0		1
3769	Space vehicle equipment, nec	0	1		1

SIC code	Description	Innovations			
		Large firm	Small firm	Not allocable	Total
3792	Travel trailers and campers	1	0		1
3799	Transportation equipment, nec	0	5		5
3811	Engineering and scientific instruments	43	83		126
3822	Environmental controls	22	10		32
3823	Process control instruments	68	93	4	165
3824	Fluid meters and counting devices	6	10		16
3825	Instruments to measure electricity	28	47	2	77
3829	Measuring and controlling devices, nec	3	45	4	52
3832	Optical instruments and lenses	12	21	1	34
3841	Surgical and medical instruments	30	36		66
3842	Surgical appliances and supplies	30	33	4	67
3843	Dental equipment and supplies	0	2		2
3851	Ophthalmic goods	9	2		11
3861	Photographic equipment and supplies	79	9		88
3914	Silverware and plated ware	3	0		3
3944	Games, toys, and children's vehicles	3	0		3
3949	Sporting and athletic goods, nec	5	15		20
3951	Pens and mechanical pencils	4	0		4
3952	Lead pencils and art goods	1	0		1
3953	Marketing devices	0	6		6
3964	Needles, pins, and fasteners	2	1		3
3991	Brooms and brushes	0	7		7
3993	Signs and advertising displays	1	2		3
3999	Manufacturing industries, nec	11	3		14
4212	Local trucking, without storage	0	1		1
4213	Trucking, except local	1	0		1
4222	Refrigerated warehousing	0	2		2
4311	U.S. postal service	1	0		1
4411	Deep sea foreign transportation	0	1		1
4613	Refined petroleum pipe lines	2	0		2
4783	Packing and crating	0	1		1
4811	Telephone communication	4	0		4
4899	Communication services, nec	1	4		5
4922	Natural gas transmission	5	0		5
4923	Gas transmission and distributions	6	0		6
4931	Electric and other services, combined	1	0		1

SIC code	Description	Innovations			
		Large firm	Small firm	Not allocable	Total
5013	Automotive parts and supplies	5	0	1	6
5043	Photographic equipment and supplies	4	3		7
5051	Metals service centers and offices	2	3		5
5063	Electrical apparatus and equipment	6	9		15
5064	Electrical appliances, TV, and radios	15	3		18
5065	Electronic parts and equipment	22	2		24
5074	Plumbing and hydronic heating supplies	1	1		2
5081	Commercial machines and equipment	2	8		10
5082	Construction and mining machinery	0	2		2
5084	Industrial machinery and equipment	0	10	1	11
5085	Industrial supplies	0	4		4
5086	Professional equipment and supplies	7	12	1	20
5099	Durable goods, nec	0	3		3
5111	Printing and writing paper	1	0		1
5122	Drugs, proprietaries, and sundries	1	2		3
5133	Piece goods	0	2		2
5141	Groceries, general line	1	0		1
5142	Frozen foods	0	1		1
5143	Dairy products	3	0		3
5146	Fish and seafoods	1	1		2
5147	Meats and meat products	0	1		1
5149	Groceries and related products, nec	0	4		4
5161	Chemicals and allied products	4	0		4
5172	Petroleum products, nec	1	0		1
5191	Farm supplies	1	0		1
5198	Paints, varnishes, and supplies	0	2		2
5199	Nondurable goods, nec	0	2		2
5311	Department stores	1	0		1
5411	Grocery stores	2	0		2
5941	Sporting goods and bicycle shops	2	0		2
5961	Mail-order houses	4	0		4
6059	Functions related to banking, nec	0	1		1
6145	Licensed small loan lenders	4	0		4
6211	Security brokers and dealers	0	1		1
6311	Life insurance	0	1		1

SIC code	Description	Innovations			
		Large firm	Small firm	Not allocable	Total
6399	Insurance carriers, nec	1	0		1
6519	Real property lessors, nec	5	0		5
6711	Holding offices	58	11	8	77
7011	Hotels, motels, and tourist courts	1	0		1
7213	Linen supply	5	0		5
7299	Miscellaneous personal services	1	0		1
7362	Temporary help supply services	0	1		1
7372	Computer programming and software	9	7		16
7374	Data processing services	7	5		12
7379	Computer-related services, nec	15	1		16
7391	Research and development laboratories	5	10	1	16
7392	Management and public relations	1	2		3
7393	Detective and protective services	1	0		1
7395	Photofinishing laboratories	1	0		1
7397	Commercial testing laboratories	1	1		2
7399	Business services, nec	0	2		2
7813	Motion picture production, except TV	1	0		1
7819	Services allied to motion pictures	1	0		1
8911	Engineering and architectural services	20	3		23
8931	Accounting, auditing, and bookkeeping	1	0		1
NA	Not allocable	4	15	3,057	3,076
	Totals	2,834	2,104	3,136	8,074

Source: U.S. Small Business Administration (Edwards and Gordon 1984).
Note: nec = not elsewhere classified.

Notes

Chapter 1

1. "The Rise and Rise of America's Small Firms," *The Economist*, January 21, 1989, pp. 73–74.

2. Tom Peters, "New Products, New Markets, New Competition, New Thinking," *The Economist*, March 4, 1989, pp. 27–32.

3. David B. Audretsch, "America's Challege to Europe," *The Wall Street Journal/Europe*, July 31, 1989, p. 6.

Chapter 2

1. For example, Scherer (1965b) and Soete (1979) included only the largest U.S. corporations.

2. For a more complete explanation of the data, see appendix A.

3. Unfortunately, no further information regarding the distribution of innovations by significance category is included in Edwards and Gordon (1984). Therefore, no comparisons across industries can be made.

4. For example, while the process control instruments, semiconductors, instruments for measuring electricity, and aircraft industries all had R&D/sales ratios in excess of 5 percent, in two of the industries the small firms were more innovative, and in the other two the large firms were more innovative. Similarly, hand and edge tools, fabricated platework, fabricated structural metal products, and plastic products are examples of industries that have a relatively low R&D intensity and in which small and large firms alternatively have the innovative advantage.

5. Further analysis comparing the results for innovations with patents can be found in our 1989c paper.

6. The employment data are from 1977 (see appendix A).

7. For a discussion of the appropriateness of standardizing measures of innovative activity, see Scherer (1965b).

8. It should be noted that there were a total of 8,074 innovations recorded, including some innovations outside manufacturing as well as some contributed by firms that could not be identified in published company directories. While some of these were subsidiaries of large firms, many more were small companies. A random sample of 600 firms (with 375 responses) was used to allocate the entire set of innovations into 55 percent from small firms and 45 percent from large firms. Such an assumption results in an innovation rate of small firms that is 2.38 percent greater than that for large firms (Edwards and Gordon 1984).

9. This pattern also existed for the earlier periods. The Gellman study determined that between 1960 and 1966, U.S. manufacturing firms with fewer than 100 employees had a mean of 3.0 innovations per $10 billion of sales; firms with between 100 and 999 employees had a mean of 2.6 innovations per $10 billion in sales; and firms with at least 1,000 employees had a mean of 1.9 innovations per $10 billion of sales. Between 1953 and 1959, U.S. manufacturing firms with fewer than 100 employees had a mean of 3.1 innovations per $10 billion of sales; firms with between 100 and 999 employees had a mean of 3.2 innovations per $10 billion of sales; and firms with at least 1,000 employees had a mean of 2.4 innovations per $10 billion of sales. One obvious explanation for the decrease in innovative activity per dollar of sales is the substantial decline in purchasing power due to inflation over this period (National Science Foundation 1975).

10. For additional explanations of the National Science Foundation study (by the Gellman Research Associates), see Scheirer (1977).

11. The classification of the innovation data listed in table 2.2 in the Gellman study (1982, 17) was made compatible with the industry group classification in table 1.5.

12. Calculation of the large-firm and small-firm innovation rates for the U.S. Small Business Innovation Data Base is explained in footnote 8.

13. The SPRU innovation data are explained in more detail in Pavitt et al. (1987), Townsend et al. (1981), Robson and Townsend (1984), and Rothwell (1989).

14. Another U.S. data source that directly measures innovation activity in several manufacturing industries, but that does not analyze differences across firm-size classes, is described in Baily and Chakrabarti (1985, 1988) and Chakrabarti (1988).

15. Armington and Odle (1982, 14) argue that the relevant unit of observation for size classification is the firm and not the establishment: "It is the parent firm that makes the business policy decisions that determine much of the behavior of the neighborhood branch of the department store, the business office of the telephone company, or the local cannery of a large food-

processing company. Similary, most government policies affecting business are directed at the legal and financial entity, the parent firm."

16. The firm itself is classified by industry according to the establishment with the greatest number of employees.

17. This calculation was based on table 1 of the 1982 *Enterprise Statistics*, published by the Bureau of the Census of the U.S. Department of Commerce.

18. For a further explanation of the development and editing of the USEEM file, see Harris (1983).

19. Other differences depend on whether the *County Business Pattern* data have been adjusted for firms that dissolve during the relevant time period, as well as on differing industry classification systems.

Chapter 3

1. For a thorough review of the empirical literature on technical change, see Kamien and Schwartz (1975) and Baldwin and Scott (1987).

2. Exceptions include our 1987b and 1988b papers.

3. Kamien and Schwartz (1975, 15) characterize this hypothesis as, "A statistical relationship between firm size and innovative activity is most frequently sought with exploration of the impact of firm size on both the amount of innovational effort and innovational success."

4. Quoted from Scherer (1980, 408).

5. For a distinction between the Schumpeterian and neo-Schumpeterian views, see Dasgupta and Stiglitz (1980) and Reinganum (1985).

6. Baumol and Willig (1981) offer an alternative definition of entry barriers. This is examined in detail in chapter 5.

7. Because the 1982 innovations were, on average, the result of 1977 inventions, the dependent variable can actually be viewed as the number of 1977 inventions, divided by employment, that ultimately proved to be commercially successful by 1982.

8. The analysis of Schumpeter (1950, 101) calls attention to the monopolist firm as an engine of economic development. The monopolist firm will generate a larger supply of innovations because, "There are advantages which, though not strictly attainable on the competitive level of enterprise, are as a matter of fact secured only on the monopoly level." While we have seen a major shift in the twentieth century, with the large firm and the industrial research laboratory playing a much more important role in innovation, individual entrepreneurs, who are not associated with established firms (Schumpeter 1934, 62), continue to survive and thrive in a number of industries (Martin 1986). Winter (1984, 295) asks, "[T]here is a cross-sectional phe-

nomenon requiring explanation: under what circumstance are new firms led by individual entrepreneurs a source of innovation?"

9. According to Winter (1984, 297), the relative small-firm innovative advantage "is likely to be roughly proportional to the number of people exposed to the knowledge base from which innovative ideas might derive."

10. The disparate effect of PILF on small- and large-firm innovation rates is perhaps implied by Scherer (1980, 422): "[T]he most favorable industrial environment for rapid technological progress would appear to be a firm size distribution that includes a predominence of companies with sales below $500 million, pressed on one side by a horde of small, technologically oriented enterprises bubbling over with bright new ideas and on the other by a few larger corporations with the capacity to undertake exceptional ambitious developments."

11. The high value of R^2 and low t-values might imply the existence of multicollinearity. While the correlation between some of the pairs of independent variables is fairly high, deleting variables from the regression equation does not qualitatively change the results for the remaining variables included.

Chapter 4

1. In fact, in his article, Lucas (1978) assumes an economy with only one market.

2. These figures are from Board of Governors of the Federal Reserve System, "Survey of Term of Bank Lending," Statistical Release E.2, December 23, 1986, and are quoted from the 1987 *The State of Small Business: A Report of the President*, table A 2.7, p. 91.

3. The hypothesis that there are scale economies in advertising has been challenged by Arndt and Simon (1983), Boyer (1974), and Simon (1970).

4. It should also be recognized that the greater the extent to which an industry offers the possibilities for producing a differentiated product, the greater are the opportunities for a small firm to develop a specialized niche. Thus, while advertising-intensive industries are generally inhospitable to small firms, markets offering opportunities for product differentiation and product niches, ceteris paribus, may actually be conducive to small firms.

5. Caves and Pugel (1980, 15) report that there does not exist any observable tendency for profitability to vary between large and small firms. This is also the conclusion of Marcus (1969).

6. The hypothesis that small firms choose more flexible production technologies, while their larger counterparts choose more capital-intensive technologies, is consistent with the empirical inverse relationship between firm size and rate of return variability observed by Alexander (1949) and Hall and Weiss (1967).

7. See also Nelson and Winter (1982).

8. It should be noted that while the entry barrier literature generally focuses on industry-specific attributes, Caves and Pugel (1980) refer to firm-specific attributes.

9. It should be recognized that the production function is not homothetic.

Chapter 5

1. For a review of the studies, see Geroski (1983).

2. More recently, Shapiro and Khemani (1987) were able to avoid this problem by using Canadian data for 143 manufacturing firms that entered de novo by constructing new plants.

3. One exception is Schwalbach (1987), who measured diversified entry between 1977 and 1982 as the share of production in 1982 by firms that have their base industry in another market. Of course, this measured only the cumulative diversified net entry by established firms, including mergers, and not entry de novo.

4. These figures are from chapter 4.

5. While Orr (1974) used net entry as the dependent variable, the dependent variable in Khemani and Shapiro (1986) was de novo gross plant entry, net of exit, plant creation by incumbents, mergers, and diversification.

6. This example was pointed out by an anonymous referee.

7. CRFSP can be thought of as a proxy for changes in minimum efficient scale (MES). For a discussion using proxy variables to measure MES, see Baldwin and Gorecki (1985, 1987) and Caves et al. (1975).

Chapter 6

1. The entire sample of engineering industries included in our analysis is listed in appendix C, and the method of classifying the industries is explained as follows:

All industries are three-digit industries according to the standard industrial classification (SIC) in SIC sectors 34–38, except

a. SIC 346 (metal forgings and stampings) and SIC 349 (miscellaneous fabricated metal products) were aggregated into a single industry.

b. SIC 347 (metal services, net elsewhere classified) was excluded since the relevant data could not be obtained.

c. SIC 353 (construction and related machinery) was disaggregated into 3530 (construction and related machinery) and 3531 (materials-handling machinery and equipment).

d. SIC 354 (metalworking machinery) was disaggregated into 3540 (machine tools) and 3541 (other metalworking machinery, equipment, and accessories).

e. SIC 355 (special industrial machinery) and SIC 359 (miscellaneous machinery, except electrical) were aggregated into a single industry.

f. SIC 372 (aircraft and parts) was disaggregated into 3720 (complete aircraft) and 3721 (aircraft engines and parts).

g. SIC 3751 (motorcycles, bicycles, and parts) and SIC 379 (miscellaneous transportation equipment) were aggregated into a single industry.

h. SIC 3811 (engineering and scientific equipment) and SIC 382 (measuring and controlling devices) were aggregated into a single industry.

i. SIC 3832 (optical instruments and lenses) and SIC 3851 (ophthalmic goods) were aggrergated into a single industry.

2. Carlsson (1984) reports that the diffusion of flexible manufacturing systems came much earlier in Sweden, Japan, and West Germany than in the United States.

3. Highfield and Smiley (1987) found that new business starts in the United States vary considerably over the business cycle. Since most new starts tend to be small firms, our model could be sensitive to the period used. Thus, we apply these three different periods.

4. Since the data for SPR, SNC, SMP, SST, and SAA are at the three-digit SIC level, the correlations are for three-digit SIC industries. Note that the regression model described in this section and estimated in the next section is based on observations at the four-digit SIC level. To implement the regression analyses, the three-digit SIC industry values for the above technology variables were repeated across four-digit SIC industries common to each three-digit SIC industry.

5. It should be noted that all of the technology variables—SPR, SNC, SMP, SST, and SAA—have been multiplied by ten in the regression analysis for presentation purposes.

6. To vary between zero and one, the dependent variable was transformed according to $SFC^* = (SFC + 100)/200$.

7. Since the OLS and logit results are identical for all equations in table 6.4, only the OLS equations are reported since they are easier to interpret intuitively.

8. In fact, the negative correlation between the presence of small firms and SNC is even stronger (-0.220) when the 1982 share of sales accounted for by firms with fewer than 100 employees is used. Similarly, there is a correlation of -0.124 between SNC and the share of sales accounted for by firms with fewer than 500 employees in 1976 and a correlation of -0.324 for this small-firm share of sales in 1982. All of these correlations are at the three-digit SIC level.

Chapter 7

1. None of these studies include the 1980s.

2. Most of the theoretical criticisms of attempts to measure industry turnover or mobility are discussed in Stigler (1956b), Mermelstein (1969, 1971), Kamerschen (1971), and Boyle (1971).

3. It should be noted that the coefficients of GR, SIE, TIE, and the intercept have been divided by 100, the coefficients of AD/S have been divided by 10,000, and the coefficients of KREQ have been multiplied by 10,000 for presentation purposes in equations 1 and 2. Similarly, in equations 3 and 4 the coefficients of K/L and CON have been multiplied by 100, the coefficients of PCM have been multiplied by 10,000, and the coefficients of KAPR by 10,000.

Chapter 8

1. Quoted in Tom Peters, "New Products, New Markets, New Competition, New Thinking," *The Economist*, March 4, 1989, pp. 27–32.

2. For a discussion and empirical analysis of the role of capital intensity, human capital, and R&D in determining U.S. trade performance, see Audretsch and Yamawaki (1988) and Yamawaki and Audretsch (1988).

3. For a review of these studies, see FitzRoy (1989).

4. Statement of Hon. Malcolm Baldridge, Secretary, Department of Commerce, in *Merger Law Reform: Hearings on S. 2022 and S. 2160 Before the Senate Committee on the Judiciary*, 99th Congress, 2nd Session, 1986.

5. For an example of changes in the antitrust law regarding merger policy proposed by the Reagan administration, see the previous footnote, as well as *Antitrust Policy and Competition: Hearings Before the Joint Economic Committee*, 98th Congress, 1st Session, 1984.

6. "Making Mergers Even Easier," *New York Times*, November 10, 1985.

7. See *Antitrust Policy and Competition: Hearings Before the Joint Economic Committee*, 98th Congress, 1st Session, 1984.

8. For example, one of the major West German daily newspapers writes that, "A glance at the most recent developments in the U.S. labor market gives Europeans a good reason for reflection. While European politicians representing every party have had overwhelming difficulties in reducing unemployment, the statistics from the Labor Department in Washington continually show new progress. . . . One asks, what has been the secret of success in the U.S. that, until now, has proven to be so elusive here in Europe?" "Erfolg unter andere Vorzeichen," *Der Tagesspiegel*, March 11, 1989, p. 1.

9. Two-thirds of the firms in the sample reported that government R&D contracts were a significant source of funding for the technological base of their

product lines. Interestingly, the share of firms that still depended upon government contracts for at least half of their revenue had fallen to less than one-third by 1986.

References

Abernathy, William J., and Kenneth Wayne. 1974. "The Limits of the Learning Curve." *Harvard Business Review* 52 (September–October): 109–119.

Acs, Zoltan J. 1984. *The Changing Structure of the U.S. Economy: Lessons from the Steel Industry*. New York: Praeger.

Acs, Zoltan J., and David B. Audretsch. 1987a. "Innovation in Large and Small Firms." *Economics Letters* 23: 109–112.

Acs, Zoltan J., and David B. Audretsch. 1987b. "Innovation, Market Structure and Firm Size." *Review of Economics and Statistics* 69 (November): 567–575.

Acs, Zoltan J., and David B. Audretsch. 1988a. "R&D and Small Firms." Testimony before the Subcommittee on Monopolies and Commercial Law, Committee on the Judiciary, U.S. House of Representatives, February 24, 1988.

Acs, Zoltan J., and David B. Audretsch. 1988b. "Innovation in Large and Small Firms: An Empirical Analysis." *American Economic Review* 78 (September): 678–690.

Acs, Zoltan J., and David B. Audretsch. 1989a. "Births and Firm Size." *Southern Economic Journal* 56 (October): 467–475.

Acs, Zoltan J., and David B. Audretsch. 1989b. "Job Creation and Firm Size in the U.S. and West Germany. *International Small Business Journal* 7 (July–September): 9–22.

Acs, Zoltan J., and David B. Audretsch. 1989c. "Patents as a Measure of Innovative Activity." *Kyklos* 42: 171–180.

Acs, Zoltan J., and David B. Audretsch. 1989d. "Small-Firm Entry in U.S. Manufacturing." *Economica* 56 (May): 255–265.

Acs, Zoltan J., David B. Audretsch, and Bo Carlsson. 1988. "Flexible Technology and Firm Size." RPIE Working Paper X. Case Western Reserve University, March.

Acs, Zoltan J., David B. Audretsch, and Richard J. Judd. 1987. "The Research University and Public Policy." Discussion Paper No. IIM/IP 87-28. Wissenschaftszentrum Berlin, October.

Adams, Walter, and James W. Brock. 1988. "The Bigness Mystique and the Merger Policy Debate: An International Perspective." *Northwestern Journal of International Law and Business* 9 (Spring): 1–48.

Aghion, Philippe, and Patrick Bolton. 1987. "Contracts as a Barrier to Entry." *American Economic Review* 77 (June): 388–401.

Alexander, Sidney S. 1949. "The Effect of Size of Manufacturing Corporation on the Distribution of the Rate of Return." *Review of Economics and Statistics* 31 (August): 229–235.

Altshuler, Alan, Martin Anderson, Daniel Jones, Daniel Roos, and James Womack. 1984. *The Future of the Automobile: The Report of the MIT's International Automobile Program*. Cambridge, Mass.: MIT Press.

Andrews, Victor L., and Peter C. Eisemann. 1984. "Who Finances Small Business in the 1980s?" In Paul M. Horvitz and R. Richardson Pettit (eds.) *Small Business Finance: Problems in the Financing of Small Business*. Greenwich, Conn.: JAI Press, pp. 75–96.

Angelmar, Reinhard. 1985. "Market Structure and Research Intensity in High-Technological-Opportunity Industries." *The Journal of Industrial Economics* 34 (September): 69–79.

Armington, Catherine, Candee Harris, and Marjorie Odle. 1984. "Formation and Growth in High-Technology Firms: A Regional Assessment." Prepared for the National Science Foundation under Grant No. ISI 8212970 and the U.S. Small Business Administration under SBA Contract No. 2641-0A-79 and reprinted in Office of Technology Assessment, U.S. Congress, *Technology, Innovation, and Regional Economic Development*, Washington, D.C., July.

Armington, Catherine, and Marjorie Odle. 1982. "Small Business—How Many Jobs." *The Brookings Review* 1 (Winter): 14–17.

Armington, Catherine, and Marjorie Odle. 1983. "Weighting the USEEM Files of Longitudinal Analysis of Employment Growth." Working Paper No. 12, Business Microdata Project, The Brookings Institution, April.

Arndt, Johan, and Julian L. Simon. 1983. "Advertising and Economies of Scale: Critical Comments on the Evidence." *Journal of Industrial Economics* 32 (December): 229–243.

Arrow, Kenneth J. 1962. "Economic Welfare and the Allocation of Resources for Invention." In R.R. Nelson (ed.) *The Rate and Direction of Inventive Activity*. Princeton: Princeton University Press, pp. 609–626.

Audretsch, David B. 1987. "An Empirical Test of the Industry Life Cycle." *Weltwirtschaftliches Archiv* 123: 297–308.

Audretsch, David B. 1989. *The Market and the State: Government Policies towards Business in Europe, Japan and the U.S.* New York: New York University Press.

Audretsch, David B. "Legalized Cartels in West Germany." *Antitrust Bulletin*, forthcoming.

Audretsch, David B., and Michael P. Claudon (eds.) 1989. *The Internationalization of U.S. Markets.* New York: New York University Press.

Audretsch, David B., Leo Sleuwaegen, and Hideki Yamawaki (eds.) 1989. *The Convergence of International and Domestic Markets.* Amsterdam: North Holland.

Audretsch, David B., and Hideki Yamawaki. 1988. "R&D Rivalry, Industrial Policy, and U.S.–Japanese Trade." *Review of Economics and Statistics* 70 (August): 438–447.

Baily, Martin N., and Alok K. Chakrabarti. 1985. "Innovation and Productivity in U.S. Industry." *Brookings Papers on Economic Activities* 2: 609–639.

Baily, Martin N., and Alok K. Chakrabarti. 1988. *Innovation and the Productivity Crisis.* Washington, D.C.: the Brookings Institution.

Bain, Joe. *Barriers to New Competition.* 1956. Cambridge, Mass.: Harvard University Press.

Baldridge, Malcolm. 1986. "The Administration's Legislative Proposal and its Ramifications." *Antitrust Law Journal* 29.

Baldwin, John R., and Paul K. Gorecki. 1985. "The Determinants of Small Plant Market Share in Canadian Manufacturing Industries in the 1970s." *Review of Economics and Statistics* 67 (February): 156–161.

Baldwin, John R., and Paul K. Gorecki. 1987. "Plant Creation versus Plant Acquisition: The Entry Process in Canadian Manufacturing." *International Journal of Industrial Organization* 5 (March): 27–42

Baldwin, William L., and John T. Scott. 1987. *Market Structure and Technological Change.* London and New York: Harwood Academic Publishers.

Baumol, William. 1982. "Contestable Markets: An Uprising in the Theory of Industry Structure." *American Economic Review* 72 (March): 1–15.

Baumol, William, and Robert Willig. 1981. "Fixed Costs, Sunk Costs, Entry Barriers, and Sustainability of Monopoly." *Quarterly Journal of Economics* 96 (August): 405–431.

Beatty, Carol A., and John R. M. Gordon. 1988. "Barriers to the Impelementation of CAD/CAM Systems. *Sloan Management Review* 29 (Summer): 25–34.

Beesley, M. E., and R. T. Hamilton. 1984. "Small Firms' Seedbed Role and the Concept of Turbulence." *Journal of Industrial Economics* 33 (December): 217–232.

Berry, C. H. 1974. "Corporate Diversification and Market Structure." *The Bell Journal of Economics* 5 (Spring): 196–204.

Bhagwati, Jagdish. 1970. "Oligopoly Theory, Entry-Prevention and Growth." *Oxford Economic Papers* 22 (November): 297–310.

Birch, David L. 1981. "Who Creates Jobs?" *The Public Interest* 65 (Fall): 3–14.

Blair, John M. 1948. "Technology and Size." *American Economic Review* 38 (May): 121–152.

Boden, Richard, and Bruce D. Phillips. 1985. "Uses and Limitations of USEEM/USELM Data." Office of Advocacy, U.S. Small Business Administration, Washington, D.C., November.

Bolton Report. 1971. *Committee of Inquiry on Small Firms*, Cmnd 4811. London: HMSO.

Bond, Ronald S. 1975. "Mergers and Mobility among the Largest Manufacturing Corporations, 1984 to 1968." *Antitrust Bulletin* 20 (Fall): 505–519.

Bound, John, Clint Cummins, Zvi Griliches, Browyn H. Hall, and Adam Jaffe. "Who Does R&D and Who Patents?" In Zvi Griliches (ed.) *R&D, Patents, and Productivity*. Chicago: University of Chicago, pp. 21–54.

Boyer, Kenneth D. 1974. "Informative and Goodwill Advertising." *Review of Economics and Statistics* 56 (November): 541–548.

Boyle, Stanley E. 1971. "Large Industrial Corporations and Asset Shares: Comment." *American Economic Review* 61 (March): 163–167.

Boyle, Stanley E., and Robert L. Sorenson. 1971. "Concentration and Mobility: Alternative Measures of Industrial Structure." *Journal of Industrial Economics* 19 (April): 118–132.

Brock, Gerald W. 1975. *The U.S. Computer Industry*. Cambridge, Mass.: Ballinger, pp. 185–207.

Brock, Gerald W. 1981. *The Telecommunications Industry*. Cambridge, Mass.: Harvard University Press.

Brock, William A., and David S. Evans. 1986. *The Economics of Small Businesses: Their Role and Regulation in the U.S. Economy*. New York: Holmes and Meier.

Brock, William A., and David S. Evans. 1989. "Small Business Economics." *Small Business Economics* 1 (January): 7–20.

Brown, H. Shelton, and Bruce D. Phillips. 1989. "Comparison Between Small Business Data Base (USEEM) and Bureau of Labor Statistics (BLS) Employment Data: 1978–1986." *Small Business Economics* 1: 273–284.

Burnes, Bernard. 1988. "New Technology and Job Design: The Case of CNC." *New Technology, Work and Employment* 3 (Autumn): 100–111.

Campbell, Duncan C. 1988. "Technology, Flexibility of Manufacturing, and Industrial Relations: A Cross-National Review of Literature." Wharton School, Industrial Research Unit, University of Pennsylvania, Philadelphia, January.

Carlsson, Bo. 1984. "The Development and Use of Machine Tools in Historical Perspective." *Journal of Economic Behavior and Organization* 5: 91–114.

Carlsson, Bo. 1987. "Flexible Manufacturing and U.S. Trade Performance." Presented at the European Association for Research in Industrial Economics (EARIE) Conference, Madrid, August.

Carlsson, Bo. 1989a. "The Evolution of Manufacturing Technology and its Impact on Industrial Structure: An International Study." *Small Business Economics* 1 (January): 21–37.

Carlsson, Bo. 1989b. "Flexibility in the Theory of the Firm." *International Journal of Industrial Organization* 7 (June): 179–204.

Carlsson, Bo. 1990. "Small-Scale Industry at a Crossroads: U.S. Machine Tools in Global Perspective." In Z. Acs and D. Audretsch (eds.) *The Economics of Small Firms: A European Challenge*. Boston: Kluwer Academic Publishers.

Caves, Richard E., J. Khalilzadeh-Shirazi, and M. E. Porter. 1975. "Scale Economics in Statistical Analyses of Market Power." *Review of Economics and Statistics* 57 (May): 133–140.

Caves, Richard E., and Michael E. Porter. 1976. "Barriers to Exit." In Robert T. Masson and P. David Qualls (eds.) *Essays on Industrial Organization in Honor of Joe S. Bain*. Cambridge, Mass.: Ballinger, pp. 39–69.

Caves, Richard E., and Michael E. Porter. 1977. "From Entry to Mobility Barriers." *Quarterly Journal of Economics* 91 (May): 241–261.

Caves, Richard E., and Michael E. Porter. 1978. "Market Structure, Oligopoly and Stability of Market Shares." *Journal of Industrial Economics* 26 (June): 289–314.

Caves, Richard E., and T. A. Pugel. 1980. *Intraindustry Differences in Conduct and Performance: Viable Strategies in U.S. Manufacturing Industries*. New York: New York University Press.

Chakrabarti, Alok K. 1988. "Trends in Innovation and Productivity: The Case of Chemical and Textile Industries in the U.S." *R&D Management* 18 (April): 131–140.

Cohen, Wesley M., Richard C. Levin, and David C. Mowery. 1987. "Firm Size and R&D Intensity: A Re-examination." *Journal of Industrial Economics* 35 (June): 543–565.

Collins, Norman R., and Lee E. Preston. 1961. "The Size Structure of the Largest Industrial Firms." *American Economic Review* 51 (December): 986–1011.

Comanor, William S. 1964. "Research and Competitive Product Differentiation in the Pharmaceutical Industry in the United States," *Economica* 31 (November): 372–384.

Comanor, William S. 1967. "Market Structure, Product Differentiation and Industrial Research." *Quarterly Journal of Economics* 81 (November): 639–657.

Comanor, Williams S., and Thomas A. Wilson. 1967. "Advertising, Market Structure, and Performance." *Review of Economics and Statistics* 49 (November): 423–440.

Connolly, Robert A., Barry T. Hirsch, and Mark Hirschey. 1986. "Union Rent Seeking, Intangible Capital, and the Market Value of the Firm." *Review of Economics and Statistics* 68 (November): 567–577.

Connolly, Robert A., and Mark Hirschey. 1984. "R&D, Market Structure and Profits: A Value Based Approach." *Review of Economics and Statistics* 66 (November): 682–686.

Cowling, K., P. Stoneman, J. Cubbin, J. Cable, G. Hall, S. Domberger, and P. Dutton. 1980. *Mergers and Economic Performance.* Cambridge: Cambridge University Press.

Crandall, Robert W., and Stephen Barnett. 1986. *Up From the Ashes: The Rise of the Steel Minimills in the United States.* Washington, D.C.: The Brookings Institution.

Dahrenmöller, Alex. 1987. *Existenzgründungsstatistik: Nutzung amtlicher Datenquellen zur Erfassung des Gründungsgeschehens.* Stuttgart: C.C. Poeschel.

Dasgupta, Partha. 1986. "The Theory of Technological Competition." In J. E. Stiglitz and G. F. Mathewson (eds.) *New Developments in the Analysis of Market Structure.* Cambridge, Mass.: MIT Press, pp. 519–547.

Dasgupta, Partha, and Joseph Stiglitz. 1980. "Industrial Structure and the Nature of Innovative Activity." *The Economic Journal* 90 (June): 266–293.

Demsetz, Harold. 1973. "Industry Structure, Market Rivalry and Public Policy." *Journal of Law and Economics* 16 (April): 1–9.

Diwan, Romesh. 1989. "Small Business and the Economics of Flexible Manufacturing." *Small Business Economics* 1: 101–110.

Dixit, Avinash K. 1980. "The Role of Investment in Entry-Deterrence." *Economic Journal* 70 (March): 95–106.

Dixit, Avinash K. 1987. "Strategic Behavior in Contests." *American Economic Review* 77 (December): 891–898.

Dodgson, Mark. 1985. *Advanced Manufacturing Technology in the Small Firm.* London: Technical Change Center.

Dodgson, M., and R. Rothwell. 1987. "Small Firm Policy in the UK." Presented at the Conference on Small- and Medium-Sized Firms in the EC, Augsburg, September.

Dosi, Giovanni. 1988. "Sources, Procedures, and Microeconomic Effects of Innovation." *Journal of Economic Literature* 26 (September): 1120–1171.

Duetsch, Larry L. 1975. "Structure, Performance, and the Net Rate of Entry into Manufacturing Industries." *Southern Economic Journal* 41 (January): 450–456.

Duetsch, Larry L. 1984. "Entry and the Extent of Multiplant Operations." *Journal of Industrial Economics* 32 (June): 477–487.

Dunkelberg, William C., and Arnold C. Cooper. "Investment and Capital Diversity in the Small Enterprise." In Zoltan J. Acs and David B. Audretsch (eds.) *The Economics of Small Firms: A European Challenge*. Boston: Kluwer Academic Publishers, forthcoming.

Economic Report of the President. 1989. Washington, D.C.: U.S. Government Printing Office.

Edwards, Keith L., and Theodore J. Gordon. 1984. "Characterization of Innovations Introduced on the U.S. Market in 1982." The Futures Group, prepared for the U.S. Small Business Administration under Contract No. SBA-6050-0A-82, March.

Evans, David S, 1987a. "The Relationship Between Firm Growth, Size, and Age: Estimates for 100 Manufacturing Industries." *Journal of Industrial Economics* 35 (June): 567–581.

Evans, David S. 1987b. "Tests of Alternative Theories of Firm Growth." *Journal of Political Economy* 95 (August): 657–674.

Evans, David S., and Byron Jovanovic. "Estimates of a Model of Entrepreneurial Choice under Liquidity Constraints." *Journal of Political Economy* 97 (August): 808–827.

Evans, David S., and Linda S. Leighton. 1989. "The Determinants of Changes in U.S. Self-Employment, 1968–1987." *Small Business Economics* 1: 111–120.

Evenson, Robert E. 1984. "International Invention: Implications for Technology Market Analysis." In Zvi Griliches (ed.) *R&D, Patents, and Productivity*. Chicago: University of Chicago, pp. 89–126.

Fazzari, S., R. Hubbard, and B. Peterson. 1987. "Financing Constraints and Corporate Investment." National Bureau of Economic Research Working Paper No. 2387. Cambridge, Mass.: National Bureau of Economic Research.

Fisher, Franklin M., and Peter Temin. 1973. "Returns to Scale in Research and Development: What Does the Schumpeterian Hypothesis Imply?" *Journal of Political Economy* 81 (January–February): 56–70.

FitzRoy, Felix R. 1989. "Firm Size, Efficiency and Employment: A Review Article." *Small Business Economics* 1 (January): 75–80.

FitzRoy, Felix R., and Kornelius Kraft. 1988. "Innovation, Rent-Sharing and Organized Labor." Discussion Paper FS IV, 88–14, Wissenschaftszentrum Berlin.

Florida, R. L., and M. Kenney. 1988a. "Venture Capital, High Technology and Regional Development." *Regional Studies* 22 (February): 33–48.

Florida, R. L., and M. Kenney. 1988b. "Venture Capital-Financed Innovation and Technological Change in the U.S." *Research Policy* 17 (June): 119–137.

Freeman, Christopher. 1971. "The Role of Small Firms in Innovation in the United Kingdom Since 1945." Committee of Inquiry on Small Firms, Research Report No. 6, London.

Freeman, Christopher. 1974. *Industrial Innovation*. Hardmondsworth, England: Penguin Books.

Freeman, C., J. Clark, and L. Soete. 1982. *Unemployment and Technical Innovation*. London: Frances Pinter.

Freeman, Richard B., and James L. Medoff. 1979. "New Estimates of Private Sector Unionism in the United States." *Industrial and Labor Relations Review* 32 (January): 143–174.

Fudenberg, Drew, and Jean Tirole. 1986. "A Signal-Jamming Theory of Predation." *Rand Journal of Economics* 17: 366–376.

Galbraith, John K. 1956. *American Capitalism: The Concept of Countervailing Power*. Revised edition. Boston: Houghton Mifflin.

Galbraith, John K. 1957. *The New Industrial State*. Boston: Houghton Mifflin.

Gaskins, Darius W., Jr. 1971. "Dynamic Limit Pricing: Optimal Pricing Under Threat of Entry." *Journal of Economic Theory* 3 (September): 306–322.

Gaston, Robert J. 1989. "The Scale of Informal Capital Markets." *Small Business Economics* 1: 223–230.

Gellman Research Associates. 1976. "Indicators of International Trends in Technological Innovation." Prepared for the National Science Foundation, April.

Gellman Research Associates. 1982. "The Relationship between Industrial Concentration, Firm Size, and Technological Innovation." Prepared for the Office of Advocacy. U.S. Small Business Administration under Award No. SBA-2633-0A-79, May.

Geroski, Paul A. 1983. "The Empirical Analysis of Entry: A Survey." Discusion Paper No. 8318, University of Southampton, October.

Geroski, Paul A. 1987. "Innovation, Technological Opportunity and Market Structure." University of Southampton. Mimeo.

Geroski, Paul A., and Alexis Jacquemin. 1985. "Industrial Change, Barriers to Mobility, and European Industrial Policy." *Economic Policy* 1 (November): 169–204.

Gerwin, Donald. 1983. "Do's and Don'ts of Computerized Manufacturing." In Alan M. Kantrow (ed.) *Survival Strategies for American Industry*. New York: John Wiley & Sons, pp. 349–362.

Gilbert, Richard J., and David M. G. Newbery. 1982. "Preemptive Patenting and Persistence of Monopoly." *American Economic Review* 72 (June): 514–526.

Globerman Steven. 1973. "Market Structure and R&D in Canadian Manufacturing Industries." *Quarterly Review of Economics and Business* 13 (Summer): 59–67.

Globerman, Steven. 1975. "Technological Diffusion in the Canadian Tool and Die Industry." *Review of Economics and Statistics* 57 (May): 428–434.

Gorecki, Paul K. 1975. "The Determinants of Entry by New and Diversifying Enterprises in the U.K. Manufacturing Sector, 1958–1963: Some Tentative Results." *Applied Economics* 7 (June): 139–147.

Gort, Michael, and Steven Klepper. 1982. "Time Paths in the Diffusion of Product Innovations." *Economic Journal* 92 (September): 630–653.

Griliches, Zvi (ed.) 1984. *R&D, Patents, and Productivity*. Chicago and London: University of Chicago Press.

Griliches, Zvi. 1986. "Productivity, R&D and Basic Research at the Firm Level in the 1970's." *American Economic Review* 76 (March): 141–154.

Grossack, I. M. 1965. "Towards an Integration of Static and Dynamic Measures of Industry Concentration." *Review of Economics and Statistics* 47 (August): 301–308.

Gudgin, G. 1978. *Industrial Location Processes and Regional Employment Growth*. Farnborough, England: Saxon House.

Hall, Bronwyn H. 1987. "The Relationship Between Firm Size and Firm Growth in the U.S. Manufacturing Sector." *Journal of Industrial Economics* 35 (June): 583–605.

Hall, Browyn H., Zvi Griliches, and Jerry A. Hausman. 1986. "Patents and R&D: Is There a Lag?" *International Economic Review* 27 (June): 265–302.

Hall, Marshall, and Leonard W. Weiss. 1967. "Firm Size and Profitability." *Review of Economics and Statistics* 49 (August): 319–331.

Hamburg, Dan. 1963. "Invention is the Industrial Research Laboratory." *Journal of Political Economy* 71 (April): 95–115.

Harrigan, Kathryn R. 1985. *Strategic Flexibility: A Management Guide for Changing Times*. Lexington, Mass.: Lexington Books.

Harris, Candee S. 1983. *U.S. Establishment and Enterprise Microdata (USEEM): A Data Base Description*. Business Microdata Project, The Brookings Institution, June.

Hart, P. E., and S. J. Prais. 1956. "The Analysis of Business Concentration: A Statistical Approach." *Journal of the Royal Statistical Society* 119 (Part 2): 150–191.

Highfield, Richard, and Robert Smiley. 1987. "New Business Starts and Economic Activity: An Empirical Investigation." *International Journal of Industrial Organization* 5 (March): 51–66.

Hilke, J. C. 1984. "Excess Capacity and Entry: Some Empirical Evidence." *Journal of Industrial Economics* 33 (December): 233–240.

Hirsch, Barry T., and John T. Addison. 1986. *The Economic Analysis of Unions: New Approaches and Evidence*. Boston: George Allen and Unwin.

Hirsch, Barry T., and Albert N. Link. 1986. "Labor Union Effects on Innovative Activity." Mimeo, June.

Hymer, Stephen, and Peter Pashigian. 1962. "Firm Size and Rate of Growth." *Journal of Political Economy* 52 (December): 556–569.

International Trade Administration, U.S. Department of Commerce. 1985. *A Competitive Assessment of the U.S. Flexible Manufacturing Systems Industry*. Washington, D.C., July.

Iwai, Katsuhito. 1984a. "Schumpeterian Dynamics: An Evolutionary Model of Innovation and Imitation." *Journal of Economic Behavior and Organization* 5: 159–190.

Iwai, Katsuhito. 1984b. "Schumpeterian Dynamics, Part II: Technological Progress, Firm Growth and 'Economic Selection'." *Journal of Economic Behavior and Organization* 5: 321–351.

Jacobson, Louis. 1985. *Analysis of the Accuracy of SBA's Small Business Data Base*. Alexandria, Va.: Center for Naval Analysis.

Jaikumar, Ramchandran. 1986. "Postindustrial Manufacturing." *Harvard Business Review* 86 (November–December): 69–76.

Jaffe, Adam B. 1986. "Technological Opportunity and Spillovers of R&D: Evidence from Firms' Patents, Profits and Market Value." *American Economic Review* 76 (December): 984–1001.

Jensen, Michael C. 1988. "Takeovers: Their Causes and Consequences." *Journal of Economic Perspectives* 2 (Winter): 21–48.

Jewkes, John, David Sawers, and Richard Stillerman. 1969. *The Sources of Invention*. 2nd edition. New York: Norton.

Johannisson, B., and C. Lindström. 1971. "Firm Size and Inventive Activity." *Swedish Journal of Economics* 73 (December): 427–442.

Johns, B. L. 1962. "Barriers to Entry in a Dynamic Setting." *Journal of Industrial Economics* 11 (November): 48–61.

Jovanovic, Boyan. 1982. "Selection and Evolution of Industry." *Econometrica* 50 (May): 649–670.

Judge, George G., E. Griffiths, R. Carter-Hill, and Tsoung-Chao-Lee. 1980. *The Theory and Practice of Econometrics*. New York: John Wiley & Sons.

Kaldor, Nickolas. 1934. "The Equilibrium of the Firm." *Economic Journal* 44 (March): 60–76.

Kamerschen, David R. 1971. "Large Industrial Corporations and Asset Shares: Comment." *American Economic Review* 61 (March): 160–162.

Kamien, Morton I., and Nancy L. Schwartz. 1971. "Limit Pricing and Uncertain Entry." *Econometrica* 39: 441–454.

Kamien, Morton I., and Nancy L. Schwartz. 1975. "Market Structure and Innovation: A Survey." *The Journal of Economic Literature* 13 (March): 1–37.

Kaplan, A. D. H. 1954. *Big Enterprise in a Competitive System*. Washington, D.C.: The Brookings Institution.

Khemani, R. S., and Daniel M. Shapiro. 1986. "The Determinants of New Plant Entry in Canada." *Applied Economics* 18 (November): 1243–1257.

Kmenta, Jan. 1971. *Elements of Econometrics*. New York: Macmillan.

Kohn, Meier, and John T. Scott. 1982. "Scale Economies in Research and Development: The Schumpeterian Hypothesis." *Journal of Industrial Economics* 30 (March): 239–249.

Koning, Cees, and Frederik Poutsma. 1988. "Automatisierung und die Qualität der Arbeit in Klein- und Mittelbetrieben." *Internationales Gewerbearchive* 36: 238–250.

Kumar, M. S. 1985. "Growth, Acquisition Activity and Firm Size: Evidence from the United Kingdom." *Journal of Industrial Economics* 33 (March): 327–338.

Kuznets, Simon. 1962. "Inventive Activity: Problems of Definition and Measurements. In R.R. Nelson (ed.) *The Rate and Direction of Inventive Activity*. National Bureau of Economic Research Conference Report, Princeton, N.J., pp. 19–43.

Langenfeld, James, and David Scheffman. 1988. "Innovation and U.S. Competition Policy." *Aussenwirtschaft* 43 (June): 45–95.

Levin, Richard C., Wesley Cohen, and David C. Mowery. 1985. "R&D Appropriability, Opportunity and Market Structure: New Evidence on the Schumpeterian Hypothesis." *American Economic Review* 15 (May): 20–24.

Levin, Richard C., Alvin K. Klevorick, Richard R. Nelson, and Sydney G. Winter. 1987. "Appropriating the Returns from Industrial Research and Development." *Brookings Papers on Economic Activity* 3: 783–820.

Levin, Richard C., and Peter C. Reiss. 1984. "Tests of A Schumpeterian Model of R&D and Market Structure." In Zvi Griliches (ed.) *R&D, Patents, and Productivity*. Chicago: University of Chicago, pp. 175–208.

Link, Albert N. 1987. *Technological Change and Productivity Growth*. New York: Harwood Academic Publishers.

Lippman, S. A., and R. P. Rumelts. 1982. "Uncertain Imitability: An Analysis of Interfirm Differences in Efficiency Under Competition." *Bell Journal of Economics* 13 (Autumn): 418–438.

Lucas, Robert E., Jr. 1978. "On the Size Distribution of Business Firms." *Bell Journal of Economics* 9 (Autumn): 508–523.

Lunn, John. 1986. "An Empirical Analysis of Process and Product Patenting: A Simultaneous Equation Framework." *Journal of Industrial Economics* 34 (March): 319–330.

MacDonald, James M. 1986. "Entry and Exit on the Competitive Fringe." *Southern Economic Journal* 52 (January): 640–652.

Mann, H. Michael. 1966. "Seller Concentration, Barriers to Entry and Rates of Return in Thirty Industries." *Review of Economics and Statistics* 48 (August): 296–307.

Mansfield, Edwin. 1962. "Entry, Gibrat's Law, Innovation, and the Growth of Firms." *American Economic Review* 52 (December): 1023–1051.

Mansfield, Edwin. 1968. *Industrial Research and Technological Change.* New York: W. W. Norton for the Cowles Foundation for Research Economics, at Yale University, pp. 83–108.

Mansfield, Edwin. 1981. "Composition of R and D Expenditures: Relationship to Size of Firm, Concentration, and Innovative Output." *Review of Economics and Statistics* 63 (November): 610–615.

Mansfield, Edwin. 1983. "Industrial Organization and Technological Change: Recent Empirical Findings." In John V. Craven (ed.) *Industrial Organization, Antitrust, and Public Policy.* The Hague: Kluwer-Nijhoff, pp. 129–143.

Mansfield, Edwin. 1984. "Comment on Using Linked Patent and R&D Data to Measure Interindustry Technology Flows." In Zvi Griliches (ed.) *R&D, Patents, and Productivity.* Chicago: University of Chicago, pp. 462–464.

Mansfield, Edwin, J. Rapoport, J. Schnee, S. Wagner, and M. Hamburger. 1971. *Research and Innovation in the Modern Corporation.* New York: W. W. Norton.

Mansfield, Edwin, A. Romeo, M. Schwartz, D. Teece, S. Wanger, and P. Brach. 1982. *Technology Transfer, Productivity, and Economic Policy.* New York: W. W. Norton.

Marcus, Matityahu. 1969. "Profitability and Size of Firm: Some Further Evidence." *Review of Economics and Statistics* 51 (February): 104–107.

Marschak, T., and Richard R. Nelson. 1962. "Flexibility, Uncertainty and Economic Theory." *Metroeconomica* 65: 42–58.

Marshall, Alfred. 1920. *Principles of Economics*, 8th edition. London: Macmillan.

Martin, Kenny. 1986. "Schumpeterian Innovation and Entrepreneurs in Capitalism." *Research Policy* 15 (February): 1–33.

Marx, Karl. 1912. *Capital.* Translated by Ernest Untermann. Vol. 1. Chicago: Kerr.

Matthews, Stephen A., and Leonard J. Mirman. 1983. "Equilibrium Limit Pricing: The Effects of Private Information and Stochastic Demand." *Econometrica* 51 (July): 981–996.

McGuckin, Robert. 1972. "Entry, Concentration Change, and Stability of Market Shares." *Southern Economic Journal* 38 (January): 363–370.

Mensch, Gerhard. 1979. *Statemate in Technology*. Boston: Ballinger.

Mermelstein, David. 1969. "Large Industrial Corporations and Asset Shares." *American Economic Review* 59 (September): 531–541.

Mermelstein, David. 1971. "Large Industrial Corporations and Asset Shares: Reply." *American Economic Review* 61 (March): 168–174.

Merrifield, D. Bruce. 1987. "Flexible Manufacturing—the New Industrial Revolution." *Research Managment* 30 (November–December): 6–8.

Milgrom, Paul, and John Roberts. 1982. "Predation, Reputation, and Entry Deterrence." *Journal of Economic Theory* 27: 280–312.

Milgrom, Paul, and John Roberts. 1987. "Informational Asymmetries, Strategic Behavior, and Industrial Organization." *American Economic Review* 77 (May): 184–193.

Mills, David E. 1984. "Demand Fluctuations and Endogenous Firm Flexibility." *Journal of Industrial Economics* 33 (September): 55–71.

Mills, David E., and Laurence Schumann. 1985. "Industry Structure with Fluctuating Demand." *American Economic Review* 75 (September): 758–767.

Modigliani, Franco. 1958. "New Developments in the Oligopoly Front." *Journal of Political Economy* 66 (June): 215–232.

Moore, Thomas. 1976. *Trucking Regulation*. Palo Alto, Calif.: AEI-Hoover Policy Study 18.

Mueller, Dennis C. 1976. "Information, Mobility, and Profit." *Kyklos* 29: 419–448.

Mueller, Dennis C. 1986. *Profits in the Long Run*. Cambridge: Cambridge University Press, 1986.

Mueller, Dennis C., and J. Tilton. 1969. "Research and Development Costs as a Barrier to Entry." *Canadian Journal of Economics* 56 (November): 570–579.

Mueller, Willard F. 1962. "The Origins of the the Basic Inventions Underlying DuPont's Major Product and Process Innovations, 1920–50." In the National Bureau of Economic Research conference report, *The Rate and Direction of Inventive Activity*. Princeton: Princeton University Press, pp. 323–346.

Mueller, Willard F., John Culberton, and Brian Peckman. 1982. *Market Structure and Technological Performance in the Food and Manufacturing Industries*. Madison, Wis.: Research Division, College of Agriculture and Life Sciences, University of Wisconsin-Madison.

Nabseth, Lars, and G. F. Ray (eds.) 1974. *The Diffusion of New Industrial Processes: An International Study*. New York: Cambridge University Press.

Nakazawa, Toshiaki, and Leonard W. Weiss. "The Legal Cartels of Japan." *Antitrust Bulletin*, forthcoming.

National Science Board. 1975. *Science Indicators, 1974*. Washington, D.C.: U.S. Government Printing Office.

National Science Board. 1987. *Science & Engineering Indicators, 1987*. Washington, D.C.: U.S. Government Printing Office.

National Science Foundation. 1986. *National Patterns of Science and Technology Resources, 1986*. Washington, D.C.

Nelson, Richard R. 1959. "The Simple Economics of Basic Scientific Research." *Journal of Political Economy* 67 (June): 297–306.

Nelson, Richard R. 1984. "Incentives for Entrepreneurship and Supporting Institutions." *Weltwirtschaftliches Archiv* 120: 646–661.

Nelson, Richard R. 1986. "Institutions Supporting Technical Advance in Industry." *American Economic Review* 76 (May): 186–189.

Nelson, Richard R., and Sidney G. Winter. 1974. "Neoclassical vs. Evolutionary Theories of Economic Growth: Critique and Prospectus." *Economic Journal* 84 (December): 886–905.

Nelson, Richard R., and Sidney G. Winter. 1978. "Forces Generating and Limiting Concentration under Schumpeterian Competition." *Bell Journal of Economics* 9 (Autumn): 524–548.

Nelson, Richard R., and Sidney G. Winter. 1982. *An Evolutionary Theory of Economic Change*. Cambridge, Mass.: Harvard University Press.

Newman, Howard H. 1978. "Strategic Groups and the Structure Performance Relationship." *Review of Economics and Statistics* 60 (August): 417–427.

Northcott, J., and P. Rogers. 1984. *Microelectronics in British Industry: The Pattern of Change*. London: Policy Studies Institute.

Office of Technology Assessment. See U.S. Congress.

Oi, Walter Y. 1983. "Heterogeneous Firms and the Organization of Production." *Economy Inquiry* 21 (April): 147–171.

Orr, Dale. 1974. "The Determinants of Entry: A Study of the Canadian Manufacturing Industries." *Review of Economics and Statistics* 56 (February): 58–66.

Oster, Sharon. 1982. "Intraindustry Structure and the Ease of Strategic Change." *Review of Economics and Statistics* 64: 376–383.

Pakes, Ariel. 1985. "On Patents, R&D, and the Stock Market Rate of Return." *Journal of Political Economy* 93 (April): 390–409.

Pakes, Ariel, and R. Ericson. 1987 "Empirical Implications of Alternative Models of Firm Dynamics." Manuscript, Department of Economics, University of Wisconsin-Madison.

Pakes, Ariel, and Zvi Griliches. 1980. "Patents and R&D at the Firm Level: A First Report." *Economics Letters* 5: 377–381.

Pakes, Ariel, and Zvi Griliches. 1984. "Patents and R&D at the Firm Level: A First Look." In Zvi Griliches (ed.) *R&D, Patents, and Productivity*. Chicago: University of Chicago, pp. 55–72.

Pakes, Ariel, and Mark Schankerman. 1984. "The Rate of Obsolescence of Patents, Research Gestation Lags, and the Private Rate of Return to Research Resources." In Zvi Griliches (ed.) *R&D, Patents, and Productivity*. Chicago: University of Chicago. pp. 73–88.

Pavitt, Keith, and S. Wald. 1971. "The Conditions for Success in Technological Innovation." OECD, Paris.

Pavitt, Keith, M. Robson, and J. Townsend. 1987. "The Size Distribution of Innovating Firms in the UK: 1945–1983." *The Journal of Industrial Economics* 55 (March): 291–316.

Phillips, Almarin. 1956. "Concentration, Scale, and Technological Change in Selected Manufacturing Industries, 1899–1939." *Journal of Industrial Economics* 5: 179–193.

Phillips, A. 1965. "Market Structure, Innovation and Investment." In W. Alderson, B. Terpstra, and J. Shapiro (eds.) *Patents and Progress: The Sources and Impact of Advancing Technology*. Homewood, Ill.: Irwin, pp. 37–58.

Phillips, Bruce D., and Bruce A. Kirchhoff. 1989. "Formation, Growth and Survival: Small Firm Dynamics in the U.S. Economy." *Small Business Economics* 1 (January): 65–74.

Piore, Michael J. 1980. "Technological Foundations of Dualism and Discontinuity." In Suzanne Berger and Michael J. Piore (eds.) *Dualism and Discontinuity in Industrial Societies*. Cambridge: Cambridge University Press, pp. 13–81.

Piore, Michael J. 1986. "The Decline of Mass Production and Union Survival in the USA." *Industrial Relations Journal* 17 (Autumn): 207–213.

Piore, Michael J., and Charles F. Sabel. 1983. "Italian Small Business Development: Lessons for U.S. Industrial Policy." In John Zysman and Laura Tyson (eds.) *American Industry in International Competition*. Ithaca, N.Y.: Cornell University Press, pp. 391–421.

Piore, Michael J., and Charles F. Sabel. 1984. *The Second Industrial Divide: Possibilities for Prosperity*. New York: Basic Books.

Porter, Michael E. 1976. *Interbrand Choice, Strategy and Bilateral Market Power*. Cambridge, Mass.: Harvard University Press.

Porter, Michael E. 1979. "The Structure Within Industries and Company Performance." *Review of Economics and Statistics* 61 (May): 214–228.

Poutsma, Erik, and Aad Zwaard. 1989. "The Effects of Automation in Small Industrial Enterprises." *International Small Business Journal* 7 (January–March): 35–43.

Pratten, C. F. 1971. *Economies of Scale in Manufacturing Industry*. Cambridge: Cambridge University Press.

Pratten, C. F. 1988. "The Competitiveness of Small Firms and the Economies of Scale." University of Cambridge, Department of Applied Economics, Working Paper.

Price Waterhouse. 1985. *Survey of Small High-Tech Business Shows Federal SBIR Awards Spurring Job Growth, Commercial Sales*. Washington, D.C.: Small Business High Technology Institute, April.

Pugel, Thomas A. 1978. *International Market Linkages and U.S. Manufacturing: Prices, Profits, and Patterns*. Cambridge, Mass.: Ballinger.

Ray, Edward J. 1981. "The Determinants of Tariffs and Nontariff Trade Restrictions in the U.S." *Journal of Political Economics* 89 (February): 105–121.

Reinganum, Jennifer. 1985. "Innovation and Industry Evolution." *Quarterly Journal of Economics* 100 (February): 81–99.

Robson, M., and J. Townsend. 1984. "Users Manual for ESRC Archive File on Innovations in Britain Since 1945: 1984 Update." Science Policy Research Unit, University of Sussex.

Rogers, Everett. 1986. "The Role of the Research University in the Spin-Off of High Technology Companies." *Technovation* 4: 169–181.

Romeo, Anthony A. 1975. "Interindustry and Interfirm Differences in the Rate of Diffusion of an Innovation." *Review of Economics and Statistics* 57 (May): 311–319.

Rothwell, R. 1984. "The Role of Small Firms in the Emergence of New Technologies." *OMEGA: The International Journal of Management Science* 12: 19–29.

Rothwell, R. 1985. "Venture Finance, Small Firm and Public Policy in the U.K." *Research Policy* 14: 253–265.

Rothwell, R. 1989. "Small Firms, Innovation and Industrial Change." *Small Business Economics* 1 (January): 51–64.

Rothwell, R., and W. Zegveld. 1981. *Industrial Innovation and Public Policy*. Westport, Conn.: Greenwood Press.

Rothwell, R., and W. Zegveld. 1982. *Innovation and the Small and Medium Sized Firm*. London: Frances Pinter.

Sands, Saul S. 1961. "Changes in Scale of Production in United States Manufacturing Industry, 1904–1947." *Review of Economics and Statistics* 43 (November): 365–368.

Scheirer, William K. 1977. "Small Firms and Federal R&D." Report to Office of Federal Procurement Policy, Office of Management and Budget.

Scherer, F. M. 1965a. "Size of Firm, Oligopoly and Research: A Comment." *Canadian Journal of Economics and Political Science.* 31 (May): 256–266.

Scherer, F. M. 1965b. "Firm Size, Market Structure, Opportunity, and the Output of Patented Inventions." *American Economic Review* 55 (December): 1097–1125.

Scherer, F. M. 1967. "Market Structure and the Employment of Scientists and Engineers." *American Economic Review* 57 (June): 524–530.

Scherer, F. M. 1973. "The Determinants of Industry Plant Sizes in Six Nations." *Review of Economics and Statistics* 55 (May): 135–145.

Scherer, F. M. 1980. *Industrial Market Structure and Economic Performance.* 2nd edition. Chicago: Rand McNally College Publishing Co.

Scherer, F. M. 1982a. "Inter-Industry Technology Flows and Productivity Growth." *Review of Economics and Statistics* 64 (December): 627–634.

Scherer, F. M. 1982b. "Inter-Industry Technology Flows in the United States." *Research Policy* 11: 227–245.

Scherer, F. M. 1983a. "The Propensity to Patent." *International Journal of Industrial Organization* 1 (March): 107–128.

Scherer, F. M. 1983b. "Concentration, R&D, and Productivity Change." *Southern Economic Journal* 50 (July): 221–225.

Scherer, F. M. 1984a. "Using Linked Patent and R&D Data to Measure Inter-Industry Technology Flows." In Zvi Griliches (ed.) *R&D, Patents, and Productivity.* Chicago: University of Chicago Press, pp. 417–464.

Scherer, F. M. 1984b. *Innovation and Growth: Schumpeterian Perspectives.* Cambridge, Mass.: MIT Press.

Scherer, F. M. 1988a. "Corporate Takeovers: The Efficiency Arguments." *Journal of Economic Perspectives* 2 (Winter): 69–82.

Scherer, F. M. 1988b. Testimony before the Subcommittee on Monopolies and Commercial Law, Committee on the Judiciary, U.S. House of Representatives, February 24.

Schmalensee, Richard. 1978. "Entry Deterrence in the Ready-To-Eat Breakfast Cereal Industry." *Bell Journal of Economics* 9 (Autumn): 305–327.

Schmalensee, Richard. 1981. "Economies of Scale and Barriers to Entry." *Journal of Political Economy* 89 (December): 1228–1238.

Schmalensee, Richard. 1986. "Advertising and Market Structure." In J. Stiglitz and G. F. Mathewson (eds.) *New Developments in the Analysis of Market Structure.* Cambridge, Mass.: MIT Press, pp. 373–396.

Schmookler, J. 1966. *Invention and Economic Growth*, Cambridge, Mass.: Harvard University Press.

Schumpeter, Joseph A. 1934. *The Theory of Economic Development*. Cambridge, Mass.: Harvard University Press.

Schumpeter, Joseph A. 1950. *Capitalism, Socialism and Democracy*. 3rd edition. New York: Harper and Row.

Schwalbach, Joachim. 1987. "Entry by Diversified Firms into German Industries." *International Journal of Industrial Organization* 5 (March): 43–50.

Schwartz, Marius, and Earl A. Thompson. 1986. "Divisionalization and Entry Deterrence." *Quarterly Journal of Economics* 60 (May): 307–321.

Scott, John T. 1984. "Firm Versus Industry Variability in R&D Intensity." In Zvi Griliches (ed.) *R&D, Patents, and Productivity*. Chicago: University of Chicago Press, 223–245.

Servan-Schreiber, J. -J. 1968. *The American Challenge*. London: Hamisch Hamilton.

Shapiro, Daniel, and R. S. Khemani. 1987. "The Determinants of Entry and Exit Reconsidered." *International Journal of Industrial Organization* 5 (March): 15–26.

Shepherd, William G. 1979. *The Economics of Industrial Organization*. Englewood Cliffs, N.J.: Prentice Hall.

Shepherd, William G. 1982. "Causes of Increased Competition in the U.S. Economy, 1939–1980." *Review of Economics and Statistics* 64 (November): 613–626.

Shrieves, Ronald M. 1978 "Market Structure and Innovation: A New Perspective." *Journal of Industrial Economics* 26 (June): 329–347.

Simon, Herbert A., and Charles P. Bonini. 1958. "The Size Distribution of Business Firms." *American Economic Review* 48 (September): 607–617.

Simon, Julian L., 1970. *Issues in the Economics of Advertising*. Urbana: University of Illinois Press.

Singh, Ajit, and Geoffrey Whittington. 1975. "The Size and Growth of Firms." *Review of Economic Studies* 52 (January): 15–26.

Smiley, Robert. 1988. "Empirical Evidence on Strategic Entry Deterrence." *International Journal of Industrial Organization* 6 (June): 167–180.

Soete, Luc L. G. 1979. "Firm Size and Inventive Activity: The Evidence Reconsidered." *European Economic Review* 12: 319–340.

Solo, Robert. 1985. "Across the Industrial Divide: A Review Article." *Journal of Economic Issues* 19 (September): 829–837.

Spence, A. Michael. 1977. "Entry, Capacity, Investment and Oligopolistic Pricing." *Bell Journal of Economics* 8 (Autumn): 534–544.

Starr, Ed. 1987. "Small Business in Manufacturing." Prepared for the U.S. Small Business Administration, July.

Statistisches Bundesamt. *Statistisches Jahrbuch für die Bundesrepublik Deutschland*. Wiesbaden: W. Kohlhammer, various years.

Stigler, George J. 1939. "Production and Distribution in the Short Run." *Journal of Political Economy* 47 (June): 305–327.

Stigler, George J. 1956a. "Industrial Organization and Economic Progress." In L.D. White (ed.) *The State of Social Sciences*. Chicago: University of Chicago Press, pp. 269–282.

Stigler, George J. 1956b. "The Statistics of Monopoly and Mergers." *Journal of Political Economy* 64 (February): 33–40.

Stigler, George J. 1963. *Capital and Rate of Return in Manufacturing Industries*. Princeton: Princeton University Press.

Stigler, George J. 1968. *The Organization of Industry*. Chicago: University of Chicago Press.

Stiglitz, Joseph E. 1987. "Technological Change, Sunk Costs, and Competition." *Brookings Papers on Economic Activity* 3: 883–937.

Stiglitz, Joseph E., and G. Frank Mathewson (eds.) 1986. *New Developments in the Analysis of Market Structure*. Cambridge, Mass.: MIT Press.

Stoll, Hans R. 1984. "Small Firms' Access to Public Equity Financing." In Paul M. Horvitz and R. Richardson Pettit (eds.) *Small Business Finance: Problems in the Financing of Small Business*. Greenwich, Conn.: JAI Press, pp. 187–238.

Stonebreaker, Robert. 1976. "Corporate Profits and the Risk of Entry." *Review of Economics and Statistics* 58 (February): 33–39.

Storey, David J., and Steven Johnson. 1987. *Job Generation and Labour Market Changes*. London: Macmillan.

Storey, David J., and A. M. Jones. 1987. "New Firm Formation—Labor Market Approach to Industrial Entry." *Scottish Journal of Political Economy* 34 (February): 37–51.

"Switching the Focus to the Buyer." 1984. *The Engineer* (May 17): 24–26.

Sylos-Labini, Paolo. 1962. *Oligopoly and Technical Progress*. 2nd edition. Cambridge, Mass.: Harvard University Press.

Tombak, Mihkil, and Arnoud De Meyer. 1988. "Flexibility and FMS: An Empirical Analysis." *IEEE Transactions on Engineering Management* 35 (May): 101–107.

Townsend, J., F. Herwood, G. Thomas, K. Pavitt, and S. Wyatt. 1981. "Innovations in Britain Since 1945." Occasional Paper No. 16, Science Research Unit, University of Sussex.

U.S. Congress, Office of Technology Assessment. 1984. *Technology, Innovation, and Regional Economic Development*, OTA-STI-238. Washington, D.C., July.

U.S. Small Business Administration, Office of Advocacy. 1980. *Case Studies Examining the Role of Government R&D Contract Funding in the Early History of High Technology Companies* (Research and Planning Institute), NTIS No. PB82 190869. Washington, D.C., July.

U.S. Small Business Administration. 1986. *The Small Business Data Base: A User's Guide*. Washington, D.C., July.

U.S. Small Business Administration, Office of Advocacy. 1987. *Linked 1976– 1984 USEEM User's Guide*. Washington, D.C., July.

U.S. Small Business Administration, Office of Advocacy. 1988. *Handbook of Small Business Data*. Washington, D.C.: U.S. Government Printing Office.

Vernon, Raymond. 1966. "International Investment and International Trade in the Product Life Cycle." *Quarterly Journal of Economics* 80 (May): 190–207.

Viner, Jacob. 1932. "Cost Curves and Supply Curves." *Zeitschrift für Nationalökonomie* 3: 23–46.

Weiss, Leonard W. 1963. "Factors in Changing Concentration." *Review of Economics and Statistics* 45 (February): 70–77.

Weiss Leonard W. 1974. "The Concentration–Profits Relationship and Antitrust." In H. J. Goldschmid, H. M. Mann, and J. F. Weston (eds.) *Industrial Concentration: The New Learning*. Boston: Little, Brown Co., pp. 184–232.

Weiss, Leonard W. 1976. "Optimal Plant Scale and the Extent of Suboptimal Capacity." In Robert T. Masson and P.D. Qualls (eds.) *Essays on Industrial Organization in Honor of Joe S. Bain*. Cambridge, Mass.: Ballinger, 126–134.

Weiss, Leonard W. 1979. "The Structure–Conduct–Performance Paradigm and Antitrust." *University of Pennsylvania Law Review* 127 (April): 1104–1140.

Weizsäcker, C. C. von. 1979. *Barriers to Entry: A Theoretical Treatment*. Berlin: Springer-Verlag.

Wenders, John T. 1971. "Collusion and Entry." *Journal of Political Economy* 79 (December): 1258–1277.

White, Lawrence J. 1982. "The Determinants of the Relative Importance of Small Business." *Review of Economics and Statistics* 64 (February): 42–49.

White, Lawrence J. 1984. "The Role of Small Business in the U.S. Economy." In Paul M. Horvitz and R. Richardson Pettit (eds.) *Small Business Finances: Problems in the Financing of Small Business*. Greenwich, Conn.: JAI Press, pp. 19–50.

Williamson, Oliver E. 1975. *Markets and Hierarchies: Analysis and Antritrust Implications*. New York: The Free Press.

Winter, Sidney G. 1984. "Schumpeterian Competition in Alternative Technological Regimes." *Journal of Economic Behavior and Organization* 5: 287–320.

Yamawaki, Hideki, and David B. Audretsch. 1988. "Import Share under International Oligopoly with Differentiated Products: Japanese Imports in U.S. Manufacturing." *Review of Economics and Statistics* 70 (November): 569–579.

Yip, George. 1982. *Barriers to Entry: A Corporate-Strategy Perspective.* Lexington, Mass.: Lexington Books.

Ziegler, Charles A. 1985. "Innovation and the Imitative Entrepreneur." *Journal of Economic Behavior and Organization* 6: 103–121.

Index